Kind Words

A THESAURUS OF EUPHEMISMS

Kind Words

A THESAURUS OF EUPHEMISMS

Judith S. Neaman and
Carole G. Silver

McGraw-Hill Book Company

New York   St. Louis   San Francisco   Bogotá
Guatemala   Hamburg   Lisbon   Madrid   Mexico
Montreal   Panama   Paris   San Juan   São Paulo   Tokyo   Toronto

KIND WORDS: A THESAURUS OF EUPHEMISMS

Copyright © 1983 by Judith S. Neaman and Carole G. Silver

Reprinted by arrangement with Facts of File, Inc.

First McGraw-Hill edition, 1985

1 2 3 4 5 6 7 8 9   FGRFGR   8 7 6 5 4

ISBN 0-07-046141-4

Library of Congress Cataloging in Publication Data

Neaman, Judith S.
    Kind words.

    Bibliography: p.
    Includes index.
    1. English language—Euphemism—Dictionaries.
2. English language—Terms and phrases. I. Silver,
Carole G.   II. Title.
PE1449.N34   1985   423'.1   84-7146
ISBN 0-07-046141-4 (pbk.)

CONTENTS

About This Book

A collection of euphemisms, complete in this volume, is none-theless a work in progress. We have not attempted to be complete and, in the course of our research, we have unearthed thousands of euphemisms on a wide variety of topics—enough for several additional volumes. We remind ourselves of the old lady carted off to the psychiatrist because her family considered her "off her rocker." When the doctor asked her why she was there, she replied, "Do you like pancakes, Doctor?" "Yes," he answered. "There's nothing abnormal about that." "Oh, good," she cried. "Come over to my house. I have trunks full!" So do we, our own and others'.

Because we have trunks full, we have been forced to omit not only individual euphemisms on the topics we do include, but also whole topics such as business, medicine and ethnicity. We have chosen to begin at the beginning with subjects we consider most basic to human thought and language—love, death, the human body. In selecting specific entries, we have considered such factors as: frequency of usage, historical interest, richness of linguistic association, unusual color or flavor and social implications. We have sometimes been capricious. If we liked a euphemism and found it interesting, we included it. But we have also attempted to be historical and informative. When we could find the date of the approximate first use of a term, we indicated it. When the etymology was accessible, we recorded it. And we have occasionally speculated on etymology, the relation of one term to another and date of use—always sharing with our readers the fact that we were speculating.

In collecting our pancakes, we have had to ask ourselves when a word is a euphemism and when it is not. We have found that vulgarisms, slang, acronyms, jargon and technical terminology may indeed be euphemistic. Much, of course, depends on the speaker and his audience. For example, a vulgarism may become a euphemism when it is less distressing to the speaker and the listener than the more orthodox term it disguises. Slang is often euphemistic when it is sufficiently arcane, that is, when it is the property of a limited group of people "in the know." In this case, the substitution of a slang word for a more widely known one that is unacceptable allows slang to function as euphemism. The same is true of jargon, which, because of its limited accessibility, is particularly effective as a concealment device. Acronyms are euphemistic when they cloak obscenities, as does "snafu" (situation normal, all fucked up), when they mask the unpleasant, as does "DOA" (dead on arrival), or when they neutralize the frightening or forbidding, as does "ICBM" (intercontinental ballistic missile). Last, the speaker who utters a word, the conditions under which it is uttered and the person to whom it is addressed will often determine whether that word is a euphemism.

VULGARISM OR EUPHEMISM?

As we have noted, it is often difficult to distinguish euphemisms from vulgarisms. The differences in tone that separate the two may be clear enough but the problems of manners and usage muddy the waters. Clearly, such words as "prick," "boobs" and "snatch" are vulgar. Nevertheless, when one asks English speakers if they are more embarrassed by saying "penis" or "prick"; "breasts" or "boobs"; "vagina" or "snatch," one hears surprising answers. Often, the formal but direct term causes speakers more discomfort than the vulgarism. This is one of the conditions in which a vulgarism may be a euphemism. Because such terms as "knockers," "bum(s)" and "exhaust pipe" strike many speakers as less offensive than the more standard names for them, we have included them in this book. They are usually marked "questionably euphemistic," "vulgar" or "vulgar euphemism." The last definition is a contradiction in terms of logic, but not of social usage.

THE TRADITION

This book could not have been written without the works of Eric Partridge, Clarence Barnhart, Harold Wentworth and Stuart Berg Flexner, David Powis, G. A. Wilkes, William Safire, and Cyril Beeching and such classics as Farmer and Henley, Grose, and Berry. In short, we are indebted to a whole tradition of amateur and professional lexicographers before us. Our largest debt of gratitude is to the second greatest story ever told, that recorded in the *OED* (*Oxford English Dictionary*). Despite its reticences and minor oversights, it remains the Omniscient Edifying Delight. Midway through the compiling of this volume, Hugh Rawson's *Dictionary of Euphemisms* appeared. We are part, therefore, of a new lexicographical tradition in the making, one that will join an older and larger tradition of dictionaries of slang, invective, jargon and bawdy.

For purposes of clarity and design, the euphemisms in the entries in this book have been set in large and small capital letters except where they occur within quotations.

without
will gave it

Acknowledgments

This book would have been impossible to write without the assistance of many institutions and individuals; all gave their help graciously and intelligently. First, we are indebted to the dedicated professionals who work in libraries great and small. These include the librarians of the Columbia University Libraries, Yeshiva University Library, the New York Public Library, the Library of Congress, the New York Police Academy Library, the United States Army Library, the British Library and the Westminster Borough Library.

Public officials on both sides of the Atlantic gave generously of their time and knowledge. The staffs of Congressman Ted Weiss and Senator Daniel Patrick Moynihan assisted us in both the local and federal spheres. In Washington, D.C., we were generously helped by Ed Hinker (USICA), Bruce Gregory (USAPCD), Philip Shipman (staff, Senate Judiciary Committee) and Lt. Colonel Gerald A. Grohowski (Public Affairs, U.S. Army, DOD). In the United Kingdom, The Honorable Peter Brooke (The Member for Westminster), Brigadier Guy

Watkins (Public Relations, Army, MOD) and the officers of the Press Bureau of New Scotland Yard were invaluable expediters and sources of information.

Our colleagues and friends in the academic world gave unstintingly of their time and skill. Among them are Professors Flavia Alaya, Nina Auerbach, (Dean) Karen Bacon, Blanche Blank, Frederick Cassidy, Michael Chernoff, Joshua Fishman, Laurel Hatvary, Lee Pederson, Walter Scheps and Carl Woodring. Yeshiva University provided a grant for the purchase of research materials, and the Institute for Research in History gave advice and technical assistance.

A great portion of our debt is that which we owe to the many friends and acquaintances who gave us their counsel, euphemisms and technical assistance. Chief among these is Lee Waldman. Valuable assistance was rendered by the following: Joseph Aloe, Isabel Balson, Lance Blackstone, the late Professor Harry G. Brown, Martin Cutts and Elaine Karpson and Chrissie Maher of the Plain English Society (U.K.), Dr. Joseph R. Dunlap, Shelley Frier, Harry Huff, Mother, Adam Neaman, Peter Neaman, Amy Page, Dr. Leonard Roberts, Merton Sarnoff, Ester Scheps, Christie Tolstoy and Laurence Urdang.

None of this would have been possible without the effort, talent and intelligence of our editors at and those associated with Facts On File. Edward Knappman begot and parented this project. Joe Reilly, Ophelia Batalion and Irma Garlick helped to mature it.

Our greatest debt is to the English language and the people who speak it and write it. We have heard it in the movies and on such television programs as "Donahue," "All in the Family", "Saturday Night Live," "The Fall and Rise of Reginald Perrin," "Fawlty Towers" and both local and national news programs in the United States and the United Kingdom. We have read it in British and American magazines and newspapers and we have relished it in the works of superb mystery writers from Agatha Christie to P.D. James, from Dashiell Hammett to Emma Latham. We have overheard it on the street corners of America and the park benches of Britain.

Introduction

Michael Flanders, of the great British comedy team Flanders and Swann, once said, "The purpose of satire is to strip off the veneer of comforting illusion and cozy half-truth, and our job, as I see it, is to put it back again." There is, perhaps, no better description of the meaning and role of euphemisms. The word "euphemism" comes from the Greek *eu*, "good," and *pheme*, "speech" or "saying," and thus means literally "to speak with good words or in a pleasant manner." Euphemizing is generally defined as substituting an inoffensive or pleasant term for a more explicit, offensive one, thereby veneering the truth by using kind words.

THE HISTORY OF EUPHEMISMS

The subject of the earliest euphemism was undoubtedly religious. Gods, whether benign or malevolent, were treated with respect amounting to terror. Since the names of gods were considered identical with them, to speak a name was to evoke the divinity whose power then had to be confronted. Such dangerous practices were reserved for priests skilled in nego- tiating with the supernatural. Even they were often forbidden to utter the real names of the powers. Consequently, priests devised indirect forms of reference to calm the spirit or avert the wrath of a deity.

Gods could be referred to by their attributes (the Thunderer), by their symbols or domains (the Rock), by their titles (the Lord), or by partial or code forms of their names, as in the famous tetragrammaton (the four-letter word composed of four phonemes of the name of the god of the Jews). Perhaps most mysterious of all the types of religious euphemism was that convoluted variety which referred to the gods by naming what they were not.

This form is exemplified in the ancient Greek terms for the Furies—the *Eumenides* or *Erinyes. Eumenides* means "the kindly ones" or "the friendly ones" and the *Erinyes,* "the revered ones." But neither of these pleasant references ac- curately describes the doglike, blood-thirsty creatures of ven- geance who stalked transgressors of tribal law. These two euphemisms served in part to tame the terrifying goddesses or at least to avert their attention. Diluted to the level of low comedy, this same practice survives in the French term for the modern Fury, the mother-in-law, who is called "the beautiful mother" (*la belle-mère).* Even today we often skirt the name of God and call the devil by a thousand titles ranging from "the Big D" to "Lord of the Flies."

The very instinct we have identified as religious extends further into the many domains of taboo that are dominated by a strong conviction about the magic power of words. Foremost of these realms is that of death, once a god in most societies. When death was lord, he was feared and euphemized for all the same reasons other deities were. To name him was to invoke him. However, conversely, knowing his many names might render the namer superior to him. Hence the multiplicity of terms for any god or his powers. Today we think of euphemisms for death as mere manifestations of our unwillingness to deal with it, but anthropologically these names are vestiges of our struggle against an adversary—a battle in which the weapons were words.

The other face of death was birth, an equally mysterious and vital event. Since birth has been associated with sex only recently in the course of human thought, the taboos surrounding it were originally social and religious rather than sexual. The now famous hypothesis of Benjamin Lee Whorf that language is a reflection of culture and carries vestigial patterns once dominant in a society[1] is especially apparent in euphemisms of birth and sexuality. For example, buried in the western European adage that the stork brings babies is the ancient belief that children are made by the contact of a woman with a totem—in this case, the stork.

Which subjects and what portions of them were acceptable or forbidden have varied both from culture to culture and from one historical period to another within a single culture. In Anglo-Saxon society, which we love to cite as the golden age of linguistic freedom and the source of our great non-euphemistic four-letter words, great care was taken not to offend political or religious leaders or the gods. Although innuendos and direct references to sex were rife, there were, indeed, also euphemistic expressions for prostitution, fertility, childbearing and successful seduction.

Many of the taboos current during the Anglo-Saxon era survived until the fourteenth century. Chaucer's Pardoner in *The Canterbury Tales* rails against those who rend the body of Christ by swearing on parts of it: "by his nailes," "by Goddes precious herte," "by the blood of Crist." On the other hand, Chaucer seems hardly to bat an eyelash at describing a woman's most intimate parts and her frank use of them for engendering. His famous Wife of Bath, though apparently bold and forthright, is actually a mistress of sexual euphemism. Chaucer's use of her illustrates one of the linguistic tendencies of euphemism that was to flower in Shakespeare. The Wife employs indirect references to sex to amplify, to multiply, to amuse and to seduce—never to avoid. What is apparently a delicacy about direct reference to sexuality is actually a delight in spicing her conversation with as many and as varied allusions to it as possible.

In the sixteenth century, Shakespeare simply begins where the Wife of Bath ended. With his genius for double entendre in a society receptive to moral and linguistic flexibility, Shakespeare was ideally placed to thrust an arsenal of sexual innuendos into each dramatic speech and sonnet. He reflects his society's panache and its strange mixture of religiosity and irreverence in his characters' words about swearing. In *Henry IV, Part I*, Hotspur urges his wife to swear "a good mouth-filling oath" instead of the meeching little expressions middle-class ladies are wont to use. In both this play and *King Lear*, there are swearing contests in which the laurels go to the hardiest and most inventive curser. What this reflects is not merely a willingness to entertain and expand invective, but also the importance of class structure in setting linguistic patterns. The swearers are aristocrats who can afford, because of their social immunity, to ape the manners of the lower classes. At the same time, the aristocracy was developing its own elaborate court language. Characterized by circumlocutions and amplifications, or, in other words, beatings around the bush, runnings around in circles, and excessive verbiage, this courtly argot was known as *euphuism* and was given its name by the author John Lyly who employed it in a satirical work called *Euphues* (1578). It is perhaps significant that, by the early 1580s, the author George Blount used the term "euphemism" in English, defining it as "a good or favorable interpretation of a bad word." Although the terms "euphuism" and "euphemism" do not have the same meaning, they both describe a manner of speaking that leans toward indirectness in the service of pleasantness.

While the aristocracy served as an inventive and even radical force in making language, the middle class was conservative, eschewing direct reference to sex, the Lord, death and the excretory functions—in fact, to nearly everything but money. James I of England, whose coronation ceremony of 1603 was dramatically interrupted by a group of petitioners from the rising Dissenters of the middle class, in 1623 signed an act levying a fine of 12d. on any blaspheming. Thus, he became the first English monarch to decree a fine against swearing. This event signaled the start of a reign of middle-class attitudes that would exercise strong restraints against not only religious but also political invective. The seventeenth century was to prove a hothouse of governmental and political, even more than sexual, euphemism.

After the Puritan revolution, with the restoration of an aristocractically oriented monarch in 1660, the restrictions against overtly sexual language were relaxed. A burst of linguistic inventiveness and a host of new and colorful terms for body parts and sexual practices were audible on the stage and legible in the new literature. But political language was still leashed and was to remain so, inspiring a continuing and growing number of political works that used elaborate circumlocutions and indirections to disguise references to political parties, policies and persons. Perhaps the best known of these is *Gulliver's Travels*, filled with undisguised dirty jokes and carefully veiled political innuendos.

With neo-classicism, euphemizing often took a Latin turn. The quest for a more decorous language promulgated a host of medical, scientific and polite expressions for vital and sexual functions. In an age that strove for classical dignity and elegance, the tendency to Latinize spilled over into perfectly innocent areas, while periphrasis became a stylistic consummation devoutly to be wished. Thus Alexander Pope would refer to fish as "the finny tribe" and scissors as a "little engine" and a "glittering forfex," and John Cleland, in writing his infamous *Fanny Hill*, would produce a world-famous pornographic novel without using a single vulgarism. But spoken language retained its bawdiness until it reached the pages of a book, whereupon it was instantly attired in peacock's feathers.

By the nineteenth century, middle- and lower-class influence had expanded and enriched the vocabulary and formation of euphemisms. Among the lower classes, the cockneys—those born within the sound of the bells of St. Mary-le-Bow in

London—were a noteworthy source of intricate and inventive language patterns.[2] Their rhyming slang drew on common experience and canny observation and called upon the speaker's native ingenuity every time it was spoken. It was and has remained a powerful force. Thieves, and criminals of every other sort, also added their cants and jargons to the language. Whereas the motives of these sub-cultures had been to create a secret language that would conceal their illicit dealings, the motives of their middle-class countrymen who were also enriching the language were more varied. Eager to escape the seamy effects of the Industrial Revolution, middle-class speakers and writers found hundreds of words that assisted them in avoiding the subjects of labor, money, sex, death and sin of every sort. Although the Victorians are constantly tarred with priggery and prudishness, this clean-up campaign was in effect long before Victoria ascended the throne in 1837.

In 1805, James Plumtre edited a Shakespearean song book in which he conscientiously whitewashed the naughty bard. Thomas Bowdler, from whose name comes our verb "bowdlerize," had been dead for thirteen years before the Queen's coronation. His expurgated Shakespeare, "suitable for the family," and the ancestor of the now familiar "family show" on television, appeared in 1818. A still more grandiose project was his expurgated version of Gibbon's *Decline and Fall of the Roman Empire*, from which the word "fall" should really have been eliminated.

Still, there can be no doubt that middle-class Victorians did perpetrate and amplify a euphemistic tradition. The Victorian lexicon of "frillies," "unmentionables" and "inexpressibles" came to reflect the shock that the general populace felt at encountering subjects never before publicized. For if language showed greater moral restraint, historical and social events revealed the beginnings of a veritable moral revolution. The middle class was to express shock and horror at the exposure of subjects that had formerly been considered private. When Oscar Wilde was publicly tried for homosexuality, a subject never before quite so widely aired, he defended his particular taste as "the love that dare not speak its name."

The reconciliation of the apparently opposed gentility of language and amorality of behavior was best summarized by the actress Mrs. Patrick Campbell. "You can do anything," (by implication, also say anything), she observed, "as long as you don't do it in the street and frighten the horses." What mattered was not the immoral act but public knowledge of it. Moral liberation was to begin to appear with such figures as D. H. Lawrence. But it is significant that this advocate of open sexuality, himself a Victorian, used fewer dirty words than euphemisms as he preached his gospel of sensuality.

In the eighteenth and nineteenth centuries, British euphemism was developing abroad as well as at home. As the British Empire expanded, the linguistic pattern of the mother country traveled with it. The British colonies were dependencies in language as well as in politics. Though Australians, Canadians, and Americans would coin euphemisms with the local color of their new lands and lives, the patterns of formation would follow those of the English middle class.

Australia, like England, often formed euphemisms by means of rhyming slang, but its special flavor is exactly what one would expect it to be: a mixture of Botany Bay prisoner cant, transplanted middle-class rancher and farmer terminology, the breezy argot of the vast outback and exotic borrowings from the aboriginal tongues. South African euphemisms take much of their special quality from Afrikaans and local dialects. But above all, they eschew indirection of any kind and an uniquely South African euphemism is a rare species. The sources of Canadian euphemism are more varied. Like America, Canada is a melting pot and draws upon a variety of cultures and languages including French, Middle European, native Indian, Eskimo, and, of course, the Queen's English. There is a constant border trade as Americanisms seep north and Canadianisms trickle south. The two countries have much in common, sharing above all a frontier background and the genteelizing tendency of their middle-class language makers.

From the beginning, American euphemisms reflected the

desires for both piety and gentility that impelled some of the earliest settlers to seek these shores. Best known for their concern with language were the Puritans, who enacted laws against profanity. The resurgence of the Puritan impulse was felt during the Great Awakening of the 1740s and its revival in 1829. One of the fruits of these attitudes was Noah Webster's expurgated Bible of 1833. By the nineteenth century, American language was showing the effects of the Industrial Revolution, which had created new types of employment with new languages and new social mobility. Now, more than ever, social refinement was considered a cardinal virtue. Sometimes the results were ridiculous. Mrs. Trollope reported that a German gentleman of perfectly good manners had offended one of America's first families by pronouncing the word "corset" aloud. This tendency to genteelize was apparently particularly prevalent among American women. As their status changed with the changing society and the growth of new territories, they came to exercise an increasingly powerful influence that led not only to genteelizing but also to sentimentalizing.

The sentimental impulse generated a large lexicon of euphemisms for both love and death. Among the great treasuries of American euphemisms are nineteenth-century graveyards. While the classic carvings of the weeping willow evade the harsh reality of the simple coffin beneath, the text or verse on such stones ranges from the pathetic to the bathetic. One epitaph reads: "Our Lamb is with His Maker." Another proclaims:

> Under this sod and under these trees
> Here lies the body of Solomon Pease.
> Only his bones are here on these leas
> For his soul is shelled out and gone to God.

Yet, while these verses were being written, America too was undergoing a linguistic revolution. Walt Whitman—who decreed that all subjects, the sensual, the unconventional, even "the kitchen," were meat for poetry—was America's D. H.

Lawrence. But these changes were not to be dramatically felt until the roar of the twenties and the bold glitter of Hollywood generated new terms, new images and new attitudes.

The greatest changes in American language were felt after World Wars I and II[3] and during the 1960s counterculture movement—itself a reaction to war. Obviously linguistic change has reflected cultural change. Someday it may amuse a linguistic historian to note that in the 1980s the richest subjects of American euphemism were money, disease, politics and war.

THE FORMATION OF EUPHEMISMS

However culturally and historically based particular euphemisms may be, the psychological and linguistic patterns underlying their formation are the same. Psychologically, if not linguistically, meaning can be defined as the sum of our responses to a word or an object. Words themselves may be seen as responses to stimuli. After a word has been associated for a long period of time with the stimulus that provokes it, the word itself picks up aspects of the response elicited by the stimulus object. When unpleasant elements of response attach themselves strongly to the word used to describe them, we tend to substitute another word free of these negative associations. In this way, psychologists tell us, euphemisms are formed.[4] Take, for example, the word "vomit." Here, the unpleasantness of the stimulus attaches to the word and, to avoid a negative response, we find new terms such as WHOOPS and FLASH for the same phenomenon. Eventually, the same unpleasant response will be evoked by these new terms and we will, consciously or unconsciously, invent euphemistic substitutes for them. In this way, the euphemistic vocabulary is constantly varied and enriched.

Joseph M. Williams suggests five general semantic processes by means of which euphemisms are created,[5] but there are others as well.

1. Most obviously, euphemisms may be made by

borrowing words from other languages—terms that are less freighted with negative associations. Thus, we use Greek and Latin expressions for many bodily parts and functions. We have coined HALITOSIS (bad breath) from the Latin *halitus* for breath and we have substituted MICTURITION for the more vulgar Indo-European "piss."

2. Euphemisms may be made by a semantic process called *widening.* When a specific term becomes too painful or vivid, we move up in the ladder of abstraction. In this way, cancer becomes A GROWTH and a girdle becomes A FOUNDATION. Sometimes, in addition to widening, we divide the negative connotations of a single direct term between two or more words. Instead of saying "syphillis" openly, we speak of a SOCIAL DISEASE. We lessen the impact of the term "feces" by referring to it as SOLID HUMAN WASTE.

3. Allied to the phenomenon of *widening* is that of *semantic shift.* This is the substitution of the whole, or a similar generality, for the specific part we do not choose to discuss. We may create such metonymies (substitutions of the whole for the part) as REAR END for "buttocks." Sometimes, as in the expressions TO SLEEP WITH or TO GO TO BED WITH someone, we use words naming the larger event in place of more precise references to the sexual relations that are part of the process.

4. Euphemisms may be made by a process called *metaphorical transfer,* the comparison of things of one order to things of another. The euphemism BLOSSOM for a "pimple" compares one flowering to another more acceptable variety. The euphemisms chosen are often romanticizings, poeticizings and softenings of the original word. But styles in language change and such current vulgarisms as "cherry" (for hymen) were once thought poetically euphemistic.

5. Euphemisms may be created by *phonetic distortion.*

When we encounter words that dare not speak their names, we *abbreviate, apocopate* (shorten or omit the last syllable), *initial, convert, backform* and *reduplicate* them. We may also *distort their sounds* and create *diminutives* and *blend words.*[6]

- *Abbreviation* is the shortening of a word and may be seen in the use of the British expression LADIES for LADIES' ROOM.
- *Apocopation* is another form of *abbreviation*, apparent in the use of VAMP for "vampire," here meaning a seductive woman.
- *Initialing* is the use of acronyms instead of their component parts, as in JC for "Jesus Christ."
- *Backforming* is the substitution of one part of speech (used in shortened form) for another, as in BURGLE (rob), which is derived from "burglar."
- *Reduplication* is the repetition of a syllable or letter of a word. Particularly common in children's bathroom vocabulary, it substitutes PEE-PEE for "piss."
- *Phonetic distortion* is the changing of a sound in a word. It is audible in such terms are CRIPES ("Christ") and GAD ("God").
- A *blend word* is a form of *phonetic distortion* in which two or more words are squeezed together both orthographically and phonetically. An example of this is GEZUNDA for a chamber pot, a term derived from the fact that this object "goes under" the bed.
- A *diminutive* is the formation of a new term by nicking or shortening a name and adding a suffix indicating affection or smallness. HEINIE, for example, is the diminutive of "hind end" and refers to the "buttocks."

Just as there are cultural and linguistic traits common to the formation of euphemisms, so there are general tendencies that shape changes in language, and these are found in all cultures. Words with neutral connotations, for example, tend to polarize, becoming either laudatory or pejorative because of the nuances they attract.[7] Often, when a word develops strong negative connotations, we create a milder, more positive term, or euphemism, for it.

Sometimes, because of an accidental resemblance between words with different meanings, one word "contaminates" another. For example, the similarity in sound between "niggard" and "nigger"—two words unrelated in origin and meaning—may lead to the avoidance of the former term[8] and its replacement by a euphemism such as THRIFTY or NEAR.

Occasionally, a linguistic tendency called *elevation* creates euphemistic phrases. A "penthouse," the magnificent domain of the rich, is really an elevated form of "pentice," a lean-to shack. In this case, a word is applied to an object more highly esteemed than its early referrent. This language change, however, also reflects the social change that preceded it. Those who lived in cities and could afford a lean-to-like structure on a rooftop were, in fact, living more elegantly. One elevation reflects another.

Degradation, the opposite tendency, appears when a formerly polite or acceptable term gradually dwindles into a negative one. In the fourteenth century, "uncouth" simply meant "unknown." It later took on the meanings of "crass," "crude" and "vulgar" because anyone who was aristocratic was obviously well known. Today, "uncouth" is a profound insult and has lost its original meaning.

As Joseph Shipley has pointed out, taboo or forbidden meanings of a word drive out its competing general or acceptable ones in a sort of Gresham's Law of language. Thus, for example, GAY, which has become the property of the homosexual community, is no longer primarily used as a synonym for "happy" or "vivacious."[9] "A gay party" is no longer a phrase used to describe a lively gathering but has the specific connotation of a social occasion for homosexuals.

The result of all these tendencies is the constant need for new terms to replace older ones that have become too specialized, loaded or negative. The numbers of euphemisms for any particular topic reflect the strength and sometimes the longevity of the taboo originally responsible for euphemizing.

THE MOTIVES FOR EUPHEMIZING

The motives for generating euphemisms are as diverse and as universal as the range of human emotions. As we said earlier, fear and a desire to placate the mysterious forces that rule the universe were probably the original reasons for euphemizing.[10] In diluted and subtler forms, these underlying impulses are still with us today; we lard our sentences with expressions like "knock on wood" without ever thinking that we do so to avert evil. We are subject to other varieties of fear as well. Afraid to flout social and moral conventions, we refer to our lovers as COMPANIONS, thus disguising the unconventional or socially unacceptable nature of the relationship. Our fear of specific diseases has led us to coin a lexicon of euphemisms for insanity and retardation, epilepsy, venereal disease, cancer, heart disease and stroke. We also suffer from a generalized terror of every sort of DISABILITY—the word itself is a euphemism—and disfigurement and, while we fear these conditions, we are equally afraid of the social rejection that might attach to us if we had them.

Another motive for contemporary euphemizing is our strong desire to avoid offending others. This fear of causing psychic pain, this desire to be well thought of leads us to use "kind words"; we prefer to DISCONTINUE rather than to "fire" employees. In our eagerness to avoid deflating our egos and those of others, we often create euphemisms that inflate them, for example by conferring overblown titles on people, places and jobs. The term "professor" has been attached to bartenders, magicians and snake oil salesmen, as well as academics. The terms "institute" and "college" have been applied to schools for auto mechanics, television repairmen, barbers, embalmers and others.

The sentimentalizing tendency we noted above is still an ever present force behind the euphemisms we create when we refer to "the wife" as THE LITTLE WOMAN and "old age" as THE GOLDEN YEARS. If, in the spirit of the new frankness of speech, this sentimental bent is on the wane, it will be replaced by new motivations for creating new euphemisms. For the nature of euphemism is change. Obviously, ours is a period of change, and it will be fascinating to observe where we next turn our linguistic attention. Will it be to war, computers, human emotion or some hitherto completely unconsidered subject?

NOTES

1. Benjamin Lee Whorf, *Language, Thought, and Reality*, ed. J. B. Carroll (New York: John Wiley and Sons, 1964).
2. Joseph T. Shipley, *In Praise of English* (New York: New York Times Books, 1977).
3. Albert H. Markwardt, *American English*, 2nd ed., rev. by J. L. Dillard (New York: Oxford University Press, 1980), p. 132.
4. Joseph M. Williams, *Origins of the English Language* (New York: Free Press, 1957), pp. 202–203.
5. Williams, pp. 200–202.
6. See Williams and Shipley.
7. Williams, p. 207.
8. James D. Gordon, *The English Language: An Historical Introduction* (New York: Thomas Y. Crowell, 1972), pp. 28, 29, also discusses *elevation* and *degradation*.
9. Shipley, p. 158.
10. See Shipley for another discussion.

1

Parts of the Body : Forbidden Territory

When Nathaniel Hawthorne died in 1864, his wife, Sophia Peabody (of the Boston Peabodys), carefully edited his journals, removing all references to the leg and substituting the word "limb." And this was no wonder in an age when even piano limbs were discreetly covered and chairs wore skirts. By the 1920s, the female leg was, for the first time since ancient Greece, on public view. Since that era the trend to expose and to discuss the more specifically sexual portions of the body has grown rapidly. But we should not think that all the varied terms for parts of the body are modern or American. In eighteenth-century England, enthusiastic lovers eulogized their ladies' bosoms and, by the nineteenth century, they and their American cousins were properly naming the intimate areas of the human body.

When terms arise and multiply tells us something about when specific parts of the human anatomy were particularly fascinating and/or forbidden. The Middle Ages seemed obsessed with the hindquarters and with the now innocent neck, chin and forehead. Shakespeare, a master but not a mincer of words, went straight for the genitalia. Each age may pick its part, but the overall ambivalence toward the "too, too solid flesh" does not melt. A delighted preoccupation shows in the vast number and variety of euphemisms of which this section can represent only a small portion. A scandalized disapproval is apparent in the deliberate vagueness and indirectness of many of the terms.

The imagery of anatomy seems to fall predominantly into five subject categories:

1. Machinery, as in COFFEE GRINDER for the vagina
2. Food and plants, as in CABBAGE PATCH for the vagina
3. Geography, as in BRISTOL CITIES (rhyming slang) and MOUNTAINS for breasts
4. Hypothetical persons, as in the infamous JOHN THOMAS for the MEMBRUM VIRILE
5. Indefinites, as in WHATCHAMACALLIT for the penis

Whatever the category, euphemisms for the specifically sexual portions of the anatomy tend to function in one of two ways. They either enhance and glamorize—as in the term GOLDEN DOUGHNUT for the vulva—or they conceal and banalize—as in THING for the male genitals. Thus the forbidden territory of the body becomes, in the hands of the euphemist, either an exotic paradise or a footworn path unworthy of notice.

NUDITY

ALTOGETHER, IN THE   This expression was first used by George du Maurier in *Trilby* (1894) to refer to the nude form in a painting. In that novel the artist's model says: "I sit for the altogether." A form of the word, ALTOGETHERY, which meant drunk, was used by Byron in a letter of 1816. Its connotation there (that a drunken man lounged about) may have influenced the later use of the term to denote the relaxed or lounging pose of a nude model. By 1895, a *New York Mercury* headline used the phrase to mean simply nudity when it asked the question: "Will the next fad be photographs of modern woman taken in the 'altogether'?" Another expression that avoids the already delicate "naked as the day he (or she) was born" is IN THE BUFF. "Buff skin" or "buff-leather" was an early term for tanned leather, especially deer hide, and by 1602 the playwright Dekker was using buff to mean bare skin when he wrote, "I go in stag, in buff." In 1591 TO GO IN STAG meant to go naked. IN THE BUFF or IN BUFF was simply a seventeeth-century replacement for IN STAG since both meant deer or deerskin.

AU NATUREL A current American phrase for "naked," this euphemism functions partially by substituting presumably elegant French for coarse English. Nevertheless, it means simply WEARING ONLY WHAT MOTHER NATURE PROVIDED. In this condition one is presumably nakeder than one would be if DRESSED IN NOTHING BUT A FIG LEAF (see **BIRTHDAY SUIT**).

BIRTHDAY SUIT, IN ONE'S This phrase possibly comes from the English custom of the king's buying a new suit of clothes for his retainers on the royal birthday. Another explanation is that it simply means what one wore at one's birth, i.e., nothing. Still in use in Britain, Canada and the United States, it has enjoyed a number of variations. According to the *OED*, a form of BIRTHDAY SUIT was introduced in 1731 and the actual phrase as we use it today was not defined in a lexicon until 1874. In 1731, Swift referred to the state of nudity as being in one's BIRTHDAY GEAR. In 1771, Smollett, in *Humphrey Clinker*, recorded the expression in its most popular form by saying "we bathed in our birthday suit." In the 1860s, the British aristocracy called the CONDITION OF UNDRESS their BIRTHDAY ATTIRE (G. and B. Wharton in *Wits and Beaux of Society*). The *Slang Dictionary* of 1874 defines BIRTHDAY SUIT as "the suit in which Adam and Eve first saw each other 'and were not ashamed.' " From the above comes the less aristocratic but equally popular euphemism—ADAM'S AND EVE'S TOGS.

FORM, YOU'RE SHOWING YOUR You are revealing your naked flesh. This American euphemism for exhibiting one's bare skin dates from about the 1930s but was used later to refer to the wearing of short shorts or a short skirt. It reveals the survival of a prudish revulsion against the UNDRAPED FEMALE FORM (see NUDE). In 1814, a writer in the *Monthly Review* railed against those who "intended to incur the contemplation of the UNDRAPED FIGURE," a sport that has remained popular ever since.

NUDE Although the word "nude" meant bare or naked as early as the sixteenth century, it was not used as a euphemism for the naked condition of the human body until the nineteenth century except in reference to art. In 1708 (*New View of London*), E. Hatton wrote, "A nude or nudity is a naked figure sculpted without drapery or clothing." By 1857, Mrs. Browning wrote in *Aurora Leigh* of "a nude as chaste as Medicean Venus." The UNDRAPED FIGURE (see FORM) had stepped out of the canvas and into the broader world of everyday life.

STITCH ON, WITHOUT A By 1825, the word "stitch" was used to mean a piece or fragment. Hence this British and American euphemism means without a piece of clothing on. Anyone appearing thus IN THE RAW was like a hide that was untanned or UNDRESSED. In 1588, UNDRESSED meant not only in a raw state but also unkempt or inelegant. By 1818, however, those who were UNDRESSED were as scantily clad as a salad without its dressing. WITHOUT A STITCH ON, now synonymous with UNDRESSED, is a simple example of metonymy: the part (stitch) used for the whole (garment).

BREASTS

BOOBS Wentworth and Flexner say that this term usually refers to "the prominent breasts of a well-developed young woman," as in "What a pair of boobs!" However, this euphemistic vulgarism may also be deprecatory for the sagging breasts of an older woman. According to Wentworth and Flexner, the term was usually used (especially during the 1950s) by a male in talking to another male about a woman. Another euphemism of that ilk is GLOBES, which is somewhat more literary than the vulgar KNOCKERS (1940s and 50s). A far more discreet euphemism is the originally English and now American WHITE MEAT, which was coined in the nineteenth century to permit gentlemen who liked the breast meat of the poultry to ask for it without using the bold term "breast." One could avoid asking for the "thigh" by requesting DARK MEAT. The terms are now used directly for poultry parts and indirectly, jocularly, and somewhat archaically for the parts of a woman's body.

BUST   As a term for "breasts," BUST entered the Engish language from the French *buste* and the Italian, Spanish and Portuguese *busto* in 1727. It was used in English to mean the upper front portion of the body and the bosom, especially of a woman. As early as 1691, the word "bust" appeared in English, but it meant the upper portion of the body, especially in a sculptural representation of the head, shoulders and breast of a person. The eighteenth century specialized its use when it readapted the term, deriving it all over again from its romance language origins. By 1819, Byron could note (*Don Juan*) without any ambiguity that "There was an Irish lady to whose bust/I ne'er saw just-ice done." A British euphemism for breasts that remains in favor is FRONT. This has its more specific but equally euphemistic American counterpart in CHEST or CHESTS.

CLEAVAGE   The area between a woman's breasts, especially when revealed by a low-cut neckline. A twentieth-century American euphemism, CLEAVAGE testifies to the enduring interest in every aspect of the bosom. Another term, GOW (which first meant opium in 1915 and from the 1930s on meant CHEESECAKE or sexually appealing photographs) came to be used for CLEAVAGE. The SWEATER GIRL of the World War II era may have concealed her CLEAVAGE under her daytime sweater, but revealed it when she donned her strapless evening gown.

ELDERS This Australian euphemism dates from about 1920 and has been used in England since 1942. Partridge (*Catchwords*) says that the term may refer to an elder tree in full leaf; it may also allude to the biblical Susannah's mysterious appeal to the lecherous elders.

EYES or BIG BROWN EYES Breasts or nipples. "Where'd you get those big brown eyes?" has been an American male on-looker's question to an AMPLY ENDOWED woman since World War II, and "She's got a nice pair of eyes" has been an expression used in England since about 1950. The euphemisms for breasts are manifold; many of them record sizes and shapes and, not surprisingly, utilize analogies to food. Among the most popular on both sides of the Atlantic are LEMONS, ORANGES and GRAPEFRUITS; APPLES, PEARS and MELONS, and, of course, COCONUTS (see the song, "I've Got a Lovely Bunch of Coconuts")—all of which indicate variations in size, shape and alimentary value.

HEADLIGHTS Among the many expressions for breasts are two that may be derived from automobile anatomy—BUMPERS and HEADLIGHTS. BUMPERS may, of course, also be derived from "bumpers of ale" or from "bumps," and it is worth noticing the relationship between HEADLIGHTS and eye-terms for breasts. The list of images and references in euphemisms for breasts is nearly endless. It includes such British terms as TONSILS and LUNGS (two anatomical substitutions) and such descriptive terms as PELLETS, MOLEHILLS, RACKS and BAGS. More ingeniously, it includes such nonsense words as MOSOB ("bosom" spelled backwards) and the mysterious GAZUNGA(S).

MAE WEST, A A breast. From World War II, when the bleached blonde movie star with the opulent bosom was still at her zenith, to 1959 this term was used for a life jacket. Later it referred to the breasts the life jacket aped and was American rhyming slang for breast, as were WOOLY WEST—a Chicago coinage from the twenties—and VERY BEST (ca.

1950s). All of the terms are now obsolescent.

NORKS The origin of this Australian euphemism is uncertain, but it is possibly derived from the wrapping on Norco butter, a brand popular in New South Wales. The wrapping shows a cow's udder. The full flavor of the expression emerges in Criena Rohan's book, *The Delinquents*, 1962, when a man remarks, "Hello, Honey, that sweater—one deep breath and your norks will be in my soup." An Australian expression, "Sheila," simply meaning a girl, is the source of several other euphemisms. The rhyming slang for Sheila, "Charlie Wheeler," came to mean both a CHARLIE (a girl) and, by 1949, breasts. TRACY BITS is Australian rhyming slang for "tits" from about 1920, and its American rhyming slang parallel is BRACE AND BITS, used on the West Coast since about 1928. Another paired and rhyming euphemism, CATS AND KITTIES, appears to be widespread throughout the English-speaking world. A South African equivalent is MAMS.

SUPERDUPERS Pendant breasts. Originating in the 1940s, "superduper" originally meant colossal. Subsequently (precise date unknown), it was used in the plural to refer to large, pendant breasts. Man's enduring obsession with the size and shape of women's breasts has coined a number of euphemisms (see, for example, **BIG BROWN EYES** and **HEADLIGHTS**) another of which is HAMMOCK for medium-sized breasts. This term was apparently based upon some simple observations about analogous shape. A more exotic term for breasts of a certain size, this time small, is CHI-CHI or CHICHI. Also meaning a sexually attractive woman, this corruption of a Japanese word meaning "little breasts" entered the American lexicon during the Korean War.

THOUSAND PITIES A nineteenth-century rhyming slang term for breasts (titties), this euphemism is now obsolete but deserves to be revived. Its popular British cousin BRISTOL CITIES or BRISTOLS is very much alive. A third British rhyming slang euphemism for breasts is TALE OF TWO CITIES. (See also **NORKS**.)

TOP The date of this evasion is unknown, but the term functions simply by generalizing, as does BOTTOM (see THE POSTERIOR, **BOTTOM**) for buttocks. It has been used to mean the upper portion of the body since 1225, when it indicated the head. Head and feet, not the breasts and buttocks, are probably implied in the lines from the *Chester Plays* (1500) which urge, "Thou takest him by the top and I by the tail." "Top" is also commonly used for chicken breasts and, like the term WHITE MEAT (see **BOOBS**), obviates the necessity of saying the taboo word. (See also **BUST**, **FRONT**, and see THE GENITALS, **TAIL**.)

THE POSTERIOR

ACRE or ACHERS *A Dictionary of Australian Colloquialisms* says that this Australian euphemism was first heard in conversation in 1938 and was popular during World War II. Frank Hardy in *The Outcasts of Foolsgarah* (1971) mentions someone "falling on his acre." Roland Robinson in *The Drift of Things* (1973) describes the practices of a group of shack dwellers as follows: "Because they used to surf in the nude and lie among the flowering tea trees . . . one shack dweller called his shack 'Sunburned Acres.' "

BOTTOM The *OED* delicately defines BOTTOM as "the sitting part of a man." In 1794, the term was used by the British writer Erasmus Darwin in *Zoonomia,* and in 1835 it was playfully and punfully utilized in J. Wilson's *Noctes Ambrosiana* when the author noted that "the dunghill cock . . . hides his head in a hole . . . unashamed of his enormous bottom." Readers of James Joyce's *Ulysses* (1922) will recognize it as one of Molly Bloom's favorite obsessions.

BUM This expression was used as early as 1387, but in 1530 it appeared not in its former euphemistic or plain-talking sense but as an insult. A character from John Redforde's morality play *Wit and Science* snaps, "I would thy mother had kissed thy bum." Shakespeare's Puck restores its euphemistic connotations in *A Midsummer Night's Dream* (1590) when he delicately describes how "then slip I from her bum, down topples she." The word BUM for posterior comes from "Johnny bum," a name for a male jackass. It is a complex play upon the word "ass" as a term for posterior (ca. 1860), which was derived from a vulgar mispronunciation of the common word for buttocks, "arse," in use in England from 1000.

BUTT   BUTT is a fifteenth-century term and is most probably a shortened form of the thirteenth century word "buttock." In 1450, the word was also used to refer to a butt of pork and it is still used to mean the end of an animal limb or the thicker end of an object. In this latter sense we use it in the expressions the "butt of a gun" or a "cigarette butt." By 1860, (Bartlett's *American Dictionary*) BUTT was frequently used in the American West in such expressions as "I fell on my butt!" It is still with us in that expression and in such others as the imperative, "Get off your butt." BUTT is interchangeable with BOTTOM (q.v.), though the latter is a shade more polite, but neither is as coy as HEINIE, a diminutive of HIND END or HINDER PART. (See also **HONKIES**.)

EXHAUST PIPE   Anus. This euphemism comes from an analogy to the automobile and therefore dates back at least as far as the 1930s, a period when comparisons between the human body and the automobile were common. Other terms for the anus (dates unknown) are: the BACK GARDEN, the BACK WAY, the DIRT ROAD, the BUCKET, the HOLE or BACK HOLE, the HOOP and the KEISTER (probably from the 1940s and used liberally by S. J. Perelman). The word "keister" originally denoted the anus as a place, familiar to smugglers and prisoners, for concealing valuables. The term comes from the argot of the underworld, from which it passed in a jocular tone to the general public. A more colorful British rhyming slang term for the same part of the anatomy is ELEPHANT AND CASTLE (arsehole). The elephant, with or without his castle, was a sign on an inn dating at least from the sixteenth century. Shakespeare alludes to it in *Twelfth*

Night (1601): "In the south suburbs at the Elephant is best to lodge." One can only wonder if he intended a double entendre!

FANNY Originally, this expression was a vulgarism for the female pudendum and probably entered the language as a tribute to the protagonist of John Cleland's erotic novel of 1749, *Fanny Hill.* Its use as a vulgarism for the pudendum was common by the 1860s in Britain and remains so. The American meaning of the word—BACKSIDE—probably originated in the nineteenth century. A jocular euphemism for it, popular in America in the 1950s, was FRANCIS—utilized in such expressions as "You're a pain in the francis."

HONKIES This current euphemism, now considered somewhat vulgar but still indirect, comes from the English expression for a squatting position—ON ONE'S HUNKERS, which dates from the late eighteenth century. HONKIES is but one of the seemingly infinite number of euphemisms for the posterior. The list includes: AFTERS, AFTER PART, BACKSIDE, SEAT, SOFT PEAT (rhyming slang for seat), BACKSEAT, RUMBLE SEAT, REAR, REAR END, REAR GUARD, BEHIND, BRUNSWICK, CABOOSE, DERRIÈRE, LATTER END or PART, HIND END, RAIL, HOOTENANNY, KEEL, LABONZA (also meaning the pit of the stomach), PARKING PLACE, PATELLAS (from the medical word for the knee bone or knees), POOP, STERN, PRAT, RUMP, RUMPUS, RUSTY-DUSTY, SOUTHERN EXPOSURE, TAIL, TAIL END, WHATSUS, SUNDAY FACE, CHEEKS and SECOND FACE. The "second face" was a term used in witchcraft rituals for the devil's REAR END, the kissing of which sealed a pact between the novice witch and Satan. We have not been able to ascertain the dates of origin.

IRELAND The POSTERIOR of a woman or perhaps the urinary and defecatory organs. In *The Comedy of Errors* (1591), we read, "In what part of her body stands Ireland?" "Marry, Sir, in the buttocks: I found it out by the bogs." In 1785, Grose, whose national slurs were cosmic, explained the connection between the euphemism and the nation by describing Ireland as "the Urinal of the Planets" because of its wet climate.

THE GENITALS

PRIVATES   External sex organs of both males and females. This euphemism is a shortening of the more formal term PRIVATE PARTS. It was first used in 1634 by Sir Thomas Herbert. Describing his travels in Africa and Asia, he speaks of natives using a cloth that should "cover those parts made to be private." PRIVATE PARTS seems to have been used in England and America as a medical term during the late nineteenth century.

TAIL   Male or female genitals, but usually the female; also (as early as 1303) the buttocks. Robert Mannyng of Brunne in his handbook on sins, *Handlynge Synne,* used the expression "Go to hell, both top and tail" about 1303. Later in the four-teenth century, Chaucer punned frequently on "tail" and "tale" or "tally" (a way of counting up money exchanged during business transactions). His most precise equation be-tween the animal tail and the genitals appears in *The Wife of Bath's Prologue* (1387) when he gives the wife a triple pun: "A liquorous mouth must have a liquorous tail" (a mouth full of liquor begets lechery at the other end). The term TAIL was elaborated on and varied so that a child's penis has been called a WAG, a term used first to describe both a roguish man and later a rascally child. Consider also the nursery rhyme: "What are little boys made of? Snakes [or "Slugs"] and snails and puppy dogs' tails."

THING, ONE'S   The genitals, male or female, the PRIVY MEMBERS or PRIVATE PARTS. In 1387, Chaucer's Wife of Bath referred to "thynges smale" (SMALL THINGS) and called her PRIVY PARTS her BEL(L)E CHOSE (modern French *belle chose,* "pretty thing"). Shakespeare used the term to mean both penis and pudendum. As the former, we find in *King Lear* (1605) the statement that "she shall not be a maid long

---

unless things be cut shorter." In modern English, the word "thing" and its meanings have been expanded to subsume whole categories of equipment or machinery. This phenomenon is reflected in such euphemisms for the genitals as: EQUIPMENT, GADGETS, PARTS, MOVING PARTS, BUSINESS, THE BUSINESS, meaning penis, vagina, and sexual intercourse, and TO GIVE THE BUSINESS, meaning to have sexual intercourse (see Chapter 7, STRAIGHT SEX, **ACTION**, BUSINESS); the RECEIVING SET (female genitals); MACHINERY, NUTS AND BOLTS (the male genitals); NUTS (the testicles, Black English for clitoris); APPARATUS, WORKS, SECRETS, SECRET or PRIVY PARTS (both male and female genitals); THE ENGINE, KIT, LUGGAGE, BAGGAGE, THREE-PIECE SET or SUIT (the male genitals).

FEMALE GENITALS

BOX Pudendum. This somewhat vulgar euphemism dates at least from 1954 and probably originated earlier. The concept of woman as container or vessel is as ancient as the female shape of prehistoric vases, and many euphemisms for the pudendum record this fact. Although BOX is the commonest, others reflect the interplay of the sexes in such terms for the pudendum as: SCABBARD, BASKET, PURSE (see MALE GENITALS, **COBBLER'S AWLS**), POCKETBOOK, BAG, CAN.

BUTTON Clitoris. This euphemism, which arose from a comparison between the appearance of the two objects, suggests a hidden pun on sewing and sowing. It originated in 1879 and has survived to the present, giving birth to many other euphemisms with the same imagery such as: BUTTONHOLE (vagina), BUTTONHOLE WORKER (the MEMBRUM VIRILE), BUTTONHOLE WORKING (coition), a BUTTON FACTORY (a brothel). There is a naval version of BUTTONHOLE—GRUMMET—which means either the pudendum or, when used as a verb, to have intercourse. A grummet is a metal eyelet in a sail that reinforces the hole through which a rope is drawn.

CAPE HORN   The pudendum. One of the many place names used to avoid direct reference to the pudendum, this clearly suggests man's triumph in successfully rounding a distant and dangerous "cape" and the word "horn" here may also be a play upon the old term for the penis. (See Chapter 7, STRAIGHT SEX, CORNIFICATION.) Many of these geographical names suggest exploration and adventure in the real world, for example: THE CAPE OF GOOD HOPE, BOTANY BAY, and THE SOUTH POLE. Others denote dreamlike or utopian locales: THE GARDEN OF EDEN, THE GATE OF HORN, THE GATE OF LIFE, THE BOWER OF BLISS (from Spenser's *Faerie Queen*), and THE MIDDLE KINGDOM. Still others are puns such as: THE FORECASTLE, UPPER HOLLOWAY, SPORTSMAN'S GAP, SPORTSMAN'S HOLE, the LOWLANDS, JACK STRAW'S CASTLE, MARBLE ARCH (all British), the WAYSIDE FOUNTAIN, the COVERED WAY (Sterne, *Tristram Shandy*, 1760), the PALACE OF PLEASURE, the ANTIPODES, the HARBOR, and the HARBOR OF HOPE, DOWNSTAIRS, the FRONT GARDEN, the FRONT PARLOR, the ALCOVE, the TEMPLE OF VIRGINITY (current gothic novels of the 1970s and 1980s), and the FIREPLACE (like the more common OVEN). The last of these is one of the many domestic references that include the KITCHEN, the CORNER CUPBOARD and the WORKSHOP (the place where WORK, a euphemism for sexual intercourse that is parallel to BUSINESS, is done). One of the BUSINESSES described is a MILLINER'S SHOP; another is the TOY SHOP, where one PLAYS GAMES just as one does in the GYM or on the FOOTBALL FIELD (1950s). Still more "far out" are the HOTEL and the familiar VALLEY OF DECISION.

CRACKLING   The pundendum. This British and American euphemism is of uncertain date but, in the American South and in Britain, crackling, rendered pig skin or poultry skin, is a delicacy. Fellatio is, then, implied in the term. Another term for the vagina is the American ACE OF SPADES; used to mean a widow at the turn of the century, it now means the pudendum. An elaboration on the term, also from the world of cards and gambling, to PLAY ONE'S ACE OF SPADES AND RECEIVE THE JACK now means to have sexual intercourse.

DOUGHNUT, GOLDEN Vulva. This Australian expression dates from the 1970s. G. A. Wilkes cites a particularly illuminating use of it in David Williamson's *The Removalists.* A character, crowing over a conquest, says "We'll be in like Flynn there tomorrow night. We'll thread the eye of the golden doughnut."

GRASS Pubic hair, usually female. One series of euphemisms for female sexual organs or for secondary sexual characteristics is based upon analogies to Mother Nature. Current American terms include GRASS, BUSHES, and BIRD'S NEST for pubic hair, THE CLOUDS for the pudendum, and THE ARBOR and THE BEEHIVE for both the *mons* and pubic hair. Other terms for the latter include BEAVER, MUFF and HAT.

HA'PENNY (HALFPENNY) Pudendum. This euphemism is used in British English and is current among women. Just as men see their sexual parts in terms of value (see MALE GENITALS, JEWELS) or a rate of exchange, so do women. Terms for female genitals include THE TREASURY, AN ORNAMENT and THE EXCHEQUER (British).

JOHN HUNT, THE The pudendum. This jocular euphemism is one of many rhyming slang phrases used to replace the vulgar FOUR-LETTER WORD. Others are SHARP AND BLUNT, GRUMBLE AND GRUNT, and BERKELEY HUNT. Similar to these are puns that, like Hamlet's reference to "country matters," play on the pudendum as the COUNTRY, BOGS and LOW COUNTRY.

LADY JANE or JANE This euphemism—a vulgarism when it was first used in about 1850—was one of the most famous of the many British proper names for the female genitals. It was popularized by D. H. Lawrence's *Lady Chatterley's Lover* (1928). Sometimes shortened to LADY, the term takes such polite and Standard English forms as LADY-FLOWER and LADY-STAR. The female genitals are also known by other women's names including BLACK BESS, AUNT MARIA (British or American), DAISY and, of course, EVE. Grose's *Dictionary* (1785) derived EVE from EVE'S CUSTOM HOUSE—"where Adam made the first entry." They are also called VENUS, VENUS'S CELL, VENUS'S TEMPLE, VENUS'S HIGHWAY, and MONS MEG (compare MONS VENERIS).

MAIDENHEAD Hymen. This euphemism is derived from the Middle English word for maidenhood, pronounced "maiden-hede" (head), which originated in 1250, when the English translations of Genesis and Exodus record that "Sichem took her maiden-hed." In 1357, the *Lay Folks Catechism* asserted that Jesus was "conceived of the maiden Mary/without any marring [or losing] of her maidenhede [hood]." These are all examples of metonymy (the substitution of the part for the whole) in which the virginal state stands for its physical manifestation, the unruptured hymen. Another term for the hymen is CHERRY. One may speculate whether it was derived not only from the red blood spilled at the moment of its breaking but also from association with the Virgin Mary, whose attribute is a cherry (see the "Cherry Tree Carol"). A far less reverent term is BUG, a euphemism derived from horse racing. A bug is a horse that has never run a race.

MONOSYLLABLE, THE DIVINE The pudendum. In use since the late 1890s, this term is a euphemistic referent to the flagrant four-letter vulgarism. It reflects a refusal to call a ROSE or BELLE CHOSE (see GENITALS, **THING**) by its own name. In the same category are: YOU KNOW WHAT, WHADDAYA CALLIT, WHATSIS (see THE POSTERIOR, **HONKIES**), WHOOSIS (the last two are also used for male genitals), UNDENIABLE (possibly Victorian), NAMELESS, NAME-IT-NOT, NONNY-NONNY, NONESUCH, FIE-FOR-SHAME (schoolgirl, British), ETCETERAS (see e. e. cummings for this usage), ABC, and POLLY-NUSSY (Black English and a disguised form of PUSSY). The DIVINE MONOSYLLABLE was obsolete by 1880 except among the cultured, who continued to use it until 1911. It came from the earlier expression (1714), the BAWDY MONOSYLLABLE. It is socially informative to note that the monosyllable (cunt) remained the same for more than two hundred years, during which time the attribute improved considerably, advancing from bawdy to divine.

MUFFIN Labia majora. This term, popular on Long Island during the 1970s and 1980s, is used in anatomical relation and verbal analogy to BUNS (meaning buttocks) in such expressions as "These jeans are too tight on my muffin." It is only one of the many comparisons between the female genitals and food, which range from HOME to gourmet COOKING (see Chapter 7, STRAIGHT SEX, **SUGAR DADDY**, HOME COOKING as an attractive girl). In 1387, the Wife of Bath said, "We wives are called barley bread," thus setting a precedent for the later euphemism for vagina—BREAD. CABBAGE is a favorite Black English term for vagina, as is CAKE, which is also British. These baking terms are garnished by those that indicate conserves, such as: JELLY ROLL (Black English from the 1890s to the 1920s) and BIT OF JAM (British); and those related to food containers and implements for COOKING (sexual intercourse) such as: HONEY POT, SUGAR BOWL (Black English), BUTTER BOAT, MELTING POT (that into which a man MELTS, i.e., emits semen), PAN, SALT CELLAR, CORNUCOPIA, and COFFEE SHOP (see the Bessie Smith song of the late 1920s "Grind My Coffee with a Deep, Deep Grind"). Two of these have an interesting history in Black English. JELLY ROLL originally meant one's lover or spouse or SUGAR MAN (see Chapter 7, STRAIGHT SEX, **COMPANION**, SUGAR, and **SUGAR DADDY**) and SUGAR has meant both love or affection and, more specifically, semen. Among the meat references are A BIT OF MEAT (British) and the Black English CRACKLIN' (q.v.).

SNATCH Pudendum. The first meaning of this euphemism—a hasty, illicit, or mercenary copulation—survived from the late fifteenth to the twentieth century. Burton, in *The Anatomy of Melancholy* (1621), described his own sexual habits, averring, "I could not abide marriage, but as a rambler, I took a snatch when I could get it." From it, at least in Yorkshire dialect, came the late nineteenth- through twentieth-century meaning of SNATCH as pudendum. A variation of SNATCH, SNATCH-BLATCH (first-order reduplicative form), was popular from about 1890 through 1915.

TOM CAT Female genitals. This somewhat precious term is a Southern dialectal euphemism used in talking to children. It is still current in Tennessee and neighboring states. Another term, also Southern dialectal and also used to indicate a child's vagina, is TOOTSIE-WOOTSIE.

MALE GENITALS

COBBLER'S AWLS Testicles. This term is a rhyming slang euphemism for the vulgar "balls." These organs are often euphemized in terms analogous to the natural objects they resemble, for example NUTS (1758) (see THE GENITALS, **THING**), BERRIES, SEEDS, MARBLES. The scrotum, linguistically described in similar terms, was called a PURSE from about 1400 or slightly after, but Chaucer may have been punning on it somewhat earlier when he wrote his "Complaint to His Purse." Shakespeare used PURSE frequently as a euphemism for the scrotum, which has also been called a BASKET, a BAG and a SACK (dates of origin unknown).

DO-JIGGERS This is one of the many nonsense words and/or coinages for the male genitalia—most of which can be rationally explained and are often versions of other, more obvious euphemisms. DO-JIGGER, for example, may refer to JIGGING—that is, having sexual intercourse—and to the Irish euphemism for penis, JIGGING BONE (see **PENCIL**). The same prefix occurs in DO-HICKEY, DO-DADS, DO-JOHNNY (a form of JOHNNY, see **JOHN THOMAS**), DO-FUNNY, and as DOODLE. Other terms are DING and DINGUS, probably from THING (see THE GENITALS, **THING**) and DONG. Others are WHANG, HICKEY, JIGGER, DUMMY, and FAG (perhaps on the basis of the resemblance of the penis to a cigarette or a stick). Among the most interesting are 4-11-44, an English Black term (possibly rhyming slang for SCORE), and BOO-

BOOS, or testicles, memorably used by Truman Capote in *The Grass Harp* (1951): "Catherine said, 'In the booboos, Colin. Kick his old booboos.' So I did. Big Eddie's face curdled." (See also **COBBLER'S AWLS**.)

HAMPTON WICK   Penis. This bit of British rhyming slang is nineteenth century in origin and has been shortened in the twentieth century to WICK and HAMPTON. In his *Dictionary of Rhyming Slang*, Julian Franklyn tells the story of a pretty and seductive young lady who insisted that her luxury apartment was furnished by Waring and Gillows whereas others believed that it was furnished by HAMPTON'S. WICK is also used in the colorful expression, "He gets on my wick." Following the same linguistic pattern is BEECHAM'S PILLS, which has been shortened to PILLS or BILLS. Both are near rhyming slang for testicles and were truncated into the shorter forms in about 1914. Two other British rhyming slang cognates for the same part of the anatomy are NIAGARA FALLS, or NIAGARA, and ORCHESTRAS', the modern, reduced form of the nineteenth-century ORCHESTRA STALLS.

JEWELS   Many of the terms for the male genitals refer to the value of these organs—thought by some to be man's most precious possessions. These include FAMILY JEWELS, JEWELRY, TRINKETS, and TREASURE (also used for the female genitals). Even the Yiddish term *schmuck* is a pejorative use of the low German term for "jewels" and implications of value shape such other euphemisms for male genitals as PRIVATE PROPERTY, LADIES' TREASURE, and LADIES' DELIGHT.

JIM DOG   Penis. This is a Southern dialectal euphemism, the male counterpart of TOM CAT (see **FEMALE GENITALS, TOM CAT**) with which it makes a full couple. It is among the terms used for and to children—like WAG for a child's penis (see **THE GENITALS, TAIL**). It is undoubtedly a combination of "puppy dogs' tails," associated with what little boys are made of, and male names like JOHN THOMAS and DICK (see **JOHN THOMAS**), which are part of a long euphemistic tradition of names given to the male genitals.

JOHN THOMAS, JOHN, JOHNNY The penis. This euphemism for the MALE MEMBER was first used as a vulgarism in the 1840s and was made famous by D. H. Lawrence in *Lady Chatterley's Lover* (1928). A large number of terms for the MALE MEMBER are references to men's names. They include such derivatives of JOHN as DR. JOHNSON, MR. JOHNSON (Black English), HANGING JOHNNY, JOHN GOODFELLOW, JACK, JACK IN THE BOX, and JACK ROBINSON—the last derived from the expression "quicker than you can say 'Jack Robinson.' " The penis is equally well known as PETER and SAINT PETER (who, as the joke goes, keeps the keys of heaven), MR. TOM (from the Black use of TOM as a woman chaser), LITTLE DAVY, DICK, DICKY, DICKY JONES, and MR. JONES. More fancifully it has been named JULIUS CAESAR (and likes her?), ROBIN (a shortening of COCK ROBIN), NEBUCHADNEZZAR, and NIMROD (a nimble ROD?).

PENCIL Penis. This term was coined on the basis of physical resemblance between the two objects. There are many other familiar terms that seem to have been engendered by similar analogies. These include: JIGGING BONE (Irish), PENCIL AND TASSEL (penis and testes), ROD, AARON'S ROD, BONE, TROMBONE, HAM BONE (Black English), ARM, SHORT ARM (a non-erect penis), LONG ARM (an erect member), TWIG AND BERRIES (penis and testes), BALLS AND BAT, PECKER (perhaps on the basis of an analogy to a bird's beak) and JOINT (perhaps a pun on a marijuana cigarette). Other familiar analogies are implied in BALONEY, SAUSAGE, BROOM HANDLE, KNIFE, BUTTERKNIFE, CHINK STOPPER, CLOTHES PROP, PESTLE, DRUMSTICK (see HAM BONE above), MIDDLE LEG, THIRD LEG. Most of these are terms (dates of origin unknown) used in America for what the British currently call the NAUGHTY BITS.

PRICK Penis. This popular vulgar term dates from 1605 or earlier. *Eastward Ho* by Marston and Jonson (1605) used the expression with a pun on "prick" as "pimple." Question: "May one be with child before they are married, Mother?"

Answer: "Ay, by 'er lady, Madam. A little thing does that. I have seen a little prick no bigger than a pin's head swell bigger and bigger till it has come to an ancome [a boil or ulcerous swelling]." Only slightly later (1608) Heywood in *The Rape of Lucrece* announces, "I wish young maids before they be sick/ To enquire for a young man that has a good prick," and the modern "beggars, benison" is "may your prick and your purse never fail you." PRICK has fathered several words of the same meaning on the basis of similarity of sound; they are STICK, which imitates both sound and physical resemblance, and DICK. DICK came to mean penis in about 1860 and was used first in military slang.

PUD Penis, seminal fluid, coitus. This is a Restoration euphemism, which first appeared in Durfey's *Wit and Mirth* (1682). It may be a shortened form of PUDDING (date unknown), a euphemism of British origin for "penis" and "seminal fluid," used especially about masturbation, as in PULLING YOUR PUD. Perhaps the word "puddinghead" (meaning a fool or idiot) originated from the old concept that masturbation makes one feeble-minded. (See Mark Twain's *Puddin'head Wilson.*)

SNAKE Penis. This Black English term for "penis" may come from voodoo and the superstition that when a snake crawls across one's trail, one has been cuckolded. It may also be a simple shape analogy. Another animal euphemism for the penis that originated in Black American English is DOG. DOG also means a man with a strong drive to roam or the humble lover of an unfaithful woman.

SOLICITOR GENERAL, THE The penis. A number of general or unusual terms for the MEMBRUM VIRILE are especially inventive and allusive—often to the various professions. These include such wry terms as the ecclesiastical RECTOR OF THE FEMALES (British), FATHER CONFESSOR, and VESTRYMAN (British and American). The full range of legal, parliamentary, religious, diplomatic, festival and sexual allusions (respectively) are embedded in: SOLICITOR GENERAL, DEAREST MEMBER (Robert Burns), THE

MEMBER FOR COCKSHIRE (British), THE BALD-HEADED HERMIT (who WORKS in the dark), THE PEACEMAKER (a pun on MAKING A PIECE, comparable to MERRYMAKER, i.e., "Marymaker"), and THE OLD MAN.

2

Parts of the Body: Neutral Territory

The old prescription for polite dinner conversation forbade any discussion of what, to many, are life's three most interesting topics: sex, politics and religion. The degree of prudery reflected in this social law can be fully understood only when we realize that, in the category of sex, was included any reference to the human anatomy—even its neutral parts or its shape and size. Some of this priggishness still survives as a vestige of earlier customs. At certain points in history, various cultures have considered almost every portion of the body highly sexual. In the ages of long skirts and buskins that concealed the foot, a well-turned ankle was taboo for the eyes and the conversation. Any discussion of the internal organs was proscribed, not because they were provocative but because they were provoking. Which of us thinks of a romantic hero or heroine as a being possessed of a full set of intestines, a healthy liver and a pair of perfect kidneys?

Modern society has relaxed many of the prohibitions against

discussing our internal organs and what medical science has done to them. "Let me tell you about my operation" is now a cultural cliché. But we often turn away or plug our ears, and squeamishness and discomfort do survive. It is these feelings that are responsible for the forced jocularity of such terms as CHEERFUL GIVER for liver and SPAGHETTI FACTORY for intestines. The fear of insult or injury accounts for avoiding such terms as "fat" or "skinny." A woman is FULL FIGURED rather than obese; when she diets, she hopes to become WILLOWY rather than emaciated.

As time progresses and cultural changes occur, the portions considered "touchy" change. But it may be a maxim that, where the body is concerned, no part is ever truly innocent. The origin of the maxim may lie in the traditional Judaeo-Christian attitude that the flesh is always suspect. It may, on the other hand, lie in the more hedonistic view that the flesh is "mighty tempting." Whatever the cause, it is certain that what Delmore Schwartz called "the inescapable animal" not only "walks with" us but also wears the concealing veil of euphemism.

BAGELS   Bulges of fat around the hips and thighs, especially used by and about women. This is a term of the last two decades probably leavened in New York. BAGELS are a form of CELLULITE (the name for fat invented by a Swiss physician and popularized by American diet programs and reducing salons in the 1970s). The West Coast equivalent of BAGELS is HIPSTERS, and both are varieties of the midline unisex complaint RUBBER TIRE(S). The most general term for excess flesh on any part of the body is BULGE. Wentworth and Flexner tells us that THE BATTLE OF THE BULGE was the humorous Americanism used after World War II to describe the perennial fight to keep a trim body. A 1970s term for BAGELS is LOVE HANDLES.

BANTING   Dieting. When a Britisher has overeaten, he or she often takes to SLIMMING by means of a diet. BANTING is an eponymous euphemism derived from William Banting (1797-1878). A corpulent London cabinet maker, he created a new method of reducing by avoiding fat, starch, and sugar.

His low-carbohydrate diet was published in 1864 and has been with us ever since. His name has also produced the verb TO BANT, and the practice of BANTINGISM, dieting. In America, a banter is a WEIGHT WATCHER, from Jean Nidetch and the corporation she formed in 1963, Weight Watchers, Inc., which had crossed the Atlantic by 1968. BANTERS and WEIGHT WATCHERS both have been known to use various types of APPETITE SUPPRESSANTS—diet pills to the uninitiated. The terms DIET PILL and APPETITE SUPPRESSANT may both additionally be euphemisms for "amphetamines."

BASIN Pelvis. This indirect and "jivey" way of referring to the pelvis actually originates in technical medical language. It first appeared in 1727, and by 1760 Brady, in the *Philosophical Transactions of the Royal Society*, described a bone found "in the pelvis or bason of man." By 1771 J. S. Le Dran, in his *Surgical Dictionary*, referred to the pelvis as "the bason" (BASIN) of the kidneys. Shape is obviously the underlying reason for the term.

BEAUTY SPOT Mole, wart or pimple. This British and American bit of politeness originated with the seventeenth- and eighteenth-century custom of placing a spot or patch on the face as a contrast with the beauty of the visage or as a foil for an especially charming feature. The patch box has disappeared, and the phrase survives to disguise, by means of a social lie, the usual attitude toward the pocks, pimples, and moles otherwise known in the world of cosmetic advertising as BLEMISHES.

CHASSIS Physique, the whole body, especially a female torso. The American writer J. T. Farrell (*Short Stories*, 1930) speaks of "those dames whose mugs and chassies were in the paper." The "figurative" CHASSIS is derived from the word (first used in 1903) for the base frame of a motor car, and women's bodies have also been called FRAMES. There is, of course, the old Ford, but an especially attractive woman is described as having a CLASSY CHASSIS.

FULL-FIGURED WOMAN Fat lady, not in the circus. The date of origin of this euphemism for an obese woman is unknown, but it was coined by the merchandising and advertising geniuses to make outsized clothes seem like high fashion. The plan was to make a virtue of necessity by implying that "fat is beautiful." A more tactful term for the sizes of clothing for the FULL-FIGURED WOMAN is HALF-SIZES. It is interesting to note that, in Western civilization, only four eras have liked their women thin. These are the Gothic age, the Mannerist era, the twenties and the present. Eras that have preferred AMPLE women have been overjoyed by the plenitude of the HANDSOME WOMAN (the nineteenth century), who was also considered A FINE FIGURE OF A WOMAN and a GRANDE DAME. The MATURE FIGURE (a term invented by corset manufacturers in the last three decades), the BIG GAL (of recent origin), and the FULL-BODIED WOMEN, all terms recently coined, are not really words of praise, but disguises for disapproval. The word "fat" has always been insulting (except perhaps when Chaucer referred to a monk as "full fat and in good point" in 1387). Hence our language is WELL ENDOWED (also meaning sexually FULSOME, large-breasted, etc.) with pleasanter words such as RUBENSESQUE, STATUESQUE, PLEASINGLY PLUMP, OF CLASSIC PROPORTIONS, FILLED OUT, STACKED (from jive talk), and BUILT.

INSIDES   Abdominal organs such as the intestines, etc.; the guts. Most of the euphemisms coined to describe the human body naturally disguise the sexual organs since, historically, this has been FORBIDDEN TERRITORY. However, a number of terms used to refer to other parts of the anatomy have originated from squeamishness about too clear a description of the internal organs. Some are geographical, some gastronomic, and some mechanical metaphors and, like all of the so-called indirect expressions in this entry, most euphemisms are nearly impossible to date. For the abdominal organs, we find: the DEPARTMENT OF THE INTERIOR (i.e., the insides described as part of "the body politic"), the INNARDS or INNERS, and the STUFFINGS or STUFFIN'S (of farmyard origin). The INNER MAN is a jocular term from metaphysical philosophy, and the INNER WORKINGS is a clockwork or mechanical euphemism. For the intestinal tract, the euphemisms are at least as numerous, including: RECEIVING SET (from telegraphy and the early days of radio), SPAGHETTI (because of the appearance of the small intestines), GRUB ABSORBERS (a jocular play on medical lore), and finally, for the liver, the SUGAR FACTORY (perhaps a euphemism from the era of "jive talk").

MARY or LITTLE MARY The stomach. This twentieth-century British personification of the stomach is used in such expressions as "I'm willing, but Mary isn't" to indicate the stomach's rejection of an eater's urge. The phrase probably comes from James M. Barrie's 1903 play, *Little Mary*, where the following saccharine lines appear: "Who is Little Mary?" "It is nobody; it is simply a nursery name that the child-doctor invents as a kind of polite equivalent to what children ordinarily allude to as their 'tum-tum.' " The quotation indicates that TUM-TUM predates LITTLE MARY as a name for the gastric organ, and the present favorite, TUMMY, is of older origin. (See also DEFECATION & URINATION, TOURISTAS.)

MIDRIFF Middle of the body. Sly evasions for the midsection of the body (particularly a woman's body) became more necessary with the advent of the revealing two-piece bathing suit in the 1930s. It actually originated in the Anglo-Saxon word for the middle of the belly—*mid hrif*—and referred to the diaphragm. A Saxon leechbook of 1000 defines the *midrif* as the "area lying between the womb and the liver." The term survived in its technical anatomical meaning for centuries. In 1596, Shakespeare has a character insult Falstaff by saying, "There's no room for faith, truth or honesty in this bosom of thine; it is all filled up with guts and midriff" (*I Henry IV*, III, iii, 175). Today, the MIDRIFF disguises the fact that there is a pleasing rift in the clothing of a woman which conceals real anatomy instead of illusory space.

MOURNING, TO BE IN To have dirty fingernails or black eyes. This nineteenth-century sporting phrase was elaborated upon by Barrère and Leland. In their dictionary, they observed that to have A FULL SUIT OF MOURNING meant to have two black eyes, while to be IN HALF-MOURNING meant to have only one black eye. In this sense, the term first appears in 1814. When it was transferred from the more quickly blackened eyelid to the more slowly blackened fingernails is unknown but the expressions are used in both England and America.

PIPE Urethra. Both the male and female urinary tubes and the internal female sexual organs are often euphemistically compared to PLUMBING. The bladder, for example, is called a WATER TANK or sometimes a BAG. In recent decades, educated Americans have resorted to medical terminology as an objective, clinical and, therefore, euphemistic way of referring to THE NETHER REGIONS, so that such terms as "bladder" are now used in polite conversation.

PRAYER BONES Knees. Although the origin of this term is uncertain, its tone and imagery are reminiscent of Negro spirituals such as "Dry Bones" and the Southern revivalist tradition. However, it may also come from a far different world. A KNEE BENDER is an underworld and hobo term for a church goer or self-righteous person. Knees, disguised for centuries under long skirts, and often considered naughty, have given rise to such British euphemisms as the rhyming slang BISCUITS AND CHEESE.

SYLPH-LIKE Slender, thin. This word originated with the corset manufacturers' promise to transform the AMPLE-BODIED WOMAN (see **FULL-FIGURED WOMAN**) of the 1950s INTO A MERE SHADOW OF HER FORMER SELF. Our present society still believes that, as Gloria Vanderbilt maintains, "There's no such thing as too rich or too thin," and even the word "skinny" has ceased to be pejorative. Women joyfully praise each other with ecstatic cries of "You're positively emaciated!" Among the many other laudatory terms for "thin" are SLENDER, WILLOWY, REEDLIKE and SLIM. But Spencer Tracy, in the movie *Pat and Mike*, probably best expressed our social ideal when he said of Katharine Hepburn, "There ain't much meat on her, but what there is is cherse [choice]."

THINK TANK Brain. When a brainy person or the "life of the mind" seems threatening, any term, even a coarser one that belittles the mind, is a euphemism. In 1908, K. McGaffey wrote in the American work *Showgirl*, "I don't believe your think tank is feeding properly," and it is surprising that the term is so early and means the brain rather than a pool of intellectuals working in a given place. Other euphemisms for the brain include THINK BOX and UPPER STOREY (1938). By 1949 the term THINKER was added to the lexicon by Raymond Chandler, who wrote in *Little Sister*, "What's on the thinker, pal?" Government panels and major industries elevated the term THINK TANK to a corporate level in the 1950s when it was particularly an IBM term for a group that originated new and exciting concepts and products.

TUMMY Stomach. This euphemism was originally a nursery pronunciation of stomach and has been used, both facetiously and politely, since at least 1868. W. S. Gilbert in *Bab Ballads* inquired: "Why should I hesitate to own/That pain was in his little tummy?" and the expression has been with us ever since. Americans by the millions have been taking "Tums [antacid tablets] for the Tummy" since the 1960s and the terms for the BELLY and its pains are numerous. The TUMMY is most often euphemistically compared to parts of a house; thus it is called the BALCONY, the BAY WINDOW, the BASEMENT, the FALSE FRONT, the FRONT EXPOSURE, the FRONTAGE, the FRONT PORCH, and the KITCHEN. Creating analogies between the stomach's shape and function and household items, people refer to it as the BAG, the BASKET, the BREAD BASKET, the DINNER BASKET, the DINNER PAIL, the POT, the FEEDBOX, the FEEDBAG, the GRUBLOCKER (or LOCKER), the FURNACE TANK, and, more generally, the CAVITY and the MIDSECTION. A drinker's protruding stomach is known as a BEER BELLY or, more colorfully, a MILWAUKEE GOITER.

3

Blood, Sweat & Tears: Secretions, Excretions & Bathrooms

Fashions in body parts and their sizes may come and go, but talking about the aromas and excretions the body produces has never been fully socially acceptable. Only in medical circles was the discussion of secretions and excretions permissible. In ancient times, doctors could diagnose not only disease but the personality of a patient by examining his blood, sweat and tears. All revealed the humors that governed one's virtues and vices. Attitudes toward secretions and excretions represent a cultural history of the world. In China, belching after a meal is *de rigueur* and indicates both satiation and satisfaction. The European hostess whose guest BROKE WIND UPWARD would consider her cuisine insulted. Knowing this, her guest would apologize profusely—the "civilized" response of Western culture to all bodily functions.

Indeed, civilization is identified, as Freud noted, with increased repression. And repression is the mother of euphemism. Even in our contemporary world there are revealing cultural variations in the specific aromas and secretions we most evade. Europeans have described Americans not only as "ugly" but as "antiseptic." The British are more relaxed about flatulation and the merriment it may produce than Americans are. However, regurgitation—especially after heroic drinking—is more acceptable in the United States than elsewhere, at least in preppy circles.

But let an excretion be related to sex and it becomes taboo in almost every culture. Menstruation and ejaculation are universally discussed in hushed tones and indirect terminology. Or they are the material of dirty jokes told on both sides of the equator and on the prime meridian. In all English-speaking cultures, the proper place for secretions and excretions is the bathroom.

As the habitat of the private parts, a sanctuary in which they may be exposed and cared for, the BATHROOM or LOO shares the mingled aura of the holy and the horrible. The term "bathroom"—itself a euphemism—came into currency in 1591 after the bathing room was moved indoors. Since the invention of the flush toilet—one of the wonders of nineteenth-century technology—literally hundreds of euphemisms have been coined to evade mentioning its existence. Yet, as Freud told us, some people love to spend time there, and perhaps it is they who are responsible for such reverent but mocking names as SANCTUM SANCTORUM.

In Britain the LOO is the butt of many jokes, and a variety of expressions has been created to avoid mentioning the real thing. American national squeamishness on the subject has taken more public forms, sometimes broadcasting itself in the kinds of signs that appear on public bathrooms. These range from the coy GULLS and BUOYS favored by seafood restaurants to the obscure refinement of LOUNGE—a term as old-fashioned as the great movie palaces that featured it.

Perhaps no one has made better use of the sexual nuances that connect bathrooms, excretions, and parts of the body than the American humorist Dorothy Parker. Distressed that she was meeting no men at her office, she hung a simple sign over her door. It said "Gentlemen." Miss Parker's office was soon inundated by a veritable stream of male visitors. Another triumph for the power of euphemism!

FARTING

BACKFIRE, A; TO BACKFIRE This is a contemporary euphemism clearly based on the analogy between the sound caused by breaking wind and that caused by a car's incomplete combustion of fuel. Another analogy based on sound takes advantage of the well-known comparison between upper and lower emissions from the digestive tract. Partridge (*Catchwords*) reports a Canadian expression popular between 1910 and 1930 and still in use: "Do you spit much with that cough?"

BREAK WIND, TO This expression was in use by 1540 and even in its early usage, it denoted both belching and farting, in other words, the expulsion of gas from either end. The dual meaning of the phrase is reflected in lines from Shakespeare's *Comedy of Errors* (1594): "A man may break a word with you, sir; and words are but wind; Ay, and break it in your face, so he break it not behind." The expression is extremely popular in British humor, in which discussions of farting are more frank than they are in American comedy. The word "fart" itself (still not used in polite American conversation) has an ancient and honorable tradition. It first appears in the medieval "Cuckoo Song" (1250), better known as "Sum[m]er is ycomen in": "Bulloc sterteth [leaps], bucke verteth [farteth]/Merye sing cuckou!" Interested readers should also see Chaucer's famous *Miller's Tale* (*The Canterbury Tales*, 1387) in which a fart, so named, is used as a weapon.

BREEZER, A A breaking of wind, especially Australian wind. This juvenile and socially accepted term has been in use since the 1970s. Its origin may lie in one of the old meanings of "breeze," to breeze or blow gently (1680). In 1974, the Australian author Gerald Murnane in his *Tamarisk Row*, reports that every boy had to write in his composition book "at the picnic I let a breezer in my pants" or else be kept in after school. A BREEZER is probably more delicate than a BEEF-HEART, late nineteenth-century rhyming slang for the obvious. An elegant and medical prelude to a BREEZER may be BORBORYGMUS, a rumbling, gurgling noise in the intestines. This windy way of describing gas is ultimately derived from a Greek term and enters the English language through the sixteenth-century French *borborygme.* By 1719, BORBORYGME had been described in medical books as "a rumbling noise in the guts."

GUNPOWDER, THERE'S A SMELL OF   Someone has farted. Partridge *(Catchwords)* notes that this expression has been in use from the late nineteenth century on. It is a British army euphemism denoting an obvious analogy between the human organ and a cannon. (See also **BACKFIRE.**) Americans too speak of a fart as a weapon when they describe it as SBD— SILENT BUT DANGEROUS—a teenage expression in use since the 1950s.

LET ONE FLY, TO   As early as 1387, in Chaucer's *Miller's Tale*, this euphemism appeared in a non-euphemistic form when "This Nicolas, anon, let fly a fart." The modern euphemism functions by merely omitting the key word and substituting for it the ambiguous "one." In a 1980 episode of the British TV comedy "The Two Ronnies" we heard another version of this euphemism, TO LET ONE OFF.

RASPBERRY TART, A   This delicious bit of British rhyming slang dates from around 1875. It should be compared with the American and British RASPBERRY—the name for a jeering or echoic sound made by sticking the tongue between the lips and then blowing vigorously. The expression THE RASPBERRY (1921) is also known as THE BIRD or A BRONX CHEER.

TOUCH BONE AND WHISTLE   The origin and date of this American phrase are unknown. Farmer and Henley, in *Slang and its Analogs* (1890–1904), suggested that it came from the custom that anyone who has BROKEN WIND backward may be pinched by his companions until he has touched a bone—

or something made of bone—and whistled.

DEFECATION & URINATION

BACK TEETH ARE FLOATING or AFLOAT, MY The expression of an intense need to urinate. Eric Partridge (*Catchwords*) says that this is a twentieth-century expression, slightly obsolete in Britain by 1960. It is still, however, commonly used by both men and women in the United States. It may be compared to the less urgent need TO GO TAP A KIDNEY. (See also KEG.)

BURN THE GRASS, TO To urinate out of doors. This Australian euphemism, dating from 1942, originates in the fact that the acid in urine will yellow and kill the grass. Its more common American equivalents imply the opposite, i.e., that urine is good for plant and animal life, so that, in the United States, when one urinates outdoors, one WATERS THE LAWN or WATERS THE STOCK (cattle). (See SWEET PEA.)

BUSINESS, TO DO ONE'S To excrete either solid or liquid matter, i.e., to urinate or defecate. Since 1645, this euphemism has been used to mean, as the *OED* so tactfully puts it, TO EASE ONESELF. It first appeared in this year in the *Sacred Decretal or Hue and Cry for the Apprehension of Martin Mar-Priest*, a propaganda pamphlet of the type popular during this period. There we read the injunction to "have . . . a care . . . that no birds build, chatter, or do their business or sing there." TO DO ONE'S BUSINESS has a later equivalent that survives: TO DO A JOB FOR ONESELF. It is questionable but possible that this expression originated in the use of the word "job" to mean a small compact piece, or portion or lump of material (ca. 1400), but more likely that it simply meant "doing a piece of work," a phrase used in this sense since the sixteenth century. An older, more elegant (and more urgent) form of DOING ONE'S BUSINESS is RELIEVING ONESELF (or GIVING ONESELF EASE). By 1375, "to relieve," meaning to give a person or a part of the body ease from physical pain or discomfort, was in common use. By

1842, A. Combe *(Physiological Digestion)* wrote that the "bowels act to relieve the system." RELIEVING ONESELF followed hard upon this association between the gastrointestinal tract and relief. The precise date at which this euphemism came into common use is at present inaccessible. In the twentieth century, those who cannot relieve their bowels are suffering from IRREGULARITY, a euphemism for constipation much used by manufacturers of laxatives.

CHAMBER LYE Urine. This euphemism was current in 1577, when it was used in medical and housekeeping sections of several books of husbandry. CHAMBER LYE has an exact Geman equivalent, KAMMERLAUGER, which appeared in Grimms' *Dictionary* (ca. 1830). CHAMBER LYE was valued for its antiseptic qualities. Although the modern medical profession is fully aware of the sterility of urine, it no longer officially recognizes that therapeutic use recorded in a recipe from 1577: "Take chamber ly, and salte, and seethe them to gether, and washe the places where the skin is cut of[f]." (See BATHROOMS, **POTTY**.)

DEW OFF THE LILY, SHAKE THE To complete the act of urination. This popular expression is from about 1930 and is still in use. Our informant, an Irish-American cleric, reported that it was often used humorously by clerics; it may be Irish in origin. The expression may be compared to the English phrase, in use since 1945 (Partridge, *Catchwords*), "It's as easy as shaking the drops off your john" or, earlier, JOHN THOMAS (see Chapter 1, MALE GENITALS, **JOHN THOMAS**)—that is, something is extremely easy. A more painful sounding variant of SHAKING THE DEW OFF THE LILY is the still current but less common SHEDDING A TEAR (date of origin unknown).

DUNG Animal or human feces. The word DUNG was used in Anglo-Saxon from the fifth century on to refer to both animal and human MANURE (ca. 1549). Now it is considered euphemistic principally when it is used to refer to human feces. A number of other euphemisms for excrement are of more mysterious origin; these include DEAD SOLDIER, WAX and BODY WAX. The euphemism SEWAGE (ca. 1834) has fairly obvious origins related to the beginnings of the large metropolitan sewage systems. There are a number of colorful terms specifically designed to be delicate about animal feces. Although their origins are unknown, they suggest rural coinage, particularly because they embody such close and accurate observations. Consider ROAD or HORSE APPLES for horse manure, RAISINS for rabbit or rodent manure, and PANCAKES and PIES for cow manure.

HOCKY, HOOKEY, HOCKEY Excrement. Flexner has suggested that this term originated in the 1960s. In *This House on Fire* (1960), William Styron referred to "great blooping hunks of dog hocky." It is one of a number of terms common to human and animal excrement, as in DO, DOG-DO, DOG-DEW, TURD, or the more general DROPPINGS. Hocky is also used to refer to semen. (See also **DUNG**.)

HONEY Excrement. The origin of this euphemism for feces is unknown. But we suspect that it is old and that the coinage of the term arose either from the resemblance between the two substances or from an ironic reference to the lack of resemblance between them. The various combined terms using HONEY seem to have been generated in either military or agricultural settings. The term HONEY-BUCKET was used in 1914 in the Canadian military to describe the container used for carrying fecal matter and continued to be used in the American and British armies during World War II. However, it seems to have been a rural expression for a fertilizer bucket long prior to this time. The current agricultural expression for a manure cart used for cleaning out barns is a HONEY WAGON. HONEY DIPPER was a common term for a latrine cleaner during the Vietnam War. The word HONEY is also a euphemism for male and female sexual emissions. (See ODDS & ENDS, **SUGAR**.)

JOHNNY BLISS Urination. This drop of Australian rhyming slang dates from 1973. One may duck out for a JOHNNY BLISS or for its English equivalent, a GYPSY'S KISS.

KEG, TO TAP A To urinate, to go to the toilet or BATH-

ROOM (American) or WC (British). This is a contemporary euphemism, used by American men, which equates the bladder with the beer keg. TAP A KIDNEY is a less subtle variation upon it.

MAKE WATER, TO   To urinate, in medical terms, to MICTURATE. To MAKE WATER, meaning to urinate, has been in use since 1375. It has a French equivalent—*faire de l'eau*. TO MAKE WATER has undergone a number of variations and exists in such forms as TO PASS WATER. The biblical prohibition against urination on walls was cited by Chaucer and provided a precedent for the passage of this euphemism into the later English translation of the Bible by Coverdale (1535) who rendered II Kings 9, 8 as "I will root out from Ahab, even him that maketh water against the wall." The expression TO MAKE WATER is now somewhat archaic in its full form but is commonly used in an abbreviated form—TO MAKE—by children and in parent-child conversations. The American parent may ask the child if he or she has TO MAKE, whereas the English parent will ask a child if he or she has TO DO. Both countries have added specific objects to the verb "make" so that one may MAKE (DO) NUMBER ONE (urinate), MAKE (DO) SALT WATER (urinate) or MAKE or DO NUMBER TWO (defecate). These phrases are among the commonest general terms in children's bathroom language.

NATURE, THE CALL OF   The need to urinate or defecate. As early as 1540, the use of the term NATURE indicated the need to go to the PRIVY (q.v.) or NECESSARY HOUSE (see BATHROOMS, NECESSARY). The elegant Lord Chesterfield speaks in his *Letters* (1747) of "that small portion of [time] which the calls of nature obliged him to pass in the necessary-house." We still announce that NATURE CALLS, but, in the past, the word "nature" has been associated with other bodily parts and functions; from the fourteenth to the seventeenth century NATURE was used to mean semen and menses, and from the fifteenth through seventeenth centuries to mean the pudendum.

NIGHT SOIL   Excrement, specifically human feces when used

as fertilizer. This euphemism for what the *OED* delicately defines as "excrementitious matter removed by night from cesspools" originated in about 1770. Alexander Hunter (*Georgical Essays*, 1770–74) notes its practical use in agronomy, where it had obviously been widely acclaimed by the time he wrote, "Night soil is found to be an excellent manure." While the euphemism has survived, the practice of using the item to which it refers is currently condemned by many Boards of Agriculture.

NUMBER ONE   Urine. This is one term in the vast lexicon of children's bathroom vocabulary. Flexner points out that this language has been carried over, semi-humorously and euphemistically, into adult usage; both children and grownups will announce that they are going to MAKE NUMBER ONE, SIS-SIS or CIS-CIS, a SISSY or CISSY, PEE-PEE or WEE-WEE or going to TINKLE. It is worth noting that these common terms are usually onomatopoetic (imitative of the sound of the action) and are often reduplicating (as in PEE-PEE).

NUMBER TWO   Defecation. This term is a major component of a child's bathroom vocabulary. The words for defecation are both more numerous and more varied than are those for urination. Many of the forms are reduplicative, as in POO-POO or BOOM-BOOM. POO-POO is now prominent in the adult vocabulary of New York dog-walkers, who refer to a dog manure shovel as a POOPER-SCOOPER. BOOM-BOOM is echoic, as is CA-CA (undoubtedly derived from German *kochen*, a vulgar verb for "to defecate") and the latter term remains the most widely understood international children's word for defecation. Just as POO and POOP may have spawned the British children's expression, "I've done POOPIE-POPS" (or POOPIE-PLOPS), so CA-CA may be partially responsible for COCKA-DOODLE-DO—a verbal elaboration of CA-CA and DO. Among other popular children's terms are GRUNT, MESS, and the perennial favorite, BM, the abbreviation of "bowel movement."

PEE   Urine. This is the most common contemporary euphemism for "piss"—a word that was considered Standard

English until the nineteenth century, when it became a vulgarism. It has, however, a long and honorable history and was first used in 1290 in *The South English Legendary*, which describes a man's CALL OF NATURE as the time "when he would [wanted to] piss." "Piss" comes from Old Frisian *pissia* and seems to be one of the universal Indo-European words. In Middle Dutch and Middle Low German it was *pissen*, in Danish, *pissa*, in Swedish, Norwegian and Icelandic, *pyssa*, in Welsh, *piso* or *pisio*; similar forms occur in Italian and Rumanian. The French street-corner urinal, the *pissoir*, takes its name from *pisser* (to "urinate"). PEE, which has replaced "piss" in polite conversation, is simply a spelling out of the first letter. As a reduplication, PEE-PEE (see **NUMBER ONE**), it is important in children's bathroom vocabulary and PEE remains one of the most common and popular prep school expressions.

PIDDLE; TO PIDDLE Urine; to urinate. Originally a children's colloquialism but now in general parlance, this word was first used in 1796 (*OED.*) Grose's *Dictionary of the Vulgar Tongue* defines it as "to make water: a childish expression." It is now used in reference both to humans and to animals and it may be compared to TINKLE and to the end product of TINKLING or PIDDLING, a PUDDLE.

PUMP SHIP, TO To urinate. This expression, current since 1788 when it was coined, was originally sailors' slang for either "to urinate" or "to vomit." By 1870, it had become a gentlemen's colloquialism. It draws upon both naval and plumbing terms, as does its more vulgar equivalent, TO SPRING A LEAK.

SWEET PEA, TO PLANT or DO A To urinate, especially outdoors. This expression, in use since the mid-nineteenth century, is said about and among women who seem to appreciate the horticultural pun. A more delicate and earlier version of it, used in the eighteenth and nineteenth centuries and cited in Grose (1785), is to PLUCK A ROSE—which means to visit the PRIVY (q.v.). The phrase alludes to the fact that rural WCs were often located in the garden.

TEA Urine. This originally British euphemism was coined as early as 1716 when John Gay (*Trivia*) noted with annoyance that "thoughtless wits . . . 'gainst [the] Sentry's Box discharge their tea." The analogy may have arisen from the color common to the two liquids, from rhyming slang, and possibly from observations of the diuretic effect of tea.

TOM TIT Bowel movement. This Australian term is not the name of a bird but, instead, one of the many rhyming slang combinations used to bury the acts and products of urination and defecation. To have THE TOMS or THE TOM TITS is to have THE RUNS (see **THE TROTS**, THE RUNS) or diarrhea. In the 1950s, THE TRAYS or TRAY BITS became favorite Australian terms for the same condition. Many have known the discomfort of A TOUCH OF THE TRAYS. A more exotic form of the same disorder is the South African APRICOT SICKNESS. This malady, consisting of diarrhea and occasional vomiting, takes its name from its cause, eating too much unripe fruit. Much earlier, craving for and getting sick from apricots was a test of pregnancy. The Duchess of Malfi in John Webster's play of 1623 betrays her delicate condition in just that way. The London *Sunday Times* in 1974 uses the expression in its modern sense as it lists it along with such other euphemisms for LOOSE BOWELS as THE TROTS, RUNNY TUMMY, and GASTRIC FLU. A more explicit but still euphemistic form of dysentery is the current British soldier's TUMMY BUG.

TOURISTAS or TORISTA(S), THE An attack of diarrhea. Flexner states that this term is replacing the older euphemism GIs (ca. 1955)—an abbreviation of the vulgarism "the GI shits" or of "gastrointestinal." TOURISTAS is based on the Spanish word for "tourists" and was probably first used by American travelers returning from Mexico. It should be compared to the even more popular and earlier term MONTEZUMA'S REVENGE (1930s). The latter expression was utilized on TV's "Sanford and Son" when Sanford proudly announced: "We got good water here that won't give you no MONTEZUMA'S REVENGE." A number of other terms for diarrhea obviously flow from tourist experiences and, therefore, reflect specific foreign locales; the HONG KONG DOG, for example, is the term used by visitors to the Far East. GIPPY TUMMY or GIPPO TUMMY comes from Egypt (and Libya) and was derived from the experiences of the British army when they campaigned there in the late nineteenth century.

TROTS, THE Diarrhea. This expression, used in Canada and America since about 1910, probably takes its name from the physical action it induces. Since to trot is to hurry or to cause to move at a pace faster than a walk, THE TROTS is the condition of the bowels that forces one to proceed rapidly to the toilet. THE TROTS are similar, nay, identical to THE RUNS. "Run" has meant a copious flowing from the thirteenth century on, and although the modern term for diarrhea is probably of twentieth-century American origin, it incorporates the medieval meaning. One has THE RUNS both because fecal matter copiously flows through the bowels and because one moves hurriedly toward a bathroom on such occasions.

MENSTRUATION

CURSE, TO HAVE THE This phrase, dating from at least the middle of the nineteenth century, is one of the many that connect menstruation with illness and evil. It is probably an allusion to the biblical curse of Eve, and it may suggest that the first sin was sex. Knowledge, both in the Bible and among primitive tribes, was frequently about sex (consider the biblical use of the verb "to know" when applied to a man and a woman). TO BE SICK, ILL, or NOT FEELING WELL are other expressions for the same condition. Menstruation has been called THE ILLNESS since 1839, and women suffering from dysmenorrhea have been described as WHITE AND SPITEFUL or SICK since the late nineteenth century. In extreme cases, where sickness becomes disaster, women have called their periods FALLING OFF THE ROOF (perhaps the source of the common I FELL OFF). What they were doing there in the first place remains a mystery.

FLOWERS, THE The monthly FLOWERS, a somewhat romantic term for a woman's PERIOD, has been used in England since the fifteenth century. It is from the Latin *fluere*, "to flow," but perhaps was mistakenly translated into the French *fleurs*. To the literary minded the expression recalls Dumas's heroine of *La Dame aux Camelias*, who indicated whether or not she was menstruating by wearing a red or white flower. To the less literary, it recalls Edith Bunker of TV's "All in the Family" coyly chirping, "It's Mother Nature come to call."

INDISPOSED, TO BE Since the late sixteenth century, INDISPOSED has meant ill, especially slightly ill. By 1623, it was sufficiently familiar that a character in Massinger's play *The Duke of Milan*, could escape an interview by sending the message that he "was indisposed." By the nineteenth century, INDISPOSED was being used to refer to a more specialized sickness, the FEMALE COMPLAINT (another contemporary euphemism), which caused one to be UNWELL.

MONTHLIES; MONTHLY COURSES; COURSES, THE These British colloquialisms for menstruation are ancient in origin. In 1563, a British author warned men to "beware that they which have their monthly courses do not come near." By 1839, THE COURSES were described as an expression in most common use among the vulgar. Have you had your MONTHLY COURSES? has been a question asked of one woman by another since the middle of the nineteenth century. The word "monthly" is a translation of the Latin and medical term *menses* (or months), which is the first part of the root of *menstruation*. Illustrating the taboo nature of the whole discussion of this normal function, the *OED* lists only one term: the extremely formal and now obsolete term CATAMENIA—in use in England from at least the 1750s. Less bashful than the *OED*, an English schoolgirl today might say that she HAS (GOT) HER RUN ON or HAS (GOT) HER RAGS ON.

RED FLAG IS UP, THE   This American expression is only one of the many that uses the color red to indicate the menstrual period. Others are: THE (BLOODY) FLAG IS UP or OUT, THE FLAG OF DEFIANCE IS OUT, THE RED RAG IS ON, THE VISITOR WITH THE RED HAIR HAS COME, SHE'S GOT THE PAINTERS IN (an oblique allusion to color). The dates of these expressions are all uncertain, but some date from the mid-nineteenth century and all are still in use. One of them, SHE'S VISITING (or HAS VISITORS FROM) REDBANK, is said to be of New Jersey origin.

VISITOR, TO HAVE A   The implication behind this expression and the many others like it is that a woman's period is an unexpected or unusual event or occasion. Some of the more colorful versions of this euphemism from about 1850 are: MY COUSINS or COUNTRY COUSINS HAVE COME (probably related to COUNTRY MATTERS, see Chapter 1, FEMALE GENITALS, JOHN HUNT, COUNTRY MATTERS), HER RELATIONS HAVE COME, A (LITTLE) FRIEND HAS COME, and I HAVE FRIENDS TO STAY. A LITTLE FRIEND has been a Canadian female euphemism since the 1920s. MY AUNTIE HAS COME TO STAY or MY GRANDMOTHER HAS COME TO STAY are British. THE CAPTAIN HAS COME or THE CAPTAIN IS AT HOME is also British and THE CARDINAL IS COME, with its pun on the red worn by a Roman Catholic cardinal, is unfortunately obsolete.

WET WEEKEND, LOOKS LIKE A   I'm about to get my menstrual period. Girls announcing the arrival of their periods have used this expression in Australia since about 1930. By about 1940, it had spread to male teenagers who reached this conclusion when they saw girls carrying the equipment requisite for such a weekend. From 1910 in England and 1920 in Australia, a girl who complained of stormy weather too frequently would be compared to THE LADIES OF BARKING CREEK. A virgin, excusing herself from sex on the grounds of menstruation, reminded her swain of "the ladies of Barking Creek [who] have their periods three times a week." Since the 1950s, American sportsmen have complained wryly, "Game called off, muddy field."

VOMITING

BUICK, TO This is a very contemporary preppy euphemism of mysterious origins. It joins certain other popular prep school terms for vomiting that originate in the even more numerous preppy terms for drunkenness. These include: LOSE ONE'S LUNCH or DOUGHNUTS, BLOW ONE'S DOUGHNUTS or GROCERIES, TOSS ONE'S TACOS, WOOF, THE TECHNICOLOR YAWN, INSTANT BOOT CAMP and KISS THE PORCELAIN GOD (see also **DANIEL BOONE, HEAVE** and **RALPH**).

CHUNDER, TO This Australian euphemism has been assigned various colorful etymologies. Some suggest that it comes from the nautical expression "watch under," the words one would yell from the upper deck of a ship to protect those below. Others believe that it is rhyming slang for CHUNDER LOO or "spew." Chunder Loo of Akin Foo was a cartoon character in a series of ads for Cobra boot polish, popular in 1909. We believe that the word may possibly be related to "chunder," the dialectal form of "chunter" (1599), meaning to murmur, grumble, mutter or complain—all noises mimicking the sound of retching. In his book on Australian colloquialisms, Wilkes indicates that after World War II and especially in the mid 1950s, CHUNDER became one of Australia's most popular words. It was used by Barry Humphries in his "Barry McKenzie" comic strip and was McKenzie's favorite term for "involuntary regurgitation." Other colorful expressions for vomiting come from American preppies who would have nothing to do with the likes of Barry McKenzie. Instead, they speak of POINTING PERCY AT THE PORCELAIN, and SPREADING A TECHNICOLOR RAINBOW.

DANIEL BOONE, TO PULL A This euphemism dates from ca. 1910 to 1935, but is still used in some locales. Flexner believes that it comes from a pun on the standard meaning of "shoot" in all Daniel Boone stories: "Daniel Boone went out and shot his breakfast." SHOOT was commonly used (from the period cited above) to mean vomit as in SHOOT ONE'S SUPPER or SHOOT ONE'S COOKIES. SHOOT A CAT or just CAT is sometimes used in Britain to mean vomit.

HEAVE, TO To gag or strain at vomiting, often unproductively. Flexner indicates that this expression has certainly been in use since the 1940s, when it was very popular, as it still is. HEAVING is often associated with overindulgence or a gastrointestinal virus. Although we do not use the expression "wet heaves," we do use the term DRY HEAVES to indicate gagging or retching without any palpable outcome. If a contemporary American college student heaves productively, or in plain language, vomits, he FLASHES. William Safire, in his *New York Times* column "On Language" (July 20, 1980), cited TO BOOT as a contemporary college term for vomiting that was more popular in the 1970s than it is in the 1980s. He suggested that the expression TO BOOT might have originated in the custom of using a boot as a receptacle. In the 1950s TO BARF was the common college expression. Other continually popular expressions for the same syndrome are: TO LOSE ONE'S LUNCH and TO TOSS ONE'S COOKIES. (Compare with **DANIEL BOONE**.)

RALPH (UP), TO Flexner says that this term originated in the 1970s. Joe Gallick ("Station House Groupies," *Village Voice*, July 11, 1974) wrote, "He ralphs up the downers [tranquilizers] and quarts of beer." An even more contemporary and preppy expression is TO DRIVE THE PORCELAIN BUS. This euphemism for vomiting may come from the resemblance in posture between the vomiter (leaning over the toilet bowl and holding onto its sides) and a bus driver. These terms are more modern forms of the still contemporary WHOOPS, which originated in the late 1920s and 1930s.

UPCHUCK, TO Flexner says that this expression has been in use since about 1925 and was originally coined by students.

During the 1930s it was considered a smart and sophisticated term—especially when applied to the results of overindulgence in the grape, the oat or the rye.

PERSPIRATION

BO Body odor, especially underarm perspiration odor. This American euphemism was popularized in about 1940 by the Lifebuoy Soap advertising campaign. It was followed, slightly later, by Veto, an underarm deodorant that said, "No, No" (to BO), but its greatest contribution to American culture came in the form of the aromatic B. O. PLENTY (ca. 1945)—a character in the "Dick Tracy" comic strip. Another advertising contribution to the lexicon of body odor and excretion euphemisms was HALITOSIS (1920s), a round about way of referring to the "horrors of bad breath." The term had been used in medical literature since the 1870s. It was formed from the Latin *halitus*, "breath," and the medical suffix "osis," which means either a disease process or an excess. Hence the new word was also a new disease—of the breath—of which there was clearly too much. British advertising less colorfully describes bad breath as ORAL OFFENSE.

LATHER, IN A or ALL OF A In a violent sweat; figuratively, agitated or extremely upset. This expression, usually applied to horses, has been transferred to human beings. In 1660, F. Brooke, in his translation of *Le Blanc's Travels*, writes, "I could not possibly bring forth a word . . . being all in a lavour with agony and distress." He must have been positively DRIPPING, OOZING and SEEPING. In the words of the modern commercials, he was OFFENDING.

PERSPIRE, TO This polite way of saying "to sweat" was in use in England by 1627. In 1656, Blount (*Glossographia*) defined PERSPIRATION as "a breathing and vapouring through the skin." The British do not seem to consider the older "sweat" a vulgar term and Swift, in *A Tale of a Tub*

(1727), used "sweat" and "perspiration" interchangeably. Americans, however, consider "sweat" a low term and have created an aristocratic hierarchy that is recorded in the Southern (American) maxim that "horses sweat, men perspire, and women glow."

ODDS & ENDS

BURP, TO   To void wind or pass gas through the mouth, to belch. This euphemism has largely replaced "belch" in popular usage. The word is clearly of echoic origin. According to the *OED*, "belch," once considered a perfectly polite word, has been in use since the year 1000, when it appeared as "Breketh he and belcheth" (see FARTING, **BREAK WIND**). In the sixteenth century, "belch" was used to mean "to vomit." By about 1706, it was also a slang word for the bad beer that caused a drinker to belch. Not until the nineteenth century did "belch" become a vulgarism.

CLARET JUG, TO CRACK THE   To have a nosebleed, an expression used in boxing circles since about 1840. The origin of this euphemism is a fascinating one. As early as 1369, the term "claret" was used to describe the color of blood-red wine. By 1604, CLARET was a colorful euphemism for blood. From 1770 on, in boxing circles, TAPPING THE CLARET meant causing an opponent to bleed, and from 1840, in England, the nose was called the CLARET JUG. A jug is a vessel, and a comparison of a blood vessel and a vessel to hold wine or water suggests yet a further comparison between the euphemism TO CRACK A CLARET JUG and those for extreme rage: TO BUST A BLOOD VESSEL and TO HAVE A HEMORRHAGE.

CREAM   Sperm or seminal fluid. CREAM, described as "father-stuff" by Walt Whitman, has been a colloquial euphemism for seminal fluid since the nineteenth century. The resemblance between the two substances is obvious and the two commonest analogies to sperm are drawn from the categories of treasure or food. CREAM is predated by CREAM-STICK, euphemism for the MEMBRUM VIRILE, in use since the eighteenth century, but it in turn has seemingly engendered MILK, BUTTER and BUTTERMILK. Other such terms are JELLY, JAM, WHITE HONEY, DELICIOUS JAM, HOME BREW, MAN-OIL (Black English, probably from the 1930s) and LOVE LIQUOR. A single drop of CREAM is called A SNOWBALL. (See also **SUGAR**.)

EXPECTORATE, TO To spit. An old general and current medical term, the word EXPECTORATE was first used as a noun (for that which causes one to spit) in 1666. By 1827, it had come to mean to spit. Lord Lytton (*Pelham*, 1828) snottily observed that "the men [at Cambridge] expectorated on the floor."

JACK Sperm. In 1922, this word was used in American slang to mean money. In 1924, Peter Marks (*The Plastic Age*) wrote: "He left us a whale of a lot of jack when he passed out [died] a couple of years ago." Flexner notes that, about this time, the word JACK was used as a verb in many senses. To "jack around" meant in college slang to fool around. To JACK OFF meant to masturbate and probably came from "ejaculate." The second term seems the likeliest origin for JACK meaning sperm; however, JACK also records the common linguistic comparison between sexuality and treasure, especially when male sexuality is involved. JEWELS and the FAMILY JEWELS (see Chapter I, MALE GENITALS, **JEWELS**) are the commonest such terms for male sexual organs, and SPENDING—a favorite Victorian euphemism meaning both expenditure and exhaustion of funds—is a common term for male orgasm. In the 1960s the Springmaid Cotton people advertised their sheets by showing a picture of an exhausted Indian brave standing beside a lissome and satisfied maiden lying in a hammock. The caption of the picture was "a buck well-spent" (see **SPEND**). Thus one would expect to find that sperm is compared to valuable currency. (For a related and possibly influential parallel to JACK, see Chapter 1, MALE GENITALS, **JOHN THOMAS**.)

SPEND, TO   To expend sexually, to discharge seminally. A British and American euphemism, this term was first used by Shakespeare. In *All's Well That Ends Well*, II, iii, 284, we read that a character is "spending his manly marrow under arms," in other words, using up his energies and his life. In 1718, Hicks and Nelson (*J. Kettlewell*) used SPEND in a specifically sexual sense when they wrote that the man was "spending himself . . . in his labours of love." SPENDING is also a noun meaning an emission or emissions. SPENDING involved the loss of vital fluids and the concept that it wasted one, as in Wordworth's famous lines: "Getting and spending, we lay waste our powers." The powers to which he referred were not sexual.

SUGAR   Sperm or seminal fluid. This Black English word has been in use since the 1920s and is one of the many terms that connects semen and food. Bessie Smith's famous rendition of the song "Want Some Sugar in My Bowl" helps clarify the numerous meanings of "sugar" and "bowl." It is worth noting that in both Black and Southern English SUGAR is used to mean affectionate behavior or its signs from either sex.

BATHROOMS

BATHROOM   The WC (British), the toilet chamber (American). In Britain the room containing the bath was first simply and succinctly called "the bath." The term first became current in 1591 after the bathing room had been moved inside the house. The term "bathroom" in England, simply means the room in which one bathes. In America, however, BATHROOM is the commonest euphemism for toilet. This major linguistic difference has confused countless British and American tourists.

BOG(S); BOGHOUSE, THE   This British euphemism seems to have originated in about 1670 and was in general use until the nineteenth century, when it was superseded by more elegant terms. In the 1940s, however, it was still common in

British schools and universities and survives to this day. It is considered vulgar.

CHAIN, EXPLAIN THE Show me to the toilet. This current British expression is a jocular and witty way of asking the host or hostess to show a guest to the WC and explain how the toilet works. The latter explanation is often necessitated by the fact that some of England's more elegant homes have toilets that are treasured antiques and are flushed by means of the old pull chain mechanism.

CHIC SALE(S) An outdoor toilet, an OUTHOUSE. This eponymous euphemism comes from the fact that American humorist Chic Sales wrote a descriptive catalogue about OUTHOUSES. The word "outhouse" itself is derived from a general term used by 1536 for any room or place outside of the main house utilized for a specific purpose. In America, farmers still refer to toolsheds, woodsheds and dairy houses as outbuildings, but the term OUTHOUSE is now used specifically for an outdoor PRIVY (q.v.). Varieties of OUT-HOUSES are distinguished from each other on the basis of size and capacity and are known as ONE or TWO HOLERS and ONE or TWO SEATERS.

COMMODE This term was an alternative to the other British eighteenth-century term for a toilet or chamber pot—the NECESSARY (q.v.). The word "necessary" originally meant commodious or convenient. The growing technology of toilets transformed a necessity into a convenience and, by 1851, COMMODE meant both a chamber pot and the often elegant article of furniture that enclosed it. The same word was earlier (1786) used exclusively to mean a chest of drawers or chiffonier. A recent informant tells us that signs in Virginia bathrooms still retain the eighteenth-century terminology; they beg ladies to "flush nothing unnecessary down the commode."

DIKE or DYKE A urinal or lavatory. This Australian euphemism especially pertains to communal WCs such as those used in schools or army camps. It came into use in the 1920s, although it is probably derived from the older English meaning of dike, a ditch or trench (ca. 893). A British term for a public lavatory is COTTAGE and a South African contribution to the genre is KLEINHUISIE or little house. The latter refers to any lavatory but is usually used to refer to an OUTHOUSE. The Australians also speak of a lavatory as a DIDEE, a borrowing from the American didy or diaper (ca. 1902). In any of these CONVENIENCES, or PUBLIC CONVENIENCES, one would need TISSUE, BATHROOM TISSUE in American, BUMF in British, toilet paper in plain talk.

DOG or HORSE, TO SEE A MAN ABOUT A Although in the late nineteenth century, to SEE A MAN ABOUT A DOG meant to visit a woman for sexual purposes, it now means to go to the bathroom. It is, of course, a traditional answer to the questions, Where are you going or What's your destination? The variations on these expressions are endless and include: GO AND SEE A DOG ABOUT A HORSE, GO AND SEE A DOG ABOUT A MAN, GO AND SHOOT A DOG, GO AND FEED A DOG, GO AND FEED THE GOLDFISH, GO AND MAIL A LETTER and GO TO ONE'S PRIVATE OFFICE (see **OLD SOLDIER'S HOME**). Among the people who may be VISITED are MRS. JONES or MY AUNT JONES—the latter is a euphemism from the 1850s or 1860s—and both are probably derived from VISITING THE JOHN. One may also GO AND VISIT SIR JOHN, SIR HARRY (ca. late nineteenth century) and the HENRY—SIR HARRY'S more modern and less aristocratic descendant.

DUNNY This is a current Australian euphemism equivalent to the British LOO (q.v.). The word was originally used to denote an OUTHOUSE in the outback. According to Australian language experts, it is derived from the Irish term for an OUTHOUSE, a DUNNEGAN.

EXCUSED, MAY I PLEASE BE MAY I GO TO THE BATHROOM PLEASE? This is one of two phrases that American schoolchildren have been taught to use to ask to go to the BATHROOM. The other is MAY I PLEASE LEAVE THE ROOM? The phrases are used jocularly by American adults who have supplemented them with more sophisticated requests such as the Southern, MAY I ADJOURN?

FACILITIES, THE This recent American euphemism is a delicate way of referring to the specific conveniences of the toilet. MAY I USE THE FACILITIES? is a common question in America and is sometimes asked in Britain.

FOURTH, THE TO KEEP A FOURTH and TO GO TO THE FOURTH or FOURTH QUAD are terms that originated in a nineteenth-century Cambridge University joke (ca. 1860). As luck would have it, there are three singularly unamusing versions of this jest. One is that the expression was first used at St. John's or Trinity College where the WCs were located in the fourth court or quad. The second is that a student's morning routine consisted of (1) chapel, (2) breakfast, (3) pipe, and (4) WC. In American terms, this is equivalent to "three to get ready and four to go." The third explanation of the phrase is that the WC was situated off the fourth staircase. From the mid-nineteenth century on, a Cambridge man would explain his temporary absence by writing GONE— meaning GONE TO THE FOURTH—on his door.

GEOGRAPHY OF THE HOUSE, WHAT IS THE This contemporary British euphemism is a polite way of asking Where is the LOO? An American might answer the question by pointing his visitor to what he facetiously calls THE SMALLEST ROOM.

GREEN MAN, THE A urinal, that is, a men's BATHROOM or WC. This twentieth-century British name for a urinal originated in pub lingo. The WCs were often painted green, and the Green Man was also a common name for a pub.

HEAD(S), THE This was originally a maritime euphemism derived from the fact that the ship's toilet was on or near the bulkhead. By World War II, the terms THE HEADS (British) and THE HEAD (American) were commonly used—mostly by men—for any BATHROOM.

JOHN, THE This twentieth-century upper- and middle-class euphemism originates from such earlier, and even less proper names for BATHROOM (WC) as: JACK, JAKES, JACQUES and AJAX. In the mid-eighteenth century, James Woodforde noted in his diary: "Busy this morning in cleaning my jack. . . ." During this period, JACK or JOCK were the more vulgar terms that were later elevated to the more formal JOHN. JAKES is perhaps the sole surviving term from a long and ancient list of such other forms of the name as JACKEUS, CLAKES etc. In the sixteenth century, JAKES meant not only the PRIVY but also filth or excrement. During this period, JAKES was also used in the form AJAX by Shakespeare and by Harrington in *The Metamorphosis of Ajax*.

LADIES' (ROOM), MEN'S ROOM, GENTS' All these terms, among the most popular euphemisms for the BATHROOM (American) or WC (British), originate from the eighteenth century practice of segregating the rooms in which men and women who attended balls or parties doffed their outer garments and FRESHENED UP. These separate cloakrooms gradually became separate WCs. British men still speak of GOING TO THE GENTS' and ladies VISIT THE LADIES' or LADIES' ROOM (American). Thus, these rooms where more private functions are now performed are cloaked in indirect terminology. Women who go to the WC speak of going to FRESHEN UP. The RESTROOM and WASHROOM, which once actually served the purpose described by the words, are now popular euphemisms for the toilet or, as we like to disguise it, the BATHROOM.

LAVATORY The word "lavatory" is from the Latin *lavatorium*, a place for washing. The lavatory was originally an apartment furnished with the necessary apparatus for washing one's hands and face and was later expanded to include a toilet. In medieval monasteries (such as the fourteenth-century Melifont Abbey in Ireland, for example) there was often a communal building for bathing called the *lavatorium*. By 1864, the pride in such modern conveniences was so great that the British *Morning Star* announced with some show that "there are separate lavatories for the men and for women and children." We use the term LAVATORY today to refer to a room in which the most important item is not the sink, the shower or the tub but the toilet.

LITTLE BOYS' ROOM, LITTLE GIRLS' ROOM These coy phrases were coined by American servicemen in about 1944 and subsequently have been understood, but not used, in Britain. By 1957, Angus Wilson could use the term LITTLE GIRLS' ROOM in his *A Bit Off the Map* with the full assurance that readers on both shores of the Atlantic would be conversant with the euphemism.

LONGS, THE The latrines at Brasenose College, Oxford. Many of the colleges of Oxford and Cambridge have endowed their latrines with in-group names. From about 1870, the LONGS was the adolescent and Oxford undergraduate name for the latrine. It was applied to the Trinity College latrines because they were long and the Brasenose latrines because the funds for them were donated by Lady Long. In Balliol College, Oxford, latrines were built on the site of an edifice donated by Lady Periam (Lord Bacon's sister): going to them has been called, since 1939, VISITING LADY PERRIAM.

LOO This most popular of British euphemisms for the WC has numerous putative derivations. According to some linguists it is derived either from the French *l'eau* (the water) or from the French *lieu* (place). Or it may have entered English from *lieu d'aisance*, a LAVATORY (q.v.). The word LOO was not in common use in English until the nineteenth century, but it may have come from the eighteenth-century French word *bourdalou(e)* used to describe a urinal or chamber pot intended "mainly for the use of ladies while traveling." *The Dictionary of Decorative Arts* (John Fleming and Hugh Honour, 1977) reports that it "was sometimes said to have been carried concealed in a muff" and was supposedly named after the famous French preacher Louis Bourdalou (1632–1704), whose sermons at Versailles were so popular that his congregations assembled hours in advance, but "the earliest surviving examples date from ca. 1720 . . . and the word—as *bourdalou* (m.)—is not recorded in print before it was defined in the *Dictionnaire de Trevoux* in 1771." Such chamber pots were made throughout Europe, including England, and even in China and Japan (for export), "usually of porcelain or rarely of faience or Japanned metal. Elaborate ones are often mistaken for sauceboats." One of the most authoritative articles on the subject is that by A. Pecker, *Cahiers de la Céramique* (1958). Still another popular theory of the origin of LOO is that it comes from the warning to passers-by in Renaissance London and Edinburgh before chamber pots or slop basins were emptied out of an upper window into the street. The cry was "Gardyloo," which was, according to the *OED*, "apparently from a pseudo-French phrase *gare de l'eau*, 'beware of the water'; in correct French it would be *gare l'eau*" (from *se garer*, "to get out of the way," "to take cover"). LOO, according to this school of thought, is that part of "Gardyloo" which was originally *l'eau*.

NECESSARY, THE This term—and the related NECESSARY HOUSE, STOOL, BOWL, or VAULT—comes from the urgently clear need to go to such a NECESSARY place. Such need was expressed in 1609 when N. Field wrote: "She showed me to a necessary vault." (see also **COMMODE** and **PRIVY**.)

OLD SOLDIER'S HOME, THE This euphemism cannot date from earlier than 1861, when the first old soldier's home was established in Baltimore. It is an example of a series of terms in which going to the bathroom is described as visiting a person or place, sometimes linguistically related to the real function and sometimes quite unconnected with it. We have heard the expression MAKE LITTLE SOLDIERS used to urge young children to defecate (see DEFECATION & URINATION, DUNG), but undoubtedly the euphemism above was created to disguise rather than reveal the event occurring. It functions in the same way as GOING TO CANNES, a jocular version of the vulgar "going to the can" (toilet, ca. 1943). A similar phrase indicates that one is GOING TO VISIT or LOOK AT THE CROPS—that is, to see if they need WATERING.

POTTY, or CHAMBERS A chamber pot (British). Both terms are abbreviations for the ubiquitous chamber pot, first described in 1608 in Withal, *Dictionary* as a "chamber stool . . . *lasanum et scaphium*" (i.e., a slops pot or bowl). In the late nineteenth and early twentieth centuries, one of the favorite kinds of CHAMBER was A DAISY. The word DAISY, used by British children and common in the midlands of England, came from the floral design of daisies that decorated the bowls of these vessels. From CHAMBER has also come the jocular euphemism for a public toilet, THE CHAMBER OF COMMERCE, so named, presumably, from the fact that one DID ONE'S BUSINESS (RELIEVED ONESELF) there (see DEFECATION & URINATION, **BUSINESS**). A North country variation of the DAISY is the GEZUNDA, so called because this chamber pot "goes under" the bed.

POWDER ROOM   LADIES' ROOM. The evolution of this term is encapsulated in the history of the room itself. In the eighteenth century, a powder closet or room was a chamber for powdering hair and wigs. By the 1920s, the POWDER ROOM had become a euphemism for the LADIES' WC where women might also actually powder their noses. Hence a discreet "modern woman" might prefer to say that she was going to POWDER HER NOSE or, more wittily, to POWDER HER PUFF. Yet another euphemism for BATHROOM (q.v.)— THE LOUNGE—is based upon a social reality. BATHROOMS, particularly LADIES' ROOMS, often contained a couch on which to recline or lounge.

PRIVY   This familar word for "a private place of easement," as the *OED* calls it, "a latrine or necessary" was first used in 1375. Barbour, in his *Bruce*, recorded the fact that "the king had . . . to . . . pass forth from his menie [entourage] when he wanted to pass to the prive."

SANCTUM SANCTORUM or HOLY OF HOLIES   This irreverent euphemism dates from about 1875 in both its Latin and English forms and is still in use. The *sanctum sanctorum* was once one's inner or private room, hence the expression was probably a jocular pun on PRIVY (q.v.). A number of other terms for visiting the WC imply acts of religious worship or public duty. They include to WORSHIP AT THE

ALTAR, to FIND A HAVEN OF REFUGE or REST, to GO TO EGYPT, and to GO INTO RETREAT.

SPEND A PENNY, TO   This British euphemism originated in the practice of spending a penny (in the United States now a dime or a quarter) to use pay toilets. Freud told us that defecation and love are both forms of spending and giving money. The many monetary metaphors for going to the bathroom seem to confirm his theory as we speak of GOING TO THE BANK and CASHING A CHECK. Both the high value of the currency expended and the contrasting fact that people are equalized since (be they emperors or beggars) they all perform the same function have led to a series of expressions: "I must go where even the Kaiser must go alone" (German), and "I must go where even the Czar must go alone" (Russian). A British version incorporates a double entendre: "I'm going where the big nobs hang out." This expression, used from the 1930s to 1945 in the British military, later spread to the general populace. One kind of nob is obvious, but equally prominent were the nobs who were nobles. "Nob" is a shortened form of "nabob."

THRONE, THE   A toilet. This term comes from the potty-throne, a raised chairlike structure for holding a chamber pot still used for children's toilet training. TO SIT ON THE THRONE is what young children are asked to do. The euphemistic abbreviation CASTLE (for "crapping castle") is perhaps related to THRONE. One folk etymology for "crapping castle," "crap," and JOHN asserts that these terms were derived from the name of the inventor of the toilet, one John Crapper. Actually, "crap" for defecate dates from as early as the eighteenth century; "crapping castle" is from the nineteenth century, and JOHN is derived from JAKES. (See JOHN.)

TOPOS   The Greek word *topos*, one of the legacies of an English classical education, means simply a place. Hence, TOPOS was used for BATHROOM (q.v.) or WC (q.v.) to avoid explicit mention of the name of the place. This practice, which probably dates from the late nineteenth century, undoubtedly gave rise to the more recent corruptions of the original word—TOPOS and DUBS—that were in common use in the 1940s. Another British school term for the WC is REARS or REAR, which came into use in 1880 and has survived to this day. TO GO TO THE REARS is TO REAR or TO DO A REAR; all three versions of the term contain double entendres. Other school terms—on a slightly higher level—are THE GROVES, used in public schools since the 1920s, and THE HOUSE OF LORDS, the urinal that twentieth-century Glasgow schoolboys are prone to visit.

WATERLOO This jocular British euphemism is an amplification of the earlier euphemism LOO (q.v.). LOO, which has its own origins, has been a popular British term for the WC ever since the late nineteenth century. WATERLOO is an obvious but humorous reference to the famous battle of 1815 where Napoleon was defeated, even brought low, when he "met his. . . ." For the humorous use of this term, see Angus Wilson, *The Wrong Set* (1949).

WC This is perhaps the commonest of all European euphemisms for the toilet. It was originally used in its full form, WATER CLOSET, and appears as such in 1755 (*Connoisseur*): "It was my office to attend him in the water closet when he took a cathartic."

4

The Seven Deadly Sins and Sundry Peccadilloes

"Think thou on sin," chided the early priests, and throughout history men have obeyed them—often with delight. This ever popular subject has spawned thousands of euphemisms. Some expressions for sin were coined to permit lecturers against it to spice their sermons with the variety that holds a listener's attention. Some were created to acquaint sinners with all the possible forms of a temptation so that they could recognize it in every guise and shun it. The most superficial of surveys, however, suggests that by far the greatest number of euphemisms for sin were products of the consumers—the sinners themselves.

By now we are all aware that the major sins far exceed the number of seven. However, medieval thinkers, who were fond of numerology, settled on the mystic seven as the ideal number of Mortal Sins and Cardinal Virtues. By the late twelfth century, the standard image of sin was a tree. The root of that tree was the subject of considerable discord. Was it pride, lust, envy, or gluttony that tempted the pair to eat the apple? However theologians decided the issue, they all agreed that one good sin led to another. Most concurred that the seven sins that killed the spirit were: wrath, avarice, sloth, pride, lust, envy and gluttony.

The thorough research and elaborate schemes to which the subject inspired the theologians were awesome. While many of their parishioners were gaily frittering away their eternal lives on forbidden pleasures, these shepherds were correlating sin with: kinds of animals, celestial constellations, body temperatures, personality types, seasons of the year and of life and mythical or historical figures.

The collected studies of sin represent a remarkable and learned history of geography, botany, zoology, medicine, astronomy and psychology. In medicine, for example, the human physiologist of the ancient world had already classified men's physiques, physiologies, and temperaments on the basis of their humors. If a person had too much black bile from his liver, he was thin, pale, dark and given to melancholy—a Greek word that means "black bile." Here was the ideal candidate for despair and, therefore, perhaps suicide. He was probably born under Saturn so that his saturnine complexion was no surprise. Like so many of his counterparts, he was likely to enter the clergy, love scholarship and/or practice the arts.

His opposite number, the sanguine type, had an excess of blood, which made him rubicund and sometimes red-haired. He was overindulgent and particularly prone to wine (gluttony), women (lust) and song. Venus was often his sign. The two remaining humoral types were the phlegmatic—who was pasty, watery and given to sloth—and the choleric—a fiery, hypertensive type whose blood pressure (had medieval men known how to take it) must have been constantly elevated by his frequent fits of rage. Such men made good soldiers, however, probably because their sign was Mars.

Though we may scoff at these primitive schemes, the wisdom of the thinkers who devised them is constantly reaffirmed. While we ask ourselves why so many artists and writers kill themselves, medieval man would have known the answer—they were melancholics. What we call nymphomania or satyriasis, they called excessive sanguinity or lust. Is it any wonder that we still describe the glutton as a hog or a wolfer of food, when a little observation reveals how apt the analogy is? Medieval people saw it too, but they were more likely to consider it a sin and we, a breach of manners. We still go red or purple with rage just as the complexion of the choleric man did. Lust is still the fancy of young men (and women), and it is no accident that Dickens's Scrooge was a SENIOR CITIZEN, for avarice was the sin of the aged.

These medieval survivals are strong and nowhere more so than in language. Anger is still associated with heat, color and bestiality. Gluttony remains an animal, and envy is still associated with the colors of a bilious temperament. The lusty are hot; the proud are cold, high and puffed up like peacocks. In general, all of the sins are to this day described in terms of the colors, temperatures, and animals with which the Middle Ages identified them.

Perhaps little has changed except for some of the forms sins take and the fact that many of these are now called sicknesses. Therefore, just as medieval authors were ingenious in adapting social and physical vices to their schemes of sin and even in expanding the number of sins to include a few variants, so have we been. Drunkenness, traditionally a part of gluttony, has been put in a separate sub-section because our culture is so fond of it. As early as Ben Franklin's day, there were already more than three hundred and fifty words for "drunk" in America alone. Despair, not always part of the seven deadly sins, was nevertheless considered mortal. Fathered by wrath, despair indicated a loss of faith in God's merciful willingness to forgive mankind. The first desperate man was Judas, whose final act, suicide, was the greatest sin of despair. We have also added sundry other more modern vices. The creative language for vice and its endless generation of new forms testify to the staying power of vice and the ingenuity both of those who commit it and of those who discuss it.

The Seven Deadly Sins and Sundry Peccadilloes   77

CHEESE PARING Stingy, niggardly, parsimonious and miserly. This indirect way of referring to the ungracious life of a "skinflint" originally meant one who would save the rind of a cheese or, by analogy, an item of no value except in the eyes of a miserly person. It was first used in its figurative sense of skimping in 1813 and had passed into adjectival form by 1857. The *Cape Natal News* of that year described "the more rigid and cheese-paring school of economists." It may be compared with the more illuminating, but even less appetizing, CANDLE PARING. A person who would pare a candle would be just as likely to STOP ONE HOLE IN A SIEVE (1616), an even more useless economic measure.

DRIVE A HARD BARGAIN, TO To haggle or bargain, usually in the interest of avarice. In its literal sense, this phrase is complimentary, for it means simply that one is a hard-headed business person. However, even in its original form—TO BEAT A BARGAIN (1664)—it had some pejorative connotations. Its uglier meaning has always been to push or prosecute a business agreement in a mean-spirited fashion.

LIVE UPON NOTHING, TO To be so parsimonious that one manages to live on little or no income. This phrase, a delicate way of referring to mean and stingy frugality, became the title of one of Thackeray's chapters in *Vanity Fair* (1848), "How to Live on Nothing a Year." In a heavily ironic tone, Thackeray offers us Becky Sharp's practical directions for achieving this feat: cheat, borrow and *never* pay your servants or your creditors. Such tactics have rarely been effective, however, and in 1824, a character in Sir Walter Scott's *St. Ronan's Well* bemoaned the rapidity with which money was gobbled up by announcing: "The law is a lick-penny, Mr. Tyrell" (ca. 1400, *London Lick Penny*). To defeat the LICK-PENNY, one must be a SAVE-ALL (1655). The latter was originally a receptacle for collecting odds and ends that might otherwise be lost, or a money box for small savings and contributions. In 1785, Grose defined a SAVE-ALL as all these practical devices and also as a miser. In 1820, this last meaning was familiar enough for John Keats to refer to "old Lord Burleigh, [as] the high-priest of economy, the political save-all." A SAVE-ALL is PENNY-WISE (compare the proverb "penny wise and pound foolish").

MAMMONISM Worship of or obsession with wealth and worldly gain. *Mammon* was the Aramaic word for riches and appeared in the Greek texts of Matthew and Luke, as well as in the Vulgate in the phrase: "Thou canst not worship both God and Mammon." Thus later readers of the Bible sometimes interpreted the passage as a reference to two gods—the latter a pagan god of wealth. Between the fourteenth and the seventeenth centuries, MAMMON was often personified as the devil of covetousness. MAMMON appears as the diabolic force of greed in Milton's *Paradise Lost* (1667). Subsequently, MAMMON fell off his pedestal and became merely money or greed. In 1706, one author wrote, "While his mammon [a jocular term for money] lasts, he's a mad fellow." In 1843, Carlyle, in *Past and Present*, popularized the word MAMMONISM as a term for the grossest and most widespread kinds of materialism. One who was a MAMMONIST might also do obeisance to wealth by WORSHIPPING THE GOLDEN CALF (see Exodus).

PINCHPENNY Miser, "skinflint." This term was used as early as 1412 by Hoccleve and, in 1577, one writer urged, "Let our wealthy pinch pence . . . leave their insatiable covetousness." In Middle English, to pinch meant to give sparingly, but also to stint. Thus the prefix "pinch-" appeared in many compound terms denoting miserliness. These include: a PINCH FIST (1580); a PINCH-BEAK or PINCHED-BEAK (1545), defined by Elyot as "a dry fellow of whom nothing may be gotten"; a PINCH-CRUST (1602); and a PINCH-PLUM (1892). Indeed, the word "pinch," which came to mean to steal as early as 1770, came from the miserly associations with pinching, i.e., squeezing or extorting money from a person. A PINCHPENNY not only wrings money out of others and stints himself, but also COUNTS

PENNIES like the king in *Mother Goose* (1603) who was always "in the counting house, counting out his money." In America, noted for its inflations, one no longer PINCHES PENNIES, but, in gambling slang or Black English, one SQUEEZES THE EAGLE—the emblem on coins of higher value up to and including gold pieces.

SCROOGE, A   A miser; a tightfisted, ungenerous person. Chaucer's Pardoner (*The Canterbury Tales*, 1387) said that cupidity (in this case, avarice) was the root of all evil, and we have translated this statement into "money is the root of all evil." But the medieval Pardoner and the modern philosophizer share the venerable view that avarice or miserliness is the besetting sin of old age. Molière's famous miser, HARPAGON (1688), was but one of the tightfisted curmudgeons to lend his name to the vice of avarice. Most of the names for misers or covetous people are those of mythical or literary characters. From Greek mythology we have MIDAS, after the legendary king who asked to have a golden touch. From the Bible we have the ungenerous rich man, DIVES, whose journey to heaven was harder than it was "for a camel to pass through the eye of a needle." SILAS MARNER, the main character in the novel of 1861, is George Eliot's contribution to the roster of misers, and the most famous of all is Ebenezer SCROOGE, the reprobate reformed in Charles Dickens's *Christmas Carol* (1843).

TIGHT   Stingy. This barely euphemistic modern Americanism for excessive frugality exists in several elaborations such as TIGHT AS THE PAPER ON THE WALL and TIGHT AS A NEW GIRDLE. Its British counterparts are NEAR (1616) and CLOSE (1712). In 1723, Defoe used both terms in *Colonel Jack* when a character bragged, "I had lived so near and so close that in a whole year I had not spent the fifteen shillings I had saved." NEAR grudgingly ground out a number of other terms including: NEAR-GOINGNESS (1774), and NEAR AS THE BARK ON A TREE (1774). CLOSE, on the other hand, seems to be an abbreviation for CLOSE-FISTED (1654). A CLOSE-FISTED fellow would now be called a TIGHT WAD—the opposite of an open-handed gentleman. By the mid-nineteenth century, English descriptiveness had expanded the terminology to CLOSE AS WAX. A typical English dig at the Scots, famous for their frugality, is to call all economical behavior SCOTTISH. The English assert that, for the Scotsman, "near" and "dear" are identical in all senses of both words.

ENVY

CONSUMED Obsessed, in this case with jealousy. The concept that envy was the embodiment of a malignant demon gave rise, as early as the thirteenth century, to words like CONSUMED. They denote the belief that one could be EATEN UP or devoured by such hostile feelings as rage or jealousy. Envy itself is from the Latin word *invidere*, meaning to envy, literally to look upon maliciously or with an (or the) evil eye. Shakespeare's Othello was warned to "beware the green-eyed monster which mocks the meat it feeds on" (see **GREEN**). In 1712, Addison (*The Spectator*) must have rejoiced that "the saint was generally eaten up with spleen and melancholy." EATING ONE'S HEART OUT, frequently used today to designate both feelings of sorrow and of jealousy, was first used in 1879 when Farrar spoke of those who were "eating away their own hearts." Today, in America, the taunt of one who wishes to point out his enviable position is EAT YOUR HEART OUT!

GREEN Pale with envy. Green complexion or eyes and pallor were considered symptoms of an excess of yellow bile, which was produced by fear, jealousy, ill-humor and sickness. Green and pale are alternate meanings of a single Greek word used in a well-known poem by Sappho to describe the complexion of a suffering lover. From 1300 on, TO GREEN (probably from the Old English *yernon*, to yearn) meant to desire, to pine after. In 1310, we find mention of the green-eye or the green sickness, probably a bilious ailment. Seventy years later, Chaucer was to follow the classical tradition of Ovid in associating green complexion with both love sickness and jealousy. By 1596, Shakespeare (*The Merchant of Venice*) had referred to "green-eyed jealousy." (See also **JAUNDICED**, YELLOW.)

HEARTBURN Rankling jealousy; discontent; enmity. The preceding definition, offered by the *OED*, suggests the many emotions associated with the physical sensation that is one of the names of jealousy. Since the days of Hippocrates, the great ancient Greek physician, emotional states and physical conditions have been considered different symptoms of the same disease. In 1621, Sandys (translating Ovid, *Metamorphoses*) correlated HEARTBURN with various forms of melancholy. Even earlier, in 1513, Thomas More, writing on Richard III, associated HEARTBURN with both hatred and envy when he wrote of "a long continued grudge and heartburning between the Queen's kindred and the King's blood." The HEARTBURN of jealousy was never considered a symptom that could be cured by bicarbonate of soda.

JAUNDICED Envious or sour. An unattractive alternative to the green complexion of the jealous is yellow skin or eyes. This is also an effect of the excess of yellow bile that may be aroused by invidious thoughts. (See **GREEN**.) Those who have known the yellow eyes of hepatitis will find it no surprise that such an affliction produces a JAUNDICED VIEW. We find it medically and historically interesting that the liver (the organ afflicted in hepatitis) was once considered the seat of love. Was the jaundiced lover a hepatitis sufferer or vice versa? Yellow has been the universal color of jealousy, and people have spoken of a JAUNDICED VIEW or LOOK from 1699 on. TO WEAR YELLOW HOSE meant to be jealous as early as the seventeenth century (Dekker and Webster). In 1602, Middleton described a jealous woman as a YELLOW LADY, and in 1611 Shakespeare varied the famous green envies of Othello and Shylock with the yellow jealousy of *The Winter's Tale*.

LONG NOSE, TO HAVE A To be jealous or envious. While the nineteenth-century fairy tale asserts that Pinocchio's nose grew longer each time he lied, English lore relates both the

---

lengthening and the swelling of the proboscis with jealousy. To MAKE A PERSON'S NOSE SWELL and TO HAVE A LONG NOSE have been colloquialisms for provoking or feeling jealousy since 1740. *The State Trials* of 1743 record that "he heard Lord Altham say, . . . 'my wife has got a son which will make my brother's nose swell.' " These emotional "nose jobs" seem to have included PUTTING SOMEONE'S NOSE OUT OF JOINT, a current euphemism for both angering and arousing jealousy.

LYNX-EYED Jealously watchful. In 1591, Sylvester wrote that "he [God] sees all secrets and [his] lynx-like eye doth every thought descry." He was drawing upon the old nature lore of the lynx, which could see at night and had yellowish eyes. Both the jaundiced color of envy (see **JAUNDICED**) and the watchful eye of a jealous person were embodied in the surreptitious lynx, which became a symbol of jealousy. Eyes, the focal organs of the lover and the jealous, have also given their names to another bestial embodiment of envy. An ARGUS-EYED person is one who is watchfully jealous. He takes his name from the Greek myth of Argus, a thousand-eyed monster selected by the jealous Hera to keep watch over the philanderings of her wily and womanizing husband, Zeus. But the best laid plans of mice, and even goddesses, oft go astray and, while Argus was watching Zeus's beloved Io, Hermes executed Zeus's order to kill the creature. According to various legends, either he was transformed into a peacock or unwillingly "donated" his eyes to the peacock's tail. The belief that a spouse who wants to philander cannot be prevented from doing so is an ancient one. To this day, the Wife of Bath's opinion that the man who thinks he has EYES IN THE BACK OF HIS HEAD is an ass survives in myriad tales of triumphant infidelity.

NUMBER ON, TO DO A To disparage, to speak of contemptuously, frequently because of jealousy. This current American euphemism originated in the older theatre or stage term "to do a number." The number in this earlier expression was one of a group of set acts or routines that any skilled

---

actor could produce on demand, either for an audition or for a burlesque or vaudeville performance. TO DO A NUMBER ON someone is to PULL AN ACT in order to manipulate the attentive victim. We might wonder exactly what the number is. If the act is directed toward provoking envy, the number is probably ten, since BREAKING THE TENTH COMMANDMENT is being envious, jealous, or covetous. Several generations of advertising companies have directed their efforts to obliterating all public memory of that commandment which enjoins us from coveting "thy neighbor's wife [or] his ox [or] his ass [or] his handmaiden."

SOUR GRAPES Jealousy disguised by detraction. In 1480, the Scottish Chaucerian Henryson translated the ancient Aesop's fable of "The Fox and the Grapes" into English, thus transforming the moral of the fable into an English cliché. Readers of Aesop will recall that the fox, because he was deprived of the delicious grapes, tried to devalue them by claiming that they were only SOUR GRAPES anyway. The fable is one of many familiar tales that associate animals and animal behavior with the sin of envy. By 950, the *Lindesfarne Gospels* had made the adder, worm or serpent of envy of the biblical Proverbs a familiar symbol of the sin. A SERPENT'S TONGUE became a traditional emblem of venomous, envious and treacherous speech. In 1374, Chaucer's Troilus (*Troilus and Criseyde*) was tormented by the "wicked serpent jealousy." In Spenser's *Faerie Queene*, the sin of envy is depicted as a figure mounted on a toad.

GLUTTONY: FOOD

EPICURE One who is devoted to the pleasures of the senses, especially eating; a gourmet, gourmand, glutton, or sybarite. The history of the English language has done the Epicurean philosophers of Rome a great disservice by distorting their dutiful acceptance of the flesh so grossly that we now think of them as hedonists. Chaucer's Franklin (*General Prologue*, 1387), a man devoted to serving and eating plentiful viands, is called "Epicurus' own son." In 1768–84, Tucker tried to correct the misunderstanding by saying, "Nobody was less of an epicure than Epicurus himself." How socially revealing it is that there are almost as many English euphemisms for undereating or starving as there are for gorging. To DINE WITH DUKE HUMPHREY means to go dinnerless. The perhaps apocryphal origin of this expression is that a part of old Saint Paul's was known as Duke Humphrey's Walk. Humphrey, Duke of Gloucester, was one of Henry IV's sons. According to popular belief, while the privileged were dining, the poor had to pass their time at DUKE HUMPHREY'S TABLE, meaning shivering either at the church or on its grounds at a nearby monument named after Duke Humphrey. In 1592, Gabriel Harvey wrote of a poor man who went "to seek his dinner in Paul's with Duke Humphrey." The Scottish colloquial variants of this expression—TO DINE WITH SAINT GILES or WITH THE EARL OF MORAY, pronounced "Murray" in the Scots dialect from which it comes—carry their own popular legends.

GOOD STOMACH, TO HAVE A   To eat voraciously. In 1596, Shakespeare (*Much Ado About Nothing*) proclaimed of a good or hearty eater: "He's a very valiant trencherman [q.v.], he hath an excellent stomach." TO HAVE A GOOD STOMACH is TO EAT WELL and the latter expression is used in 1709 by Addison (*The Tatler*) to refer to a hearty eater and, jocularly, to a voracious one. Like many euphemisms for gluttony, TO EAT WELL politely understates what today we call "pigging out" and may be an index of the more tolerant attitudes of the sixteenth through nineteenth centuries toward overindulgence in food.

GOURMAND   One overfond of eating, glutton. In 1491 when Caxton speaks of "gourmands and gluttons which eat more than is to them necessary," he is using the word in its pejorative sense. By 1890, the word also meant a delicate or choosy eater. Now, in our diet conscious age, we again use it as a synonym for "glutton," although in French it retains positive connotations. The similar terms GOURMET (1820) and GAS-

TRONOME (1823) both imply exquisite discrimination in eating, but they are sometimes ironically used to imply an obsession with food.

HIGH OFF or ON THE HOG, LIVING or EATING   Living, and therefore eating, extremely well and abundantly. An equivalent is LIVING or EATING HIGH ON THE JOINT. These euphemisms are of Southern origin and refer to the fact that the choicest cuts of ham and bacon come from high up on a hog's sides. Flexner (*Dictionary of American Slang*) suggests 1949 as the date of origin, but we believe that a date of twenty to thirty years earlier is more probable. HIGH, pertaining to eating, means very well from 1628 on when Bishop J. Williams (*Sermons at Westminster*) speaks of "a lucious kind of meat [which] feeds very high." (Consider the relation to PRIDE, **HIGH AND MIGHTY.**)

HOLLOW LEG, TO HAVE A   To eat voraciously. In 1362, Langland (*Piers Plowman*) used the word "hollow" to mean hungry or starved looking. To eat as if one HAS A HOLLOW LEG is a later euphemism for eating as if one were hollow. Hollow legs, of course, did exist as wooden legs and seem to have been found quite often among seamen. It amuses us to speculate that these men might have STOWED IT AWAY (q.v.) in their hollow legs.

LIVE FOR FOOD or TO EAT, TO   To have an excessive interest in food, to be a glutton. Both expressions grow out of an ancient tradition that is moral and reformist. In the fourteenth century, Chaucer's Pardoner summarized an already old admonition when he warned against making one's belly one's god. We are all acquainted with the later Puritanical saw: "Eat to live; don't live to eat"—a sentiment that would send a chill down the spine of any French gourmet.

PLAY A GOOD KNIFE AND FORK, TO   To eat heartily. This British euphemism appears in Malkin's translation of *Gil Blas* (1809). By 1812, the British *Sporting Magazine* referred to KNIFE-AND-FORK MEN, and by 1845 the term had become so literal that a hearty eater could be called a KNIFE-AND-FORKER.

STOW or PUT or TUCK IT AWAY, TO   To eat voraciously or have a hearty appetite. This jocular expression for eating up quantities of food was used in Britain as early as 1692. Its origins are naval, and it came into being simultaneously with the same term ("to stow it away") in its more literal meaning—to fill the hold of a ship with supplies. (Compare this with the expression "stow it" [invective for "shut up," 1567].) To TUCK IT AWAY, a somewhat more discreet euphemism for gorging, was defined by Holloway in his *Dictionary of Provincialisms* (1838). His example was: " 'He has a pretty good tuck of his own' means that man is a great eater." In 1847–78, Halliwell (*Dictionary*) defined TUCK as both the verb "to eat" and the noun "appetite." To PUT IT AWAY appears to be later form of these expressions.

SWEET TOOTH, TO HAVE A   To have an excessive appetite for sweetmeats, sweets or sweeties (British). In the fourteenth century, the word "tooth" commonly meant taste or appetite. Chaucer's Wife of Bath says, "I will keep it [my body] for your own tooth." By 1390, Gower (*Confessio Amantis*) writes, "Delicacy his sweet tooth has fostered." Principal among the delights and delicacies that evoked a SWEET TOOTH in the Middle Ages were sensuality and HIGH LIVING (see **HIGH OFF THE HOG,** and consider the relation to PRIDE, **HIGH AND MIGHTY**). In the twentieth century we use the term occasionally with sexual inference, but most often to describe a lust for candy and desserts. What a sad fall!

TRENCHERMAN   Hearty eater. Greene, in 1590 (*Never Too Late*), wrote that "Millidore tried himself so tall a trencherman that his mother perceived he would not die for love." This term for a hearty eater is often qualified by the adjective "good," "stout," or "valiant." By 1891, Hardy (*Tess of the D'Urbervilles*) had struck a blow for equalization of gluttons when he described a GOOD TRENCHERWOMAN. From 1576 on, "trencher" was the name for a wooden square or circle on which one cut one's meat. However, earlier forms of trenchers were popular in the Middle Ages, when a hunk of stale bread often served the dual purpose of plate and gravy-sopper.

GLUTTONY: DRINK

ARISTOTLE, AN A bottle of liquor. This cockney and Australian expression is one of many rhyming slang terms concerning drink. Its origins are quite logical if one considers A. E. Housman's couplet:

> And malt does more than Milton can
> To justify God's ways to man.

Compare this expression, for example, with: ELEPHANT'S (ELEPHANT'S TRUNK, meaning drunk), THE JOES (short for THE JOE BLAKES, meaning the SHAKES or DTS [delirium tremens]) and THE JOHN HALL (or alcohol). Who would ever guess that TIDDLY is from TIDDLY-WINKS, which stands for "drinks"?

BEND AN ELBOW, TO To drink. When one sits at a bar, traditionally one BENDS AN ELBOW on it. When a person was drunk in 1833, he was BENT, today a word for GAY but then implying "walking at an angle." The current American preppy term is BENT OUT OF SHAPE. Perhaps these terms explain the origin of the word BENDER for a drunken spree. A less violent or more controlled and elegant form of a BENDER has, since 1915, been a PUB-CRAWL. A less elegant term is a DRUNK (since ca. 1862). To HAVE A BUZZ ON is to be drunk, and a BUZZ was an earlier euphemism (1950) for a bout of drinking, which is now more commonly called A SPREE.

BEVERAGE ROOM Beer parlor. This Canadian expression is the polite name of a room in a hotel licensed to sell beer. Canadians have long believed that:

> 'Bar' is a nasty, a horrible word
> 'Taprooms' and 'taverns' and 'pubs' are absurd;
> Give us a name with a resonant boom,
> A respectable name like 'Beverage Room.'
> (Scott and Smith, *Blasted Pine*, 1936)

One clearly does not get properly INKED, SHICKERED, or HIT AND MISSED in a BEVERAGE ROOM. INKED, meaning fully drunk or incapacitated, has been used in Australia since 1898. HIT AND MISSED is British rhyming slang for "pissed" (extremely drunk) and SHICKERED is, of course, Yiddish for "drunk." SHICKERED is an international euphemism and has been in use in Australia since 1859 and even earlier in America. It appears in various forms such as: TO SHICKER (to drink, to get drunk) and SHICKERY (drunk).

BLIND Thoroughly drunk. In 1933, J. T. Farrell wrote, "I was blind last night," and Philip Wylie (*A Generation of Vipers*, 1942) wrote, "She loses count of drinks and gets a little blind." Maiming, sickness and physical incompetence—even to the point of loss of consciousness—are common metaphors for drunkenness. Thus we have: BLINDED, BLUE AROUND THE GILLS (sick from drinking), HALF-UNDER (nearly unconscious from DROWNING YOUR SORROWS), ABOUT GONE (dead), OVERCAME, and, just before being OVERCOME, TANGLE-FOOTED and TANGLED. TANGLE-LEG was a nineteenth-century American term for liquor, especially cheap whiskey—and for the physiological effects of drinking it. From 1860 on TANGLED meant drunk and was associated with the Western term, TANGLE-FOOT.

BLITZED Overcome by alcohol, extremely drunk. BLITZED is a post–World War II expression for drunk which has its parallel in the synonym BOMBED. The origin of both phrases is obvious, but since 1945, BOMBED, in Australian English, has also referred to doping a racehorse. BLITZED and BOMBED belong to the larger category of expressions that associate excessive drinking with weaponry, war and devastation. This is no surprise to anyone who has ever seen a pugnacious drunk or one who is GASSED (one of the earlier of these phrases and clearly from World War I), ZONKED (dead drunk), SMASHED (possibly from SMASH, Black English for cheap wine), HALF-COCKED and LOADED (as in a gun), and SHOT (also from gun imagery). Among the most interesting terms is BLOTTO (ca. 1905), meaning fuddled with liquor. P. G. Wodehouse described a man in this condition as "oiled, boiled, fried, whiffled, sozzled and blotto," and Americans have been using it since 1919 to indicate one who has SOAKED IT UP. *Blackwood's Magazine* (1921), however, may have taken the expression as far as it can go when it depicted a British gentleman whose "evening's potations [had] left him . . . somewhere between blotto and blithero-blotto." Intoxicated American preppies are currently RIPPED, WRECKED, SQUASHED (a variation of the earlier SMASHED) or WASTED (an earlier gangster term for killed, adopted in the 1960s by the drug culture to mean doped or overdosed).

BOOZE, TO BOOZE Drink; to drink alcoholic beverages. This ubiquitous expression has a number of apocryphal origins. The most famous of these is that it was popularized by (or originated with) a nineteenth-century Philadelphia vintner or distiller whose name was Mr. Booze. In fact, the term is English and dates from the fourteenth century, when it was used to refer to a drinking vessel, alcoholic drinks and excessive drinking. It appears at various times as "bouse," "bowse," "boose," "bouze" and "booz." It probably comes either from the Dutch *buizen* (to drink) or from the Low German *busen* (to drink to excess). By the nineteenth century it was also used in the form of BOOZED to mean drunk. In a fourteenth-century English poem, we read "deep can ye booze [drink]." In 1819, Wolcott (*Works*) defined A BOOZER as "one who drinks heavily." In 1824, *Blackwood's Magazine* warns: "Never bozzify a second time with a man whom you have seen misbehave himself in his cups" (see CUPS). BOOZE is still one of the commonest expressions for TIPPLING, THE TIPPLED and the TIPPLER.

BOTTLE MAN Heavy drinker. Since the 1920s, various forms of this expression for drinking and drunkenness have been current in America. Among them are: WELL-BOTTLED (TIPSY), HIT THE BOTTLE or THE RED-EYE or THE SAUCE (drink heavily), BOTTLE BABY (habitual drinker or drunkard), A BOTTLE-A-DAY MAN or A FOUR-BOTTLE-A-DAY MAN. Although all of these terms may have been related to the prohibition euphemism for a drinking place—A BOTTLE CLUB—it is interesting to speculate on associations with infantile oral urges, as well as their more literal origins.

BULLET-PROOFED Drunk. The similes that compare the state of inebriation to sleep or death are legion. William Safire, in his *New York Times Magazine* column, "On Language," has listed a number of them including: STIFF, HAMMERED, BUZZED, LAID-OUT, PASSED OUT, STRETCHED and TIRED. While these American euphemisms for "drunk" refer to states of consciousness or unconsciousness, still others allude to a variety of subjects. FACED, for example, from ONE'S BACK FACE or buttocks is scatological. GIFFED is a fanciful abbreviation of THANK GOD IT'S FRIDAY—a traditional American call to weekend celebration. A POWER DRINKER or HEAVY DRINKER alludes to the prowess of the person who imbibes. Any enthusiast who WATCHES THE ANT RACES (is immobilized by drink) probably knows such names for a shot of liquor as NOGGIN (TASTE), A LITTLE RUB OF THE RELIC, A MITE, A DROP, A SWAP OF THE MOP (rhyming slang for "drop") or a L'IL DAB (a half shot). All of the above'll do you.

BUN ON, TO HAVE A To be drunk. Common since 1925 in various forms such as BUNNED (drunk, 1938), and A BUN (a drinking SPREE or JAG), this expression may come from BUNGEY, an eighteenth-century (ca. 1730) expression for "drunk." It probably arose from "bung," a word that originated in the seventeenth century for the stopper in a sherry—or any other—cask. When one HAS A BUN ON, one HAS FALLEN OFF THE WAGON, which one is on (ON THE WAGON) when one is sober or has renounced drink. Whether the wagon in question is a farm, brewery or police vehicle is still a mystery.

CONSOLATION Liquor, especially the dram brought out from the tavern to mourners after a funeral. A clearly jocular reference to the comforts of religion—and the bottle—this euphemism is still current in rural Ireland (see Frank O'Connor, *Traveller's Samples*, 1951). It may be compared to: DUTCH COURAGE, DUTCH CHEER (q.v.), and BALM (see also EMBALMED).

CUPS, IN ONE'S or IN THE   Thoroughly drunk. Wyclif (1382) first called a vessel *and* the liquor it contained a CUP. This euphemism has been used since in a number of variations such as AMIDST ONE'S CUPS, AT ONE'S CUPS, and OVER ONE'S CUPS. In 1406, Hoccleve wrote that "in the cups it is seldom found that any man commends his neighbor." The image seems a bit incongruous, as does TANKED, probably implying that one has fallen into one's tankard. TANKED is originally an American expression and appeared in A. H. Lewis, *Wolfville Days* (1901), as, "Higgins is in here tankin' up." (See also SAUCED.)

DUTCH CHEER   Liquor; the merry mood associated with drinking it. A noteworthy series of terms linking drinking and drunkenness with the Dutch was one of the legacies of the seventeenth-century war between England and Holland. Best known among these today is DUTCH COURAGE, the false courage or bravado inspired by drink. A DUTCH FEAST is a drinking party. (See also BOOZE and JUNIPER JUICE.)

EIGHTY-SIX, TO   To BOUNCE or throw a drunkard out of a bar for misbehavior. This term, which also means to reject, disqualify or insult, originated among American jazz musicians who used it to mean drunk.

EMBALMED   Drunk, extremely inebriated. One of the many and most permanent preserving images is encased in the word EMBALMED. Whiskey has been called EMBALMING FLUID in America since the 1920s perhaps because the embalmed reveler FEELS NO PAIN. It is probable that EMBALMED grew out of a nineteenth-century British expression for drunk, BALMY, which now means insane. Another such image that links excessive drinking and insanity appears in the word LOOPED, a late nineteenth- through twentieth-century term meaning mad. Its newest variations are the recent preppy terms, TWISTED and SCHIZZED OUT (schizophrenic). Back in the 1850s one became BALMY in America by drinking liquor, which was ironically called the BALM OF GILEAD.

This was a jocular allusion to the spiritual: "There Is a Balm in Gilead to Heal the Sin-sick Soul." (See **MEDICINE**.) There is an even more interesting etymology for BARMY (which we think of as a cockney corruption of "balmy") meaning crazy or LOOPY in Britain and crazy or drunk in the United States. From 1000 on, "barm" was the word for the froth that forms on the top of fermenting malt, and one may have become BARMY or BALMY from drinking too much of it.

FRENCH CREAM   Brandy. This euphemism, in use by about 1788, is one of the many pet names for brandy, which include: the indefinite FRENCH ARTICLE (1821), FRENCH ELIXIR and FRENCH LACE. Other wines and liquors have had their own terms of endearment and disguise. Rum, made from sugar brought round from the Indies by ship, has been called CAPE HORN RAINWATER. Champagne has tickled linguistic wits as ANGEL FOAM, CHAMOIS, MINNEHAHA or LAUGHING WATER, GIGGLE WATER, and, most popularly, BUBBLY. Whiskey has been called BARLEY BROTH and SCOTCH SOUP, while beer has names, like BREW, too numerous and declassé to list. Nothing demonstrates this better than the British euphemism, ALLS, for beer. This comes from the fact that customers were supposed to throw the remains of their drinks down special holes (cockney " 'oles") in the bar counter. Popular superstition—and suspicion—maintains that these collections of slops were used in preparing the house draught, hence the sneering response to foul-tasting beer: "This must be ALLS." (See also **JUNIPER JUICE**, COLD CREAM, CREAM OF THE VALLEY.)

HAPPY   High or inebriated. The association between drink and joy and conviviality is an ancient one, as are so many of the polite terms for the JOLLY state of the drinking reveler. Like Old King Cole, many an imbiber has been described as MERRY, CHEERFUL, MELLOW, GLOWING, CHIPPER, FEELING GOOD, or, at times, GAY or GAYED. The STUFF that causes this effect has been called JOY-JUICE (see **JUICED**), and the place in which one may imbibe it will often advertise a HAPPY HOUR (cocktail hour).

HIGH Intoxicated. The *OED* indicates that, since 1627, HIGH has meant excited with drink. From about 1860 on, TO FLY HIGH has meant to get or be drunk, and the American expression, HIGH AS A KITE, has been in use since the 1930s. Perhaps the earliest use of the word "high" comes from the noble quality of the beverage consumed. Wyclif in 1384 uses the expression "high wines"—that is, those rich in flavor or quality. In seventeenth-century English ELEVATED was an elegant substitute for HIGH.

HOLY COMMUNION Hard liquor or the drinking of it. Originally, this was a British World War II term for rum collected by the coxswain for the chief and petty officers' Sunday messes, where it was imbibed "quite illegally." Until 1970, a given number of measures of rum constituted part of every British sailor's provisions.

JOHN BARLEYCORN or **SIR J. B.** Liquor, grain alcohol. This common euphemism for drink has been in use since the seventeenth century and was the subject of Robert Burns's tribute in *Tam o' Shanter* to Scotch whiskey—a substance with which he was well enough acquainted to praise:

> Inspiring bold John Barleycorn!
> What dangers thou canst make us scorn!
> Wi' tippenny [two pennies' worth], we fear nae evil;
> Wi' usquebae [whisky], we'll face the devil!

Barleycorn is the English name for grain used to make malt liquor, especially malt drink. Familiarity has led many sentimental drinkers to personify THE SAUCE OF LIFE as JOHN HALL (rhyming slang for alcohol) and MAMIE TAYLOR (origin unknown).

JUICED Drunk. Although the word JUICED, meaning drunk, originated in the 1930s, the concept underlying it is probably earlier. It may derive from an analogy to electricity (as in "battery juice") or the excitation it produces, or from the act of drinking a refreshing liquid as one does when WETTING ONE'S WHISTLE. From JUICED have come JOY JUICE (compare with the "kickapoo joy juice" in Al Capp's comic strip, "L'il Abner"), JUICE, or JUICE BACK (to drink liquor), JUICE HEAD (a drunkard, Afro-American slang) and a JUICE JOINT (a bar since the 1930s). JUICE is also sometimes called LIQUID FUEL, LAUGHING SOUP or WATER, GIGGLE WATER (especially when it is champagne), GIDDY WATER, LIQUID JOY, OIL OF JOY, STAGGER JUICE, TIGER MILK or NECTAR. NECTAR, from the drink of the gods, has meant a delicious wine or other drink from 1583 on.

JUNIPER JUICE Gin. Juniper berries are, of course, the major flavoring ingredient in gin and gave their name to the product from about 1720 to 1910. The word "gin" itself is from the French *geniévre*, meaning juniper, which is related to the Dutch name for that plant, *genever*. In 1717, Mandeville charmingly explained it thus: "The infamous liquor, the name of which derived from juniper berries in Dutch, is now in frequent use,—from a word of middling length shrunk into a monsyllable, Intoxicating Gin." By 1854 gin, long the most popular drink of the British lower classes, for whom it was "mother's milk," had spawned a large number of popular synonyms. *Household Words* explains: "For . . . gin, we have ten synonyms: max, juniper, . . . cream of the valley, white satin, and old Tom." The same magazine defines a YARD OF SATIN as a glass of gin in 1854, and SATIN was in common use from about 1860 on. Gin is also known as GORDON and GORDON WATER— from the name of one of its manufacturers—and as COLD CREAM, a less elegant form of CREAM OF THE VALLEY.

LOW BLUE FLAME, TO BURN WITH A To be extremely intoxicated. This graphic twentieth-century American expression is perhaps the most scientifically accurate of the many heat and light images for drunkenness. These include: to HAVE A NOSE TO LIGHT CANDLES AT (sixteenth to twentieth century, British), to HAVE A CROWN-FIRE (loggers' slang for a severe hangover), and to BE LIT UP LIKE A CHRISTMAS TREE, LIT UP LIKE TIMES SQUARE, LIKE BROADWAY, LIKE A STORE WINDOW, LIKE A CHURCH etc. When one is drunk one IS FIRED UP or LIT (because liquor was called FIRE-WATER), LIT UP or HAS A GLOW ON. Liquor was called FIRE-WATER in Hollywood films featuring Indians, and these films, which continue to be shown, have preserved the use of the term. This term also encapsulates the fact that liquor heats or reddens the face of a drinker. One asks of a red-nosed person, "Been in the sun [i.e., drinking] lately?"

MEDICINE Drink, alcoholic beverages. Since antiquity and the Middle Ages, TAKING ONE'S MEDICINE (i.e., the punishment one deserves) has often been a pleasant experience when that medicine was a cordial (liquor for stimulating a weak heart) or some wine to warm the blood. Eighteenth-century ladies kept their little flasks of ratafia or brandy for use when they had the "vapours" (headaches and fainting fits). In 1851, Mayhew (*London Labour*) wrote of "young men . . . fond of taking their medicine." In 1891, Farmer noted that "What's your medicine?" was American slang for "What would you like to drink?" With a less salutary perspective, Americans now say, "Name your poison." Those Americans who chose to dwell on the virtues of liquor called it ANTI-TOX, an expression that had reached England by 1885. Liquor has been called PHYSIC, BALM, PAIN-KILLER, PRESCRIPTION, SOOTHING SYRUP, COUGH MEDICINE or SYRUP, MOUTHWASH and SERUM. When liquor is MEDICATION it's GOOD FOR WHAT AILS YOU; when it's POISON the drinker gets POLLUTED.

MOUNTAIN DEW Contraband whiskey, homebrew. Because of the song "Mountain Dew," most Americans would swear that the euphemism originated in the southern mountains of the United States. It was actually first used by Sir Walter Scott in 1816 and became Standard English in 1860. It has, of course, come to be associated with MOONSHINE as celebrated in the song: "They call it that good old mountain dew/and them that refuses [it] is few/Now I'll shut up my mug/If you'll fill up my mug with that good ole mountain dew." MOONSHINE is indeed American and was first used to mean smuggled spirits in 1785. It is also used in

England and became Standard English in 1890. Occasionally, the term implies adulterated, homemade alcohol. Other domestic or regional names for the same home-distilled product are: HOMESPUN, PRAIRIE DEW, SQUIRREL DEW, SWAMP ROOT, YELLOWSTONE WATER, and KENTUCKY CORN FIRE.

NELSON'S BLOOD   Rum. Beeching's *Eponyms Dictionary* tells the now popular story of the demise of Admiral Nelson (1758–1805). After his death at the Battle of Trafalgar, his body was preserved in rum for shipment back to England and NELSON'S BLOOD has been a nautical euphemism ever since. Another British admiral who contributed his pint to the lexicon of inebriation was Edward Vernon (1684–1757), affectionately known as "Old Grog." In 1740 he ordered his sailors' issue of rum diluted with water, thus creating GROG. GROGGY, or half-drunk, a euphemism for mildly drunk, alludes to the effect of a plentiful intake of GROG. The rum issue to British sailors ceased in 1970, but the words to describe its effects remain. Equally colorful are the words that have attached to beer. BISHOP BARKER, the distinguished Anglican bishop of Sydney (1845–81), unwittingly contributed his name to the long Australian glass of beer because he stood six feet, five and one-half inches tall. Other Australian names for sizes of drinks are: a CRUISER (a twenty ounce beer glass), a SCHOONER (one size smaller and derived from a Yankee schooner), a LONG SLEEVER (so tall you can dip your long sleeves in it), and a DEEP SINKER (you can sink a lead deep in it or sink yourself in it).

NIGHTCAP   Drink; drinking spree; the last drink or the last of many drinks. In 1818, a NIGHTCAP was literally an alcoholic drink taken to induce sleep. Happily, the *OED* offers us two early recipes for this cure for insomnia: "A pint of table beer (or ale, if you make it for a 'Night-Cap')" or "A pint of hot brandy and water." A NIGHTCAP served the opposite function of the much-favored drinker's term for a morning stimulant—AN EYE OPENER. On less cheerful mornings, when you are feeling HANG-DOG (HUNG-OVER), you may

---

require A HAIR OF THE DOG THAT BIT YOU or A PRAIRIE OYSTER. The recipe for the latter is too disgusting to repeat; we recommend that the needy consult a cookbook.

NINETEENTH HOLE, THE A period of drinking; the bar at an American country club or British golf club. After the eighteenth hole, all good golfers seek the NINETEENTH— which is to be found at the bar in the clubhouse. A person engaged in drinking is said to have reached or to be at THE NINETEENTH HOLE. This expression belongs to the sports terms for drinking that include the baseball reference to a heavy drinker—a LONG HITTER.

OWL-EYED Drunk. This euphemism is part of a veritable zoo of animal terms for drunkenness. It was used in one form in 1764 when Horace Walpole wrote a letter describing "the noise which made me drunk as an owl." This phrase is still dialectal in some parts of England and America. OWL-EYED was in student use in America as early as 1905, and the meaning of the expression may lie in man's observation of the owl's glazed stare. The fact that WALL-EYED (glazed or staring eyes) and FISH-EYED also mean drunk supports this supposition. Another form of the word is PIGEON-EYED, first used in the *Pennsylvania Gazette* in 1737. PIE-EYED, yet another variant, probably refers to a magpie rather than a lemon chiffon. SKUNKED joins the menagerie by alluding politely to the fact that one is STINKING DRUNK or DRUNK AS A SKUNK. A more mysterious-sounding and anthropomorphic expression is the 1980s preppy euphemism, FACED, a polite abbreviation of SHIT-FACED.

PETRIFIED Drunk, extremely inebriated. In 1667, this term was commonly used literally to mean changed into stone. By the seventeenth century, John Donne had begun to use it more figuratively to mean hardened by conscience. In the twentieth century it is commonly used in America to mean drunk. The relation between being PETRIFIED and being STONED, OSSIFIED, and ROCKY (see **ROCKY SOCKS**) is obvious.

ROCKY SOCKS, WALKING ON Drunk. This contemporary

expression, in common use on Long Island, is a newer version of ROCKY, meaning UNSTEADY ON ONE'S FEET. ROCKY is connotatively but not etymologically related to STONED, OSSIFIED and PETRIFIED (q.v.).

SAUCED Drunk. SAUCED appears to be a modern form of SOUSED, a term that once meant pickled, usually in vinegar or brine. It implied not only pickling but also preserving and was in use from 1387 on. Although some lexicographers suggest that SAUCED (meaning drunk) is related to the Australian and New Zealand term OFF ONE'S SAUCER (meaning ill-disposed, crazy), we think it is more closely related to the many cooking and preserving terms for drunkenness. In 1550, "soused" meant steeped in pickle or pickled. In 1613, it meant soaked in liquor. About 1890, PICKLED came to mean drunk, hence ON THE SAUCE. In the nineteenth and twentieth centuries, the terms CROCKED, SALTED, STEWED, CORNED (preserved as in "corned beef"; British, "salt beef"), FRICASSEED, CANNED, JUGGED, PRESERVED, POTTED, CORKED, COOKED, BOILED and STEAMED have all been used to describe drunkenness. STEAMED probably comes from the 1920s word for bootleg liquor or a drink of it—STEAM. One step beyond being cooked and preserved is being PETRIFIED (q.v.).

SHELLACKED Extremely intoxicated, drunk. SHELLACKED is an American term most familiar as a synonym for "beaten up." It has also meant drunk, at least as early as the 1920s. SHELLACKED belongs to a set of drunkenness metaphors that may best be identified as industrial processing terms. Most of these date from the late nineteenth and early twentieth centuries. They include: PLASTERED, GLUED, SHINED, OILED and LUBRICATED. Clearly, the human machine functions better when it is WELL OILED or LUBRICATED, but it is likely to be STIFF when it is PLASTERED or SHELLACKED. Automobile imagery dominates such expressions as LUBRICATED, GEARED-UP, GREASED, TUNED, VULCANIZED (like rubber tires) and the concept of liquor as FUEL or ANTI-FREEZE.

TIE ONE ON, TO To get drunk. Partridge suggests that this

---

expression is derived from HANG ONE ON (ca. 1935), which originated in the United States and was later adopted in Canada. It is clear that a HANGOVER—more politely, the MORNING AFTER—is the miserable memento of having HUNG or TIED ONE ON. We are uncertain as to why drinking is described as TIEING, HANGING or BELTING (as in BELT ONE DOWN or A BELT of rye).

TIGHT Drunk, tipsy. A deliciously verbose entry in the British periodical *Household Words* (1853) proudly asserts that "for the one word *drunk*, besides the authorized synonyms *tipsy, inebriated, intoxicated*, I find unauthorized or slang equivalents . . . thirty-two, viz.: in liquor . . . half seas over, far gone, tight, [etc.]." TIGHT, first used in the United States in 1843, was amplified by the British into their own TIGHT AS (or FULL AS) A TICK. The Australians have created new variants including FULL AS A GOAT and FULL AS AN EGG (ca. 1925). A more exclusively British expression for drunk is SCREWED. In 1838, Barham (*Ingoldsby Legends*) wrote:

Alone it stood, while its fellows lay strew'd
Like a four-bottle man in a company screw'd
Not firm on his legs, but by no means subdued.

UNDER THE WEATHER Drunk, under the influence of alcohol. Between the mid-nineteenth and twentieth centuries, this was an Australian euphemism for "drunk." It entered British English in 1942 and is still used in Britain and America, where it means drunk or ill. A parallel form is UNDER THE INFLUENCE, short for UNDER THE INFLUENCE OF ALCOHOL or, as it is more comically and indirectly phrased, UNDER THE AFFLUENCE OF INCOHOL. Nautical analogies for drunkenness, like this weather expression, are extremely common, presumably because sailors had a reputation for heavy drinking. With this fact in mind, consider: A FULL CARGO, THREE (or FOUR) SHEETS TO THE WIND (land-lubbers should know that a sheet is a rope for controlling a sail), HALF-SEAS OVER (1737), and DECKS AWASH. KEEPING ONE'S SAILS UP, NOT HEELING OVER, and SAILING A CLEAR SEA all mean that ONE CAN TAKE IT, DOES NOT SHOW IT or HANDLES (or HOLDS) ONE'S LIQUOR WELL. A still longer voyage on the seas of inebriation is suggested by the contemporary American preppy expression for drunk—GONE BORNEO. We do not know its origin, but it suggests being FAR OUT or OUT OF IT (dissociated or crazy, 1960s) or having GONE WILD or NATIVE (1920s) and acting like a "wild man of Borneo" (1930s slang for sloppy and disheveled).

WASSAIL; WASSAILER Drink, particularly a celebratory one; drinker, particularly a merry-maker. In 1208, Layamon (*Brut*) records the toast *waes haeil*, meaning "be healthy," to which the proper response was *drink haeil*. In the fourteenth, seventeenth, eighteenth and nineteenth centuries, "wassail" was used in English to refer to the liquor in which toasts were drunk and especially to the spiced ale used at Christmas and New Year's Eve celebrations. In the seventeenth century, WASSAILERS begins to be a general term for revelers.

WET ONE'S WHISTLE, TO To take a drink, particularly of liquor. Chaucer, in *The Reeve's Tale* (1387), describes a woman as having "wetted well her jolly whistle," and, by the eighteenth century (1719), a WET meant an alcoholic drink. One addicted to drink or primed with liquor was then called a WET QUAKER (originally, ca. 1713, a name for a drunkard of that sect, which was used later to mean any drunkard). WET GOODS, the opposite of dry goods, was a popular term for liquor by 1779 and, by 1888, American towns that permitted the sale of alcoholic beverages were called WET TOWNS. Aitken described a typical one: "It's a very wet town and the voters are wet too." Expressions similar to WET ONE'S WHISTLE are: to MOISTEN or WET ONE'S CLAY (1708). Addison, in the *Spectator* of 1711, spoke of those who "moisten their clay and grow immortal by drinking," and Fielding in 1754 asked, "How should he return to dust who daily wets his clay?" To WET THE OTHER EYE (1745) means to drink one glass after another. To be SOAKED is to be drunk, as is to be SATURATED. To DROWN ONE'S SORROWS is often considered the happy effect of being SOAKED. (See also **CONSOLATION**.)

WOODSER, A JIMMY or **JOHNNIE** A person who drinks alone. This Australian term for a solitary drinker was first used in 1892. Its eponymous source is supposedly a sheep shearer of the 1880s by the name of James Wood, famous or infamous for going to bars by himself. Although he may have indulged in an occasional COROBOREE—an aborigine word for a get-together that was adopted into Australian rhyming slang, where it means a drunken spree—or been ON THE BATTER—British slang for the same phenomenon—he was never known TO SHOUT, that is, to buy drinks for anyone else (Australian, 1853).

LUST (See Chapter 7.)

PRIDE

AIRS, TO PUT ON To assume a haughty or affected manner. In 1704 Addison wrote, in his *Italy*, about "the airs they give themselves." In 1850, Harriet Beecher Stowe (*Uncle Tom's Cabin*) described a woman who drew herself "up with an air." Clearly, PUTTING ON AIRS was a lighter occupation than PUTTING ON THE DOG (q.v.). But the burden became heavier when, in 1938, one began to PUT ON THE RITZ. The date of the expression and of the song "Puttin' on the Ritz" probably coincided. The concept behind both the phrase and the song originated in 1898 when the Ritz Hotel opened in Paris, where it became a synonym for "luxury." In 1940, an anonymous book entitled *Better English* recorded the expression: "Put on the dog and give him the Ritz."

BACK SEAT TO NO ONE, TO TAKE A To refuse to defer to anyone; to be proud or haughty. "Back seat" originally indicated a seat towards the rear of a hall or vehicle, hence a position of relative obscurity or inferiority. The phrase TO

TAKE A BACK SEAT was first used in the American *Southern Historical Society Papers* (1863). Writing of the men who stayed by the hearthside, the proud authors asserted that "those able-bodied men who are sleeping in feather beds tonight, . . . must be content to take back seats when we get home."

DANDY(ISH) Conceited; foolishly proud of or concerned with appearances. This direct hit at the DANDY had been institutionalized in England by 1672. Between 1672 and 1676 the passage up the center of the pit (orchestra) in the opera house where DANDIES congregated was commonly known as "Fop's Alley." The *OED* suggests that "fop" may be derived from "fob off"—meaning to cheat or to pretend to be better than one is. The synonym for "fop" was in use as both DANDY and JACK-A-DANDY by 1659, but was not in full vogue in London until 1813, when it was used as a substitute for an EXQUISITE (probably from the French term for a fop, *un exquis*) or for the English SWELL (q.v.).

DOG, TO PUT ON (THE) To assume pretentious airs. Kipling, in his *Fringes of the Fleet* (1915), was the first to use this colloquial expression in the form TO PUT ON DOG. In 1924 W. J. Locke, in *The Coming of Amos*, wrote: "I don't want to put on dog, but the Lord didn't give me physical strength for nothing." To symbolize their power and royalty, the high kings of Ireland surrounded themselves with noble Irish wolfhounds. Later, the ladies of King Charles's court announced their aristocratic standing by carrying their lapdogs with them. In European society, the practice of putting on the dog's leash and walking out with one's carefully groomed animal announced to the world that one was a personage of note. Now, in Europe and America, anyone who surrounds himself with the accoutrements of wealth—including pedigreed pets—PUTS ON THE DOG.

GASCONADE, A; TO GASCONADE A braggart or boaster; to boast. The men of Gascony were notorious for their pride and *braggadocio*. Smollet recorded this fact in 1771 when he described a man as "a peacock in pride . . . in conceit a Gascon" (see **PEACOCKISH**). Dumas immortalized the swaggering Gascon in his *Three Musketeers*.

HIGH AND MIGHTY This phrase formerly indicated dignity, but it is now a colloquial term for "arrogant" or "imperious." It was first used in 1564 by Whitlock in *Zootomia* where he described "book-learned physicians, against whom they bring in their high and mighty word, experience." HIGH AND MIGHTY is just one of the many euphemisms for pride that employ the imagery of height (see also **TALL IN THE SADDLE**). These terms have an ancient pedigree. The earliest among them is ON A HIGH HORSE or HIGH HORSED, first used in 1380. This phrase draws upon the fact that a tall or great horse was the standard mount of a lordly man. The term was used pejoratively for a person who affected superior airs or acted pretentiously. The next is HIGH-MINDED, which also has the laudatory meaning of "moral." HIGH-SIGHTED was used in Shakespeare (*Julius Caesar*) in 1601 to mean supercilious (see **NOSE IN THE AIR**), in the exclamation, "Let high-sighted tyranny range on." HIGH-HANDED was first used in 1631 to designate overbearing or arbitrary behavior. Gradually, the number of euphemisms descended from "high" has mounted to include: HIGH, ON THE HIGH ROPES, HIGH FLOWN (see **HIGH-FALLUTIN[G]**), HIGH FLYER, WALKING TALL (see **TALL IN THE SADDLE**), HIGH HORSE, HIGH SEAT and ELEVATED (as in "an elevated opinion of oneself"; compare **UPPITY, UPPISH** and TOP LOFTY [1823].) In 1824, Jane Carlyle (*Letters*) described an unbearable lady as "quite intolerable with her fine-lady airs and toploftical notions."

HIGH-FALUTIN(G) Pompous, pretentious in behavior or speech. This American term, which was originally slang, was familiar by 1848 when L. Coombs, writing of New York festivities, described "a regular built fourth-of-July . . . [with] Jefferson speech-making gestures to suit the high falutins." Although the origin of "high" is obvious, the origin of "falutin" is less so. The *OED* suggests that it may have come from "high fluting" or HIGH FLOWN. (See also

HIGH FLYING   Lofty, pretentious. This term was first used as HIGH FLYER by Pepys (*Diary*, 1663) when he spoke of an overambitious person with LOFTY notions. In the late seventeenth and early eighteenth century it was often used specifically to mean a churchman who made lofty claims on behalf of the church. The concept behind HIGH FLYER in all its forms comes from the mythical Icarus, whose pride compelled him to fly too near the sun. Pepys's ideal woman was no Icarus, but "a widow . . . a woman sober, and no high flyer . . . ." Closely related to this term is the phrase used for overblown rhetoric, HIGH-FLOWN. Also related is ON THE HIGH ROPES meaning elevated or disdainful, first used in 1700 in the *Dictionary of the Canting Crew.* Its lexicographer might well have been referring to circus tricks when he spoke of being or living "upon the high-ropes, cock-a-hoop." (See also **HIGH AND MIGHTY.**)

HIGH HAT, TO   To act superior to; to snub. The term was first used as a noun in America in 1899. As late as 1924 (P. Marks, *Plastic Age*), the expression was being used as an adjective to mean supercilious: "Christmas Cove's a nice place; not so high hat as Bar Harbor." Now we use the expression in verb form when we HIGH HAT (snub) someone.

INFLATED   Proud, puffed up, self-important. In 1526, Tyndale, in his translation of the Bible, wrote "knowledge puffeth a man up, but love edifyeth." The image of a proud person as one INFLATED with air or wind comes originally from an early medieval work, the *Psychomachia* by Prudentius, in which pride is personified as a woman who wears a high-crested headdress, sits on a tall horse, and has a cloak puffed out with the wind. This figure was carved on scores of cathedrals, and the association between pride and inflation became common and familiar. Orgoglio, the proud giant of Spenser's *Faerie Queene* (1590), is described as a bag of wind whose flesh and pride are deflated by the hero. We suspect that all of these images were derived in part from the observation of animal behavior, especially that of the peacock (see **PEACOCKISH**). The peacock appears as a symbol of pride in classical mythology and medieval bestiaries, partly because it struts and partly because it spreads or puffs out its tail. INFLATED and PEACOCKISH are more polite forms of the more literal "swollen," "swelled-up," and "puffed-up."

KUGEL A proud, wealthy young woman. This light and airy South African expression derives from the equally fluffy Yiddish word for noodle or potato pudding, KUGEL. It is used to describe a rich young woman whose interests are men, money and fashion and who speaks in a recognizable drawling accent. The British equivalent is COUNTY, that is upper class or affecting the manners, dress and speech of the upper class. The expression first used in the 1850s was COUNTY FAMILIES and referred to aristocratic families with their love for the country and its pleasures. PRINCESS, the American equivalent, is a snipe at the predominance of a moneyed rather than a landed aristocracy. It has been in use at least since the 1950s and is often preceded by an ethnic qualifier such as Jewish-American, Puerto Rican, Polish, Afro-American. The authentic Afro-American adjective for such an affected and spoiled young woman is HINCTY (Black English for UPPITY [q.v.], "snobbish" and "conceited"). In Australia, since about 1882, when affected people have adopted affected speech or manners, they have PUT ON JAM.

MR. BIG A conceited or self-important man. Originally an American underworld term used to describe a gangster, this expression is now applied generally and often ironically to a person who gives himself AIRS (q.v.). It was originally applied to a gangland leader of such importance that his real name was kept secret. It probably dates from the late 1920s or early 1930s.

NOSE IN THE AIR, TO HAVE ONE'S To be arrogant or supercilious. It is physically almost impossible to be supercilious (from the Latin for "eyebrow") without having ONE'S NOSE IN THE AIR. The oldest form of the phrase appears in 1579 in a translation of John Calvin's *Sermons*, which warns: "Let women hold up their noses no more: all their presumption is sufficiently beaten down." In 1818, Byron's haughty maid, Antonia (*Don Juan*), was seen TURNING UP HER NOSE in disdain. By 1882, Floyer notes that in *Unexplored Baluckistan* "there was a general nose-in-the-air defiant kind of aspect." History happily assures us that the Empire TOOK THEM DOWN A PEG.

OFF-PUTTING, TO BE To be disconcerting or disturbing, particularly by condescension. OFF-PUTTING was first used in 1909 and PUT OFF was a verb form of it that originated in about 1930. In Britain (ca. 1920) to PUT OFF meant, to the boys of Bootham School, to annoy or to be distasteful. An earlier abbreviated form of these expressions is OFFISH, meaning proud, aloof or condescending. The term OFFISH was used by C. A. Davis in 1830 and later by J. Downing (1833) when he noted that "others are a little offish." STAND-OFFISH originated in England in 1837 and was later effectively used in *All Year Round* (1860). "We are . . . not aristocratic, perhaps, but decidedly rich, and on that account rather high and stand-offish," remarks a character. It is now in common use throughout the English-speaking world to describe a person who KEEPS HIS DISTANCE.

PEACOCKISH Proud as a peacock. PEACOCKISH is another form of the proverbial simile "proud as a peacock." Anyone who has ever observed this native bird of India strut, bob its crest, or spread its ostentatious tail must immediately think of vainglory just as Chaucer did in 1374 when he used the phrase. By 1872, in England, the word PEACOCKERY meant foppery. (See also **DANDY[ISH]** and **INFLATED**.)

SWELL, A A vain person; a socialite. This colloquial expression was originally English slang for a fashionably or stylishly dressed person who, for this reason, was often considered a highly distinguished person. In 1804, The *Times* (of London) wrote: "They were dismissed . . . having formed an expensive club under the title of 'The Swell.' " By this time, a swell was a gentleman, so that in 1812 J. H. Vaux, in the *Flash Dictionary*, defined "a swell" as "a gentleman, but any well-dressed person . . . emphatically termed a 'swell' or a 'rank swell.' " (See DANDY[ISH].) The term later came to mean a person who affected social prominence.

TALL IN THE SADDLE Managerial, imperious, proud. Since 1660 (Pepys's *Diary*) the term "in the saddle" has meant in a position of power. TALL IN THE SADDLE is undoubtedly an American Western expression derived from it and parallel to ON A HIGH HORSE (see **HIGH AND MIGHTY**). "Tall" is the Americanism equivalent to the British "high"; and TALL IN THE SADDLE is part of traditional American terminology, which also includes TALL TALK (U.S., 1846) or exaggerated and HIGH-FLOWN (see **HIGH FLYING**, HIGH-FLOWN) language like that used in TALL TALES (exaggerated stories). A similar Americanism, to WALK TALL, popularized in the hit movie of the 1970s *Walking Tall,* means to carry one's head high or exhibit a proud bearing. It entered American English in 1846 when T. B. Thorpe (*Mysteries of the Back Woods*) proclaimed: "I will walk tall [among] varmint and Indian."

TICKETS ON ONESELF, TO HAVE To be conceited, to be a showoff. Self-advertising people have been described in various ways in English-speaking countries. In Australia, one HAS TICKETS ON ONESELF (1915), a term derived from the practice of advertising high-priced merchandise on sales tickets or flyers. In America, such conceit is also known as BLOWING ONE'S OWN HORN or TRUMPET, that is, sounding one's own praises, an expression that has been in use in England since 1447 and the age of heralds. Americans have also been accused of GRANDSTANDING (ca. 1950) or PLAYING TO THE GRANDSTANDS. A talkative, boastful person is described in South Africa as a GROOTKEH; an Anglo-Indian would call such a person a BUCK. All the above are addicted TO GIVING IT ALL THAT (British slang for bragging or showing off) and most are attracted to CAKES AND ALE (British for HIGH LIVING since at least 1600).

UPPITY, UPPISH Proud or snobbish, displaying airs inappropriate to one's station. The British form, UPPISH, was used as early as 1734 to characterize one who affected superiority or acted GRAND. The United States form of the term,

UPPITY, is a typically "colonial" response to affectation; Americans have always met it by PUTTING (IT) DOWN with folksiness. The eighteenth-century English were particularly sensitive about exceeding the bounds of rank and about the appropriate behavior of each gradation of each social class. In 1766, for example, Oliver Goldsmith (*The Vicar of Wakefield*) had one character complain of another: "She's too grand to see me now." In 1863, an affected manner was called a GRAND AIR. By 1893, Americans had colloquialized this social sin by referring to those who made a great display as DOING THE GRAND; this phrase was a transformation of the much earlier British expressions PLAYING THE GRANDE DAME (or GRAND SEIGNEUR) and ACTING LORDLY (1377).

SLOTH

EAT ONE'S OWN FLESH, TO This description of how any inhabitant of *The Castle of Indolence* (the title of a poem by James Thomson, 1748) behaves was first used in the Bible. Ecclesiastes, 4:5 asserts that "the fool foldeth his hands together and eateth his own flesh."

EYE TROUBLE Sloth, the inability to remain awake. This is a euphemism for another euphemism—SLEEPY—for slothful. SLUG-A-BEDS (q.v.) or SLEEPYHEADS have been called BED-STEADERS, in an analogy with homesteaders. Such somnolent types are more fancifully referred to as VALE OF RESTERS. They are people who like to PUT A SLEEP JOB because they HAVE NO GET-UP-AND-GO and are devoid of PEP or PEPLESS.

FAINEANCE This term may be considered euphemistic primarily because it is French and thus sounds acceptable in any company. In French, it is an allusion to the *rois faineants* or do-nothing kings, a term applied to the later Merovingian rulers. FAINEANT, for an inactive, indifferent, or apathetic person, was first used as a noun in English in 1619 as a substitute for the more vulgar "idler" or what we call a DO-NOTHING. The term DO-NOTHING entered the language in

1597, and variations upon it, DO-NOTHINGNESS (Jane Austen, *Mansfield Park*) and DO-NOTHINGISM (the British *Saturday Review*), entered the language in 1814 and 1891, respectively. The Do-Nothings was a pejorative name for an American political party. The Italians have contributed to this lexicon of laziness the *dolce vita*, "the sweet life," from the older commonplace *dolce fa niente*, "the sweetness of doing nothing"; utter relaxation has been called GREEK EASE, and sleep has been dubbed EGYPTIAN PT (physical training) or BLANKET PRESSING by the British.

GOLD BRICK A person who loafs on the job. This slang expression originally designated a World War II soldier who did not fully exert himself. To GOLD-BRICK is to shirk one's duty. Other professions have spawned their own special terms for unauthorized coffee breaks. New York policemen have been known to indulge in COOPING, pulling their patrol cars to the side of the road in order to sleep or CATCH A CATNAP while on duty. One COOPS in a coupe or an enclosure (i.e., cage or chicken coop). (See also Chapter 6, CRIME & PUNISHMENT, **BATTING AVERAGE**.)

LAZYBONES, A This colloquialism dates from 1590 and is one of a group of expressions, perhaps not fully euphemistic, that use "lazy" as their first element. They include: LAZY-BOOTS (ca. 1830), LAZY-LEGS (ca. 1830 and a favorite expression of Charles Dickens), LAZY AS A TINKER (a shortening of the more vulgar "lazy as a tinker who laid down his budget [pack] to fart"), and LAZY LAURENCE. LARRENCE, LAWRENCE, or LAURENCE was the incarnation of sloth from about 1650 on. The name may refer to the distinguished saint who, martyred by being toasted on a griddle, was too inactive to move in the flames. It may also allude to his feast day, August 10, which was generally quite warm and thus conducive to somnolence.

LEISURE, LADY or GENTLEMAN OF The word "leisure" has indicated freedom from occupation since 1375 in English, and it was used even earlier in French. By 1794, *The Gentlemen's Magazine*, a publication directed to those who did not labor for a living, had referred to LEISURED MORTALS. By 1845, *The Athenaeum* described the rich as THE LEISURE CLASSES. Thorstein Veblen immortalized the phrase in his book, *The Theory of the Leisure Class* (1857), and the term is now used rather ironically both for those who cannot work and for those who do not choose to do so. LADIES and, especially, GENTLEMEN OF LEISURE are not merely prone to idleness, but often literally prone. Hence, they have been described in the jazzier argot of the 1920s and 1930s as LOUNGE LIZARDS, LOUNGE HOUNDS or simply LOUNGERS, clearly the ideal population for smoking jackets, hostess gowns· and lounging pajamas or jackets.

LENTITUDINOUS Slow, sluggish or lazy. This euphemism conceals the bald truth in polysyllabic and Latinate form. LENTITUDE was first used in 1623 but perhaps best described in 1832 by J. Taylor (*Saturday Review*), who depicted the slothful character by observing, "There is a serenity—might we say a lentitude of the physical temperament." In 1862, Mrs. Speid spoke of "the struggle between English punctuality and Oriental lentitude." The adjective form, LENTITUDINOUS, seems to have originated in 1801.

LIFT A FINGER, DOESN'T This is a variant of the British DOESN'T STIR A FINGER (1854). To STIR A FINGER means to make a small effort or the least effort. On the heels of these expressions, slowly, of course, came further amplifications such as LIFT (UP) A HAND, THE HANDS, AN ARM (all ca. 1890). The most contemporary version is also the oldest, dating from 1377, and found in Langland's *Piers Plowman*—a poem about labor and "doing." It tells of someone who DOESN'T STRAIN HIMSELF. Advice given in 1580 is still applicable today: "Keep thy house with as much ease as thou mayest and strain not thyself in any wise."

LUDLAM'S DOG, LAZY AS This expression for bone lazy utilizes LUDLAM'S DOG, (DAVID LAURENCE'S DOG or, in Sussex dialect, LUMLEY'S DOG) as mythical beasts who personify sloth. It originated ca. 1660 and described a household pet who leaned against a wall to bark. A later version of it meta-

---

morphoses the dog into JOE, the British marine, who laid down his musket to sneeze. Although both expressions were obsolescent but still in dialectal use by 1900, we recommend their resuscitation.

OBLOMOVISM Overwhelming sluggishness, inertia, sloth. Although Barnhart calls this an American euphemism, it is a rare and highly literary eponym. Oblomov, in Ivan Goncharov's (1812–91) novel of the same name, was a wealthy Russian landowner who simply took to his bed early in the novel and, in an act symbolic of the indolence of his class and of the passivity of the Russian character as conceived by the author, stayed there until the end. A far less elegant but more indirect Australian euphemism for an idler is a SOONER (ca. 1892). In the Australian view, these shirkers would "sooner" loaf than work or fight.

PHLEGMATIC Although the phlegmatic temperament is older than the English word for it, the word has been in use in the language since 1320. The *Agenbite of Inwit* tells us that "the devil assaileth most strongly the choleric with ire and with discord . . . the phlegmatic with gluttony, and the sloth." The signs of THE PHLEGMATIC are lethargy and apathy. "Lethargy," used first in English in 1390, was initially employed to describe a medical condition ("the sleeping evil") that we would call unconsciousness or coma. Today, we are being kind, if not medical, in describing a lazy person as A BIT LETHARGIC. "Apathy"—indolence of mind, indifference to what should incite interest—is a later addition to the language, dating from about 1733.

SKIVER, A; TO SKIVE SKIVING became British army and school slang for dodging a duty by 1919 when it was listed in *The Athenaeum* as military slang. The *OED* traces the origin of this euphemism to an older meaning of the dialectal word "skive" (to move quickly or dart) current in 1854. If this is the origin of the current slang word SKIVE, then British military men who want to malinger have to move fast to avoid their duties. Those of more phlegmatic temperament GOLD-BRICK (q.v.) by SWINGING THE LEAD or LEAD SWINGING, a term derived from British nautical slang for taking soundings with a lead line. By 1919, *The Athenaeum* list defined to SWING THE LEAD as "to malinger, go sick with the object of escaping an irksome duty."

SLUG-A-BED or LIE-A-BED SLUG-A-BED comes from the Norse *slugg* (a person with a large heavy body) and *sluggje* (a heavy, slow lout). A similar form, "sluggard" for the slow and lazy, was used in English as early as 1485. It is interesting to note that the snail is named after the sluggard, for it is not called a slug until after 1704. One who, because he is lazy, lies long in bed, was called a SLUG-A-BED by Shakespeare's time. Juliet's nurse, in *Romeo and Juliet* (1597), cries, "Why lamb, why, lady, fie you slug abed," not realizing that her mistress is drugged rather than SLUGGISH (ca. 1440). Other forms of SLUG-A-BED are LOLL-A-BED and LIE-A-BED. The latter was used by Washington Irving in 1832 to denounce one of the many vices of a woman who was "a little of a slattern, something more of a lie abed, and above all, a gossip." Her twentieth-century equivalent is someone who "lies on the couch eating chocolates and watching the idiot box."

TAKE IT EASY, TO This expression, meaning to do no more than one must, is the contemporary form of the older expression TO TAKE ONE'S EASE. The phrase AN EASY LIFE dates from 1380 and its contemporary variant, ON EASY STREET, appeared at least as early as 1903. One who is ON EASY STREET is in comfortable circumstances, wealthy enough to be called leisured rather than lazy (see **LEISURE, LADY or GENTLEMAN OF**).

TEN O'CLOCK SCHOLAR Lazy or tardy person. Generations of British and American children have learned the *Mother Goose* (English translation, ca. 1744) rhyme:

> A diller, a dollar, a ten o'clock scholar,
> What makes you come so soon?
> You used to come at ten o'clock
> And now you come at noon.

By 1862, English and American schools had established "late books," and in some cases late fees, to record and punish tardy students, often considered lazy and teased for being TEN O'CLOCK SCHOLARS. An adult who behaves in the same way is said to KEEP BANKER'S HOURS. This expression, which has been current for at least eighty years, may be a reference to the more leisurely nineteenth-century practice of keeping banks open to the public for a relatively brief portion of the normal working day.

WRATH

BLACK LOOKS; TO LOOK BLACK An angry, irritated, threatening facial expression; to wear such an expression. Anger and depression can both cause a darkened complexion or gaze. A Jane Austen character in *Mansfield Park* (1814) remarks with trepidation, "My brother-in-law . . . looked rather black upon me." Even earlier, in 1789, we are told that a gentleman "swore himself black in the face." Today, being RED IN THE FACE usually denotes embarrassment, but it may also indicate anger.

BLOW or BLOW YOUR FUSE, TO To explode with anger, to express violent feeling. Although the first of these euphemisms—TO BLOW—may be as old as the nineteenth-century whaling cry "Thar she blows" for citing the spout of a whale, the second dates from about 1880. There are numerous and more mechanical variations on BLOWING ONE'S COOL (1960s and 1970s for losing one's composure). They include: BLOWING ONE'S LID (ca. 1940s), ONE'S TOP (1950s) or ONE'S GASKET (1949 or earlier) and BLOWING UP, BLOWING OFF STEAM or LETTING OFF STEAM. William and Mary Morris suspect that the grandfather of all these terms is BLOW ONE'S STACK. This euphemism refers to the smoke stacks on old riverboats. If the ship's boiler overheated, it would indeed blow the stack, creating confusion and causing widespread damage. The implication here, of course, is that anyone who is present when someone BLOWS HIS or HER

STACK is likely to be a wreck after the explosion. There are many other expressions for this eruptive way of LETTING OFF STEAM or VENTING SPLEEN (see **SPLEEN**). The terms are all physically graphic. A cork pops off a bottle if the pressure within is too great, and a lid blows off a pot if there is enough steam within etc. Many of these expressions commemorate technological inventions. To BLOW OFF STEAM, for example, dates from about 1830, the age of the steam-powered engine. At this time, it meant talking, swearing etc. vigorously as a safety valve against a more serious BLOW UP, an expression that has been used, chiefly in the United States since 1809, to mean a verbal explosion. In New Zealand TO BLOW UP means to scold. "Blow up" was, in fact, a very early expression and, when it was coined in 1225, it meant to excite or fan the flames of discord or passion. BLOWING or BLOWING ONE'S COOL are more contemporary American euphemisms that are just as violent but much less literal.

BOILING POINT, AT THE About to become enraged. AT THE BOILING POINT is one of the many expressions that link anger and cooking, particularly cooking with water. The reason is obvious: the physical similarity between the disruption of composure and the agitated surface of boiling liquids. The analogy between anger and cooking also reflects the medieval theory of humors (see introductory essay to this chapter), according to which anger was caused by overheating or cooking the yellow bile, a feat accomplished by the rising temperature of heated blood. THE BOILING POINT has been used in a general sense since 1579 and remains a "hot item" in the contemporary lexicon of euphemisms. Other anger/cooking images appear in such expressions as to BE IN A STEW (also meaning to be anxious or alarmed since 1806, and overheated, 1892), and SEETHING—a euphemistic abbreviation of "seething with rage."

CALL SOMEONE DOWN, TO To reprove someone, to challenge a person angrily or sharply. This American euphemism dates from 1899. It was used in George Ade's *Dr. Horne*, in which a character folksily remarks, "I'll call anybody down on them statements." To CALL SOMEONE DOWN (American) is to TICK HIM OFF (British, see **TICKED OFF**) or to GIVE HIM A PIECE OF YOUR MIND.

CROSS-EYED, TO LOOK AT To stare at angrily, to be angry at. The original form of the expression was probably TO LOOK AT SOMEONE WITH A CROSS-EYE SQUINT, that is, with a taunting or disgusted expression. TO CROSS or betray someone may have been an earlier and abbreviated form of both the current and original "cross-eyed" expressions. Both TO LOOK AT CROSS-EYED and TO LOOK AT CROSSLY stem from the word "cross" used to mean perverse, ill-tempered and irritable as early as 1639. When one is looked at crossly, one's NOSE IS PUT (or THRUST) OUT OF JOINT. In other words, one is irritated, annoyed, or disconcerted. This expression, though used as early as 1591, is most effectively employed in 1662 by the gossipy Samuel Pepys (*Diary*), who wrote, "The King is pleased with her: which, I fear, will put Madam Castlemaine's [his present mistress] nose out of joint." TO LOOK AT CROOKED is a much later American variation of the many euphemisms for the indirect TO LOOK ASKANCE AT.

FED UP, TO BE To be angry and/or disgusted. This expression, meaning to be filled with rage to the point of vomiting (see **SPLEEN**), has a number of variations also associated with eating and regurgitating. All seem to date from the last decades of the nineteenth century and the beginning of the twentieth. FED (UP) TO THE TEETH, and its intensified form, FED TO THE BACK TEETH, date from about 1910. FED UP TO THE EYELIDS is another variation on this theme. SPITTING NAILS, BULLETS or NICKELS is the result of being FED UP, and SPITTING BUTTON STICKS is a military Britishism for using angry or invective language. If one has reached or drawn the LAST STRAW—from the fable about "the straw that broke the camel's back"—one is likely to be FED UP (especially if one was forced to EAT ONE'S WORDS [i.e., take back what one has said]). In *Dombey and Son* (1848), Dickens used THE LAST STRAW to mean FED UP.

FLY OFF THE HANDLE, TO   To get violently angry or out of control. This colloquialism dates from about 1843 in the United States and is now common throughout the English-speaking world. The image embodied in it is derived from woodcutting, during which too violent a blow would cause an ax blade to fly off its handle. Similarly, to GO OFF THE HANDLE means to die. To FLY OFF THE HANDLE suggests the image of breaking or dissevering parts because the force of emotion has made one lose the control that holds one together. A number of other expressions for anger also suggest this image of loss of control (to LOSE CONTROL) including to FLIP ONE'S LID.

GET ONE'S OWN BACK, TO   To exact revenge. TO GET SOMEONE, in the sense of annoying or bothering someone, became a part of American English in 1867 (*Dictionary of American English*). TO GET BACK AT was a popular United States colloquialism by 1888. The reflexive form of this expression dates from ca. 1910, but was probably popularized by Bernard Shaw's *Pygmalion*. Henry Higgins: "You have wounded me to the heart, Eliza." Eliza Doolittle: "I'm glad I got a little of my own back!"

GOAT, TO GET ONE'S   To make someone angry. This mysterious American euphemism, now also common in Britain, dates from 1912. C. Mathewson, in *Pitching in a Pinch*, describes a tense baseball scene: "Then Lobert . . . stopped at third [base] with a mocking smile on his face which would have gotten the late Job's goat." "The late Job" is the proverbially patient man from the Bible whose flocks were destroyed to try his forebearance. Even Job must have been tempted to RAISE CAIN or FLIP HIS RASPBERRY (become enraged) when his last goat was taken.

GRASSFIGHTER, A   An angry person, a brawler and a bruiser (Australian). This Australian term has been used since 1930 and possibly indicates that a man who gets sufficiently angry knocks his opponent down on the grass, where they struggle.

HACKLES UP, TO PUT ONE'S or TO SHOW ONE'S

HACKLES To become enraged or to be willing to fight. This expression, in use by 1881, compares an angry human being to a fighting cock. Hackles are the feathers on the back of the neck of a bird or the hairs on the back of a dog that become erect when the animal is angry or threatened. The expression, probably derived from both cock fights and fox-hunts (the hound's hackles are up when he is about to kill the fox), is most often applied to people. Other versions of it are: GETTING ONE'S DANDER UP (1848; dander is flecks of dried skin), GETTING ONE'S BACK UP (1728; like the back of an angry cat), GETTING ONE'S QUILLS UP (like a porcupine) and GETTING ONE'S BRISTLES UP (like a wild boar). One may also BRISTLE (1533) and discover that irritation is RUFFLING ONE'S FEATHERS. The assumption underlying all these euphemisms is that uncontrollable anger transforms man into a beast.

HUFF, TO BE IN A A huff is a fit of petulance of offended dignity and was used, at first, in the now obsolete phrase TO TAKE HUFF, or offense. Fanny Burney, in *Evelina* (1778), thus describes an angry woman: "She went out of the room quite in a huff." A person IN A HUFF has, since the seventeenth century, been MIFFED, possibly from an instinctive angry explosion or sound of disgust; another possible source for the word is the German *Muff, Miff* or *Miff-muff*, meaning a sound, sign or feeling of disgust. Originally, an angry person TOOK A MIFF. In seventeenth-century English script f's and s's looked very similar; hence "to take a miff" became TO TAKE AMISS. "Miff," "tiff," "huff," and "amiss" are all etymologically related.

INCENSED, TO BE This expression for being inflamed with wrath, angry, or enraged, was used by Shakespeare in *Richard III* (1594). With a number of other phrases, it suggests the heating or boiling of the blood and/or yellow bile (see **BOILING POINT**). It is parallel to HEATED (1593), HOT-TEMPERED, and HOT UNDER THE COLLAR (1920). TO BE HOT, meaning angry or excited (see also Chapter 7, STRAIGHT SEX, **HOT FOR**), has been used since 1225. Other expressions for anger that come from the medical tra-

---

dition's culinary references to the humors include: TO FUME, TO BURN, TO DO A BURN, TO SIZZLE. The more serious medical consequences of "overheating" may be cracking or breakage, so that too warm a temper may make those incapable of "burning with a hard gem-like flame" BUST A BLOOD VESSEL and HAVE A HEMORRHAGE.

IRISH UP, TO GET or PUT ONE'S   This expression, from as early as 1834, politely associates temper and nationality. The Irish have been perhaps rightly accused of having red hair and perhaps wrongly accused of having the temper to go with it. This Americanism, first used in Crockett's *Narrative Life* (1834), describes a woman's fit of passion by saying, "Her Irish was up too high to do anything with her." Although both men and women have been considered subject to Irish tempers, the DONNYBROOK is a particularly male manifestation of them. This term for a fight or brawl entered the language in 1900. It immortalizes the name of an Irish town famous for its riotous, uproarious annual fair.

JIMMY BRITS or JIMMIES, THE   An anxiety attack or temper tantrum. This Australian expression for a fit of either nerves or rage is rhyming slang for "shits." It is derived from the name of a boxer, Jimmy Brit, who toured Australia in about 1918. When an Australian is TOEY (1940s), nervous, restive or touchy—possibly in analogy with a nervous horse pawing the ground—he has THE BRITS UP.

LARRY DOOLEY, TO GIVE SOMEONE   To express anger; to beat someone up. No one knows who Larry Dooley was, but some say that this Australian expression for a verbal or physical assault is derived from the name of a boxer, Larry Foley. A BARNEY, on the other hand, is not derived from the name of a person but from a British term of the 1880s for a prize fight. It now simply means an argument. If one is not quite up to a BARNEY or GIVING SOMEONE LARRY DOOLEY, one may GIVE SOMEONE CURRY, GET ON ONE'S QUINCE, or GO TO MARKET. The first of these Australian terms, used in the 1940s, is an elaboration of MAKING SOMETHING HOT FOR SOMEONE, that is, expressing anger toward or assaulting another person. The second of them, also from the 1940s, means to annoy or irritate someone, analogous to GETTING ON ONE'S NERVES. The last term, GOING TO MARKET or TOWN is from about 1898 and means, in Australia, to behave in a violent or angry way. In America, the expression has several meanings and may indicate either anger or enthusiasm ("You sure went to town on that roast beef!"). In a wonderful cross-cultural mix, K. S. Pritchard in *Golden Miles* (1948) has a character say: "She goes to market when I get *shickered* [Yiddish for 'drunk']."

LAVENDER, TO LAY OUT IN   To be angry enough to knock someone down or to kill him. To LAY OUT IN LAVENDER comes from the older, more punitive meaning of LAYING OUT, i.e., prostrating an opponent in wrath. It was combined with another of the term's meanings, that is, stretching out a body while preparing it for burial. To LAY UP IN LAVENDER (1822) meant both laying out and embalming a body with herbs (e.g., lavender) and putting someone out of the way of doing harm by, for example, putting him in prison. It is probably the antecedent form of to LAY OUT IN LAVENDER, but does not imply the same violence. To LAY SOMEONE OUT, or LOW, or ON HIS BACK was used as early as 1655 to mean to knock down. Gurnall, in *The Christian in compleat armor or the saints war against the devil* (1655), said of unrepentant sinners, "They never look up to heaven until God lays them on their back." Other forms of the expression are: TO LAY IN (1809), which became TO LAY INTO (1838), that is, to deliver a blow or to thrash, and the euphemism based on farming imagery, TO PITCH INTO, that is, to attack with a pitchfork.

LIVID, TO BE or BECOME   To get very angry or enraged. There is no agreement on the exact shade a person turns when LIVID with rage, but the term has denoted intense, painful emotion since 1720, when Gay used it. Whether it means purply red, pale, blue or black and blue is not entirely clear; however, all these colors reflect the connection between lividness and one's liver, the seat of violent feeling.

OWL, TO TAKE THE Popular in England during the late eighteenth through mid-nineteenth centuries, this euphemism is now obsolete. However, the association between owls and anger may arise from the fact that owls are night birds who live in blackness, or from their long identification with war deities, or from their predatory and carnivorous nature. We believe that the expression, TO TAKE THE OWL, should be revived, and that is why it appears here.

PET, TO BE IN A To take offense at one's treatment, to be angry, to sulk. The expression TO TAKE THE PET was used as early as 1590 in Lodge's "Rosalynde. Euphues Golden Legacie." It equated an angry person with a pet animal or a spoiled, overindulged child. The latter equation may seem strange to Americans but, in England, a PET has long meant a spoiled brat. The expression to BE IN A PET may be compared to the early to BE IN A TIFF (1727), probably from the word "tiff," meaning a slight puff of air or gas (1727). This expression has survived as to HAVE A TIFF (a temporary disagreement or quarrel). In 1754, Richardson (*Sir Charles Grandison*) used the expression when he wrote, "My lord and I have had another little tiff."

PIECE or BIT OF ONE'S MIND, TO GIVE SOMEONE A To give an angry retort or scolding. This expression should be compared with the more direct TO TELL SOMEONE OFF. Although it originally meant giving someone your candid opinion about something, by 1861 it had come to indicate a highly uncomplimentary opinion. In 1864, the London *Times* described a parliamentary debate in which a gentleman "had given the House what was called 'a bit of his mind' on the subject." In the process, he probably CALLED SOMEONE DOWN (q.v.).

ROW, KICK UP or MAKE A Cause a commotion or a violent quarrel. This expression is an example of the conversion of a vulgarism into a euphemism. When first used in 1781 in Britain, it was considered a very low expression, but by 1880, it had become socially acceptable. Its origin is obscure. Similar to it are KICK UP A ROUGH and BUCK UP A ROUGH,

---

which come from the still earlier "roughshod." "To ride roughshod over someone," meaning in its figurative sense to tyrannize, was in use by 1688. A roughshod horse (or person) wore shoes from which the nails projected. The angry person implied in this expression is compared to a violent animal kicking up the ground beneath his feet. The form "rough" is an earlier one, and we suspect that "row" was simply the product of that change in pronunciation so common in the development of Old and Middle English to Modern English. The gutturals and glottals of the Germanic words were swallowed and the result was a blend. In this way *thoghte* became "thought," *knyghte*, "knight" etc. A third expression of the same meaning is KICK UP (British) or CUT (American) A SHINDY. The latter was in use in England in 1845. This expression may have come from the nautical game of shindy—a spree of noisemaking or a rough dance among sailors (1811).

SCENE, TO MAKE or THROW A To create a disturbance; to exhibit strong feeling or anger. The expression, parallel to the French *faire une scène*, was current by 1761. The eighteenth century was a golden age of theatre, from which we suspect the metaphor was derived. The folly of MAKING A SCENE was discussed by Aubrey in 1831, and the combined form THROWING A SCENE probably associates the act of throwing a chair, dish or fit in the presence of others with MAKING A SCENE.

SPITFIRE, A A hot-tempered person, usually a woman. From 1680 on, this expression has been used to describe those of quick temper and irascible, fiery disposition. Richard Baxter, in *Catholic Communion Defended* (1680), reports that "malignant spit-fires do already write books full of palpable lies against other men." The expression was later used (1825) to describe a cat with her back up. It is best known to Americans through dozens of vintage 1930s and 1940s movies; in *The Untamed*, for example, red-haired Paulette Goddard smacks her master and is angrily called "you little spitfire." The Spitfire fighter aircraft, taking its name from the term for a tempestuous woman, has become a legend in Britain since its use in World War II. Other such terms that insist upon the connection between choler and fire include FIRE-EATER (1804), an expression first used for a man fond of fighting and dueling and, before the United States Civil War, for a violent partisan of the Southern cause. Still others are HOT-TEMPERED (see **INCENSED, HOT TEMPERED**) A FLARE UP, and FIERY.

SPLEEN, TO VENT   To express violent anger, to give expression to one's feelings of rage. The spleen was once regarded as the seat of the melancholic and choleric humors (i.e., the black or yellow bile). SPLEEN, meaning rage, was first used in English in 1390 (Gower, *Confessio Amantis*). Shakespeare uses it frequently to mean hot or proud temper. In *Romeo and Juliet* (1597), he writes of "the unruly spleen of Tybalt" and in *Richard III* (1594), of "damned spleen." VENTING SPLEEN became a euphemism only after people had become unfamiliar with the older equation between spleen and rage. Whereas VENTING SPLEEN is a purgative process, WAXING WROTH (growing angry) has been interpreted humorously as a polishing or refining one. We never forget that Groucho Marx, when told that a Mr. Jones, whom he had kept waiting, was WAXING WROTH, said, "Well, tell Roth to come in and let Jones wax someone else for a while."

TICKED OFF, TO BE; TO TICK OFF   To be angry, to arouse anger; to reprimand (British). In a 1919 article in *The Athenaeum* magazine on British war slang, TO TICK OFF is defined as "to reprimand." According to Partridge this is, in effect, to check off (or tick off, British) a name on a list, thus to give someone a bad mark. Americans have adopted the phrase but changed its meaning to indicate anger rather than censure. The world is apparently divided into aggressors (those who TICK others OFF) and victims (those who are TICKED OFF). Since World War II, both tickers and tickees have accepted TICKED OFF as the polite substitute for "pissed off."

TOOTH AND NAIL or TOOTH AND CLAW, TO GO AT

SOMEONE To argue or fight violently with someone. This phrase, originally, TO GO AT IT WITH TOOTH AND NAIL (or CLAW), means literally using one's teeth and nails for biting and scratching an opponent. Now, however, it is almost always used figuratively to mean to attack with vigor. By 1562, it had become proverbial. An expression from the same family and with a similar meaning is TO LOCK HORNS. This originated in the observation that embattled cattle frequently entangle horns during their charges at one another. It was American and was effectively used in 1888 in Bryce's *American Commonwealth* when he described "the boss of Tammany with whom Mr. [Grover] Cleveland had . . . 'locked horns.' " Within the last decade, an informant described a meeting between two men named Bullock and Gilgore by telling us that "Mr. Bullock and Mr. Gilgore really locked horns." He did not name the victor but the match was at least nominally even.

UMBRAGE, TO TAKE; TO GIVE UMBRAGE To be angry, annoyed; to give offense. Originally spelled "ombrage," the word appears in English as early as 1620. In the form TO TAKE UMBRAGE AT, the phrase appears in about 1680. Umbrage is literally shade or shadiness, and the word in this expression suggests either the blackness of a rage (see **BLACK LOOKS**) or the shadow crossing the face of an angry person.

WORDS, TO HAVE To engage in a heated argument. This current expression derives from the older HAVE HIGH WORDS in which "high" meant in a raised or loud voice (ca. 1205). LETTING SOMEONE HAVE IT is a similar expression, recorded in America as early as 1848. It was in use in England by the 1880s. HAVING IT OUT, expressing one's grudge or anger against someone, is also American in origin and dates from the mid-nineteenth century.

DESPAIR: SUICIDE

BLUE Depressed, unhappy. As early as 1550 to LOOK BLUE

meant to look dispirited and unhappy. BLUE LOOKS referred to the darkened face that was an outcome of an excess of melancholy humors (see WRATH, **BLACK LOOKS**). By 1833, A BLUE LOOKOUT meant depressing affairs, circumstances and prospects and, when things LOOKED BLUE (Trollope, 1858), they looked equally unpromising. The BLUE DEVIL, meaning a condition of melancholy or sorrow, is even earlier. Robert Burns, in 1787, speaks of "blue devilism," and Washington Irving, in 1807, uses BLUES as an abbreviation for "blue devils." The BLUE DEVILS themselves are the apparitions seen during the DTs and, where we may see PINK ELEPHANTS, they saw BLUE DEVILS. All these associations between blueness and grief were reinforced by the American songs of the 1920s called THE BLUES. We now speak of SINGING and CRYING THE BLUES when we mean grieving or complaining. That no one, regardless of age, sex or race, is immune to the BLUES has been asserted by a host of song titles from the twenties to the present: "Mama's Got the Blues, Papa's Got the Blues," "Young Blues," "Downhearted Blues," "Black and Blue," "St. Louis Blues," "Talking Blues," "Union Blues" and, finally, "Am I Blue?" To this much sung question, there are literally thousands of answers because a simple yes or no has never satisfied the craving for SINGING SONGS OF WOE.

BLUE FUNK, TO BE IN A   To be affected with fear or anxiety, to be dismayed, perturbed, miserable, or depressed. (See **BLUE.**) The BLUE FUNK, a state of extreme nervousness and dread, seems to have been first used in the British *Saturday Review* in 1861 as "we encounter . . . the miserable Dr. Blandling in what is called . . . a blue funk." The term was certainly popular and, in 1871, a certain Maxwell (*Life*) created an erudite anachronism when he noted that "χλωρὸν δεζος is the Homeric for a blue funk." A funk is, according to both Noah Webster and Funk and Wagnalls, a fright. It may be described, as well, as an extreme form of the mythical emotional condition known as THE BLAHS. THE BLAHS was a disease—invented by ad writers in the 1960s—that could be

---

cured only by taking Alka Seltzer: "Plop plop, fizz fizz, oh, what a relief it is!"

BROKEN UP Upset, actively depressed, weeping etc. To be BROKEN UP, CUT UP, BROKEN-HEARTED (1526), BROKEN-DOWN, and BROKEN-SPIRITED (1824) are all variations of the same experience and the expression of it. They suggest GOING TO PIECES or FALLING APART or COMING UNGLUED, as well as the more severe CRACKING UP, images of the dissociation and fragmentation that comes from despair.

CREPE HANGER, A A depressed person, pessimist. CREPE HANGING or venting one's depression comes from the use of the fabric crepe for ladies' mourning dresses and men's hatbands and armbands. The tradition of literally hanging crepe around one as a sign of grief is as early as 1763. Wreaths of crepe were also hung on the doors and in the rooms of a house of mourning. A CREPE HANGER, now meaning a professional pessimist, is a SAD SACK who RAINS ON EVERYONE'S PARADE. The term SAD SACK clearly comes from demonstrating one's grief by wearing sackcloth and ashes, the traditional biblical mourning gear.

CRESTFALLEN, TO BE or TO LOOK To be or look disheartened, saddened, depressed. CRESTFALLEN, like CHAPFALLEN and CHOPFALLEN, indicates the physical signs of a DROOPY or DROOPING SPIRIT. A bird with a drooping crest is CAST DOWN in spirits, confidence and courage. In 1589, Pappe W. Hatchet described such a sad fowl when he wrote, "Oh, how meagre and lean he looked, so crestfallen that his comb hung down to his bill." This expression, like the others mentioned, was later applied to human appearance and behavior. The "chops" or "chaps," the jaws or the areas on the cheeks, were also known to fall when a person or animal was dejected or dispirited, as was the tail (TO HAVE YOUR TAIL DOWN). In 1608, Day spoke of pouring "the spirit of life . . . into the jaws of chapfallen scholarship." CHAPFALLEN was used again in 1794 by Wolcott to describe the condition of a lover: "But if his nymph unfortunately frowns,/Sad, chapfall'n low! he hangs himself or drowns."

Those whose crests or chaps have fallen HAVE A LONG FACE. To HAVE A LONG FACE or to PULL A LONG FACE has been in use in English since 1786. Another version of the LONG FACE is the mysterious FRIDAY FACE (1592), perhaps derived from the fact that Friday was a fast day in Catholic countries and Good Friday is the day of mourning preceding Easter Sunday. A FRIDAY LOOK AND A LENTEN FACE (ca. 1681) has become a proverb. A FRIDAY LOOK is a gloomy expression. Friday itself has a long history as an ill-omened day. A famous medieval apostrophe (Geoffrey of Vinsauf, twelfth century) refers to it as the day of Richard I's death, and Chaucer's Nun's Priest mourns it as the day that almost brings death to the comic hero of his tale. December 6, 1745, a Friday, brought a panic to London as the landing of the Young Pretender was announced. May 11, 1866, another Friday, was the day of a great British commercial panic. Remember Friday the 13th!

DO AWAY WITH ONESELF or DO ONESELF IN, TO A number of euphemisms for suicide utilize reflexive forms of verbs, suggesting self-murder (German, *Selbstmord*; Latin, *suicidium*). One may DO AWAY WITH ONESELF, LAY VIOLENT HANDS ON ONESELF, TAKE ONE'S OWN LIFE, DO ONESELF HARM and DIE BY ONE'S OWN HAND. All the terms combine the reflexive with a general impersonal expression, such as "to do," "to end," "to take." TO DO AWAY WITH ONESELF, for example, comes from the earlier DO AWAY WITH, used in 1230 to mean destroy. Another form of the expression, TO DO FOR, meaning to injure fatally or to destroy, was current by 1752. This was later shortened to TO DO, as in I'LL DO HIM (I'll kill him). The same pattern may be recognized in TO TAKE THE LIFE OF. It was used as early as 1300 (*Cursor Mundi*), in the phrase "his life shall from him be taken," to mean to kill another or, in this work, to be killed by another. It later became reflexive as TO DO ONESELF IN or to DO AWAY WITH ONESELF. LAYING VIOLENT HANDS ON ONESELF comes from the earlier (1380) LAY HANDS ON, meaning to punish or kill. By 1662, it had also

---

The Seven Deadly Sins and Sundry Peccadilloes   127

assumed its reflexive form to refer to harming the *self*. *The Book of Common Prayer*, in its "Service for the Burial of the Dead," speaks of those who have LAID VIOLENT HANDS ON THEMSELVES. TO MAKE AN END OF or TO (another person) is found as early as 1340 and follows the same pattern. Thus there is an historical "grammar of suicide" in which the earliest forms were simple active verbs for murder. These developed into reflexive verbs indicating murder of the self. All these expressions for DOING ONESELF HARM reflect the convoluted syntax that perhaps embodies the religious, legal, ethical and social Western attitudes that suicide is a perverse act.

DOWN   In despair, depressed, melancholy. To be DOWN or IN LOW SPIRITS comes from "to down" or put in a state of depressed spirits, used as early as 1330 by Robert Mannyng of Brunne. DOWN is probably a shortening of "downcast," but it appears in its shortened form as early as 1645. One is often DOWN IN THE MOUTH (depressed) when one is DOWN AND OUT (unsuccessful, destitute and thus miserable). The latter phrase is an Americanism dating from 1889 and immortalized in the later song "Nobody Loves You When You're Down and Out" and the still later English account *Down and Out in Paris and London* by George Orwell (1933). To be LOW is used as early as 1744 and seems to be a shortening of "low-spirited." Bishop Berkeley in 1744 speaks of "lives which seem hardly worth living for bad appetite, low spirits, [and] restless nights." The expression, "I'm feeling mighty low" was popularized on American radio in the 1930s but it originated much earlier. Again, geography and the literary use of it dictate that, on the pilgrimage of life, one must inevitably pass through lowlands—THE VALE OF TEARS and SLOUGH OF DESPOND (see **PITS**)—and end in THE VALLEY OF THE SHADOW (of death).

EASY WAY OUT, TO TAKE THE   The OUT or THE GREAT OUT is death. As early as 1560 TO PUT SOMEONE OUT OF THE WAY meant to kill him. The WAY is, of course, the way or path of life. TO TAKE THE WAY OF DEATH meant to die as early as 1586. Each of these phrases incorporates the elements of our later, more current EASY WAY OUT and its less complimentary variations, the COWARD'S WAY OUT and THE GREAT OUT.

END IT ALL, TO   This euphemism comes from TO END or kill a person, an expression first used for murder in 1340. In *Henry IV, Part I* (1596), Shakespeare reports that "this sword hath ended him." Hamlet (1602), clearly alluding to suicide, immortalized the phrase in English when he spoke of the desire "to take arms against a sea of troubles and, by opposing, end them." "Them" (the troubles) become "it" (the life that causes them), and we FIND A WAY OUT of pain by ENDING IT ALL. In current parlance, we "shuffle off this mortal coil" by OFFING ourselves.

GORGING OUT   This exotic euphemism for committing suicide comes from Cornell University, located in the hilly town of Ithaca, New York. According to the *New York Times* (William Safire, "On Language," July 18, 1980), GORGING OUT is a current expression for student suicides committed by jumping off the bridge that spans one of "Cayuga's waters." The act is ostensibly a result of the despair that comes from failing college examinations. This new practice is an academic form of the older LOVER'S LEAP—a result of frustrated or rejected romantic passion. A milder form of GORGING OUT, used at other colleges, is VEGING OUT. TO VEG OUT is to turn into a vegetable (to become almost catatonic) after one fails, flunks, or BLOWS an examination.

HAPPY DISPATCH   This English term is a jocular name for the Japanese HARI KARI (also spelled "Hara Kiri," "Hurry-Curry"). The Japanese colloquial expression, of which the more elegant form is *suppuku*, means literally "cut" (*Kiri*) "belly" (*Hara*), a reference to ritual disembowelment. In 1859, the *Times* of London translated the expression when it explained that "the Japanese are . . . taught the science, mystery, or accomplishment of 'happy dispatch.' "

JOES, THE   A fit of depression. THE JOES (ca. 1915) is the

Australian form of THE WILLIES (q.v.). A place or person might give an ordinary Australian THE JOES, but a wealthier and more dignified "silvertail" (Australian slang for a rich upper cruster) would, under the same circumstances, become A DEAN MAITLAND. This character appears in the novel of 1914 *The Silence of Dean Maitland*, and in the 1934 film based on it, as a silent, tense person, weighed down by care. R. S. Whitington in *The Quiet Australian* (1969) notes the following: "The twenty-two players were far too tense to talk during the twenty-minute break. Twenty-two Dean Maitlands sipped their tea in silence."

PIP, TO GIVE THE   To depress. TO GIVE THE PIP has been a British euphemism for to depress since about 1890. Its contemporary American version is IT GIVES ME THE PIP or I HAVE THE PIP. From about 1918 on, TO PIP OUT has been a colloquial expression for "to die." "The pip," the name of a disease of poultry and other birds, has been applied, usually humorously, to various diseases in human beings and especially to the depressed state of mind since the late Middle Ages. Thackeray speaks with some disgust of "children ill with the pip or some confounded thing."

PITS or DUMPS, IN THE   Depressed, low, DOWN (q.v.). TO BE IN or FALL IN THE PITS is derived indirectly from the Bible. The pit, in the parable of Dives and Lazarus, is hell, and a PITFALL is an error or temptation serious enough to cast one into such a literal depression. Robertson, in his *Sermons* (1850), speaks of "the cold damp pits of disappointment," and the phrase clearly developed from its association with John Bunyan's SLOUGH OF DESPOND. Also called the SLOUGH OF DESPONDENCY, this famous topographical landmark was created in 1678 by Bunyan in *The Pilgrim's Progress*. Thomas Twining in *Recreations and Studies of a Country Clergyman of the Eighteenth Century* (1776) records: "I remember slumping all of a sudden into the slough of despond, and closing my letter in the dumps." One who is IN A SLUMP goes from the SLOUGH to the DUMPS to the PITS, falling into the sin of despair. The term DUMPS was first used in 1529 to mean not a place but a fit of melancholy. Later, through its association with refuse or garbage dumps, it took on an association with a physical place that is LOW and DOWN.

PLANNED TERMINATION This contemporary euphemism for suicide comes from *A Guide to Self-Deliverance*, published in 1980. Along with SELF-DELIVERANCE (q.v.) and SELF-TERMINATION, it joins a number of more colorful terms that describe processes and methods of killing oneself. These include: TO TAKE THE PIPE (meaning either the gas pipe or the opium pipe), TO TAKE AN OVERDOSE (of drugs) or, more commonly, TO OD, and TO MAKE THE GREAT LEAP (DEFENESTRATE oneself). Other terms for suicide hint at the sensations of dying. TO TURN OUT THE LIGHTS and TO DOUSE THE or ONE'S LIGHTS (see *Macbeth*, "Out, out brief candle" and *Othello*, "Put out the light, and then put out the light") equate life with light and suggest the fading of the dying person's vision. SOLITAIRE, the Black English expression for suicide (1940s), clearly derives from playing the card game that must be played alone.

SELF-DELIVERANCE SELF-DELIVERANCE and SELF-TERMINATION (see **PLANNED TERMINATION**) are two of the most recent euphemisms for suicide. Both are used in a current book called *A Guide to Self-Deliverance* (1980). In their reflexive forms they are more current and less pejorative versions of the older terms "self-slaughter," used in Shakespeare's *Hamlet* ("Oh that the everlasting had not fixed his canon 'gainst self-slaughter") and "self-murder," first used about 1586. SELF-VIOLENCE, a more delicate term for "self-murder," was used in about 1671, and SELF-EXECUTION and SELF-IMMOLATION are more recent popular forms. It is worth noting that some of the terms (especially SELF-DELIVERANCE) have substituted secular, neutral meanings for earlier religious connotations. "Deliverance" was originally used to mean God's freeing of the soul from the weary body.

SUTTEE This term, which, in 1786, meant an Indian woman who immolated herself on her husband's funeral pyre, has

---

taken on a broader meaning. By 1813, SUTTEE referred not only to the unfortunate, if dutiful and pious, woman but also the act itself. It has lost its once specifically national and positive connotations and its gender identification, so that it may now be performed by a person of "any sex, age, or marital status." Another term, similar in its national reference is THE DUTCH ACT. This euphemism, which implies TAKING THE COWARD'S WAY OUT, comes from the period of the English-Dutch conflicts and is only one of the many anti-Dutch slurs that were coined at this time (see Chapter 4, GLUTTONY: DRINK, **DUTCH CHEER**). Three hundred years later, it has lost most of its pejorative associations with nationality and now both SUTTEE and the DUTCH ACT suggest the more general GOING WITHOUT A PASSPORT. As Lytton said in 1833, "This gaiety of 'suicidalism' is not death a la mode with us." The choice of foreign terms and locales (see **HAPPY DISPATCH**) indicates the British feeling that "it's simply not done."

THROW IN THE TOWEL, TO   This expression comes from American boxing slang, in which it originally meant to admit defeat. In 1915, Corri (*Thirty Years a Boxing Referee*) related an incident in which the seconds in a boxing match " 'threw the towel' in literally." The expression comes from the earlier THROW IN, THROW UP or CHUCK UP THE SPONGE. In 1860, *The Slang Dictionary* explained that TO THROW UP THE SPONGE came from the boxing practice of throwing up the sponge used to clean the boxers' faces as a signal that the "mill" (match) was over. The expression TO THROW UP THE SPONGE appears in Dickens's *Great Expectations* (1861) when the hero defeats Herbert Pocket in a fight. This term and its variations came first to mean to be defeated and to give up the struggle and, later, TO GIVE UP THE FIGHT for life. "To chuck" and "chucking" are again boxing terms (dating from about 1875) for "to defeat" or "defeat."

WATERS OF LETHE, TO DRINK THE   This euphemism contains a classical allusion to the river of oblivion, one of the five rivers of Hades, the Greek underworld and home of the dead. To GO TO LETHE and LETHEWARDS were used poetically in English from 1602 on, and Keats, in the "Ode to a Nightingale" (1820) speaks of feeling "as though of hemlock I had drunk . . . and Lethe-wards had sunk." In mentioning hemlock, Keats draws upon another group of classical euphemisms for death. To TAKE HEMLOCK, to DRINK HEMLOCK and to QUAFF THE CUP come from the use of hemlock as a powerful sedative and, in large doses, as a poison. It is, of course, most famous as the drink used to execute Socrates. In 1635, Swann noted that "hemlock . . . is meat to storks and poison to men," thus adding to its lore. To QUAFF THE CUP means not only to DRINK HEMLOCK but, more metaphorically, to DRAIN THE CUP OF LIFE or the BITTER CUP (OF AFFLICTION; 1633).

WATERWORKS, TO TURN ON THE To have a fit of weeping. THE WATERWORKS is a jocular euphemism for a flood of tears similar to A CLOUDBURST. In use in this sense since 1647, it implies that the weeper's eyes are "copious fountains" (Herbert, 1593–1633), since the term "waterworks" meant an ornamental fountain or cascade from 1586. Other expressions for the weeping that comes from grief include: TO TUNE ONE'S PIPES (to begin to cry, 1818), and TAKE A PIPE (to weep, 1817). Both are Scots in origin and probably use the word "pipe" to refer to the human voice as it is used in singing, and to the sorrowful tones of the bagpipe. However, TO PIPE YOUR EYE (cry), thus TO PIPE, has been cockney rhyming slang since the nineteenth century.

WILLIES, TO HAVE THE To be nervous, upset, afraid, morbid. TO HAVE THE WILLIES, also known as THE WHIM-WHAMS, THE JIMMIES and THE JIM-JAMS, is to be in a state of considerable depression, fear, and upset. The JIM-JAMS, a fit of depression, came into the language in England in 1904 and THE JIMMIES, a more familiar and personal form of it, meaning gloomy fits, entered the language in this sense in 1921 (it had meant the DTs in 1885). THE WILLIES, however, does not seem to be derived from a human name but from a willow tree, which has long been a symbol of grief. The willow (Middle English, *wylaugh*) appears among the trees at a funeral in Chaucer's *Knight's Tale* (1387). As early as 1584, the expressions TO WEAR THE WILLOW or THE WILLOW GARLAND or THE GREEN WILLOW meant to grieve for the loss of a loved one. In Shakespeare's *Othello*, Desdemona remembers a poor forsaken maid called Barbary, who sat sighing "by a sycamore tree, /Sing all a green willow;/Her hand on her bosom,/Her head on her knee,/Sing willow, willow, willow." In the nineteenth century, Gisele, the betrayed and maddened heroine of the ballet of that name, is possessed by the Willis, the spirits of other deserted maidens. "Willy" is the early dialectal form of "willow." One who HAS THE WILLIES may appear possessed, as he shows the signs of fright and nervous fidgeting.

SUNDRY PECCADILLOES

BANANA OIL Insincere or foolish talk. This American euphemism for hypocritical, nonsensical bulling is a great deal younger than the name of the fruit (1563). It probably dates from the twentieth century, as do its equivalents, APPLESAUCE and BALONEY. It may originate in the expression BANANAS, an interjection used to indicate craziness or incoherent dither.

BABBITT, A A self-satisfied conformist. The American satirist Sinclair Lewis added a word to the language by describing the hero of his novel (*Babbitt*) in 1922 as a narrowminded, insular bastion of the ordinary. Since that time, those who practice conformity, rigid bourgeois attitudes and dull complacency have been guilty of the sin of BABBITTRY.

BENT Dishonest, crooked or criminal. (See also Chapter 7, GAY SEX, **CROSS**, BENT.) This originally British expression used of a crooked or criminal person dates from about 1905. TO GO BENT for "to turn criminal" entered the language in about 1901, yet both expressions ultimately come from much older sources all relating to the biblical warnings about STRAYING FROM THE STRAIT (originally meaning confined but later interpreted as "straight") AND NARROW PATH or GATE of virtue.

BIND, A or RIGID BIND, A A bore or hearty bore. It has been said that the greatest sin is to be boring, and the British have tactfully concurred by coining the gentle euphemism, A BIND and the more direct one, A YAWN. The latter expression was put to pointed use in 1964 by Harold Wilson speaking of an opponent: "Sir Alec had become a yawn, . . . tedious repetition alternated with repetitive tedium, depending on which of two speechwriters was writing his speeches" (*Manchester Guardian Weekly*, April 9, 1964).

BUTTER (UP), TO To flatter, praise unctuously, fawn upon. The *OED* cites the first use of BUTTER as "unctuous flattery" as occurring in 1823. But Congreve, in *The Way of the World* (1700), had already indicated the meaning of the expression when he announced, "The Squire that's buttered still is sure to be undone." Soft or sweet substances, especially foods, seem to be connected with sycophancy, and TO HONEY has meant to coax or flatter since 1604. The original fruit of sin, the apple, has generated such terms for flatterers as APPLE POLISHERS (American at least since 1925, but we suspect from the nineteenth century). The idea is far older, but the most obvious source of the term is the rural American practice of bringing a shined apple to the teacher as a token of good will. This was a way TO SHINE UP TO or be ingratiating to the figure in authority. The term dates from the 1880s. Allied to the expressions above by texture if not by taste is the phrase TO SOFT SOAP, used in America since 1830 and shipped to England by the 1860s. SOFT SOAP (flattery or BLARNEY) derives from potash soap or "soft sawder," as it was often called. An earlier term for a flatterer was A SOFT SAWDER or SAWDERER.

COPROLOGY Obscenity. The *OED* defines coprology as "filth in literature or art," as early as 1856, but has refused to define the lover of this material, the COPROPHILIST. It is particularly ironic that, in the 1880s, Swinburne, known to his detractors as "the libidinous laureat of a pack of satyrs," wrote: "All English readers, I trust, will agree with me that coprology should be left to Frenchmen."

DECK, NOT PLAYING WITH A FULL   Being dishonest, specifically, cheating at cards. As early as 1593, Shakespeare (in *Henry VI*) spoke of stealing a king from a deck of cards. While the term "deck" for a full pack of cards became dialectal in the north of England, it was standard in America by the 1850s—after which time this American expression must have blossomed. Cheating or card sharping, the gamblers' sin, is called GREEKERY, from the ancient idea of the Greeks as shrewd and wily in their dealings. Thus, since 1528, a card sharper has been called A GREEK. He may have cheated by NOT LAYING ALL HIS CARDS ON THE TABLE, or by hiding cards UNDER THE TABLE or SUB-ROSA (under the rose), meaning in secret since 1654. All of these expressions now have expanded to mean dishonesty in general rather than card sharping in particular. In recent years, the phrase has been applied to persons of questionable sanity or intelligence.

GRANGERIZE, TO   To mutilate a book. Formerly, this British eponym meant making a collection of clippings, often cutting them out of other books. It honors, or disgraces, James Granger (1723–76) who published the *Biographical History of England*, leaving pages blank so that his readers could insert appropriate prints or clippings. Thus he helped to found an eighteenth-century hobby, GRANGERISM. Its modern meaning, libracide, records the contemporary feeling that this is a GROTTY thing to do. GROT and GROTTINESS, from GROTTY (a recent but short-lived British slang term meaning mean, wretched, miserable, junky), were exalted to the dizziest heights by Reginald Perrin, the comic hero of British TV's "The Fall and Rise of Reginald Perrin" (1970s), when he went into the GROT business, selling useless, ugly things to silly people. However, even the Anglo-Saxons had *grot,* for Aelfred uses the term as early as 888, when it meant an atom or particle.

HOLY FRIAR   Liar. This piece of British rhyming slang was a

---

common and popular euphemism for a liar as early as the nineteenth century. After the advent of the automobile, the euphemism DUNLOP TIRE was spawned on analogy. "Friar" and "tire" are joined by an equally common cockney term of more recent vintage: DAILY MAIL (after the newspaper) delicately masks a lie or tale. A British soldier who tells tall war stories may also be lying, but he is accused of SWINGING THE LAMP. The literal meaning of the expression is particularly interesting when one considers how appearances are altered by a moving light. As early as 1671, however, A SWINGER was a big or bold lie. A more innocent deception is A BIT OF FIDDLE, the British version of "a white lie." In 1850, "fiddle" meant "cheat" or "swindle" (see Chapter 6, FLIMFLAMS, FELONIES AND MISDEMEANORS, **FLY GEE**, DOING A FIDDLE), a sense transferred to PREVARICATING in general and to the expression for nonsense or falsehood, FIDDLE-FADDLE.

IRVING, AN A boring person. This American euphemism records the dull character of the perpetrator of one of the worst sins, that of boring others to death. It is synonymous with A MELVIN, an obnoxious or boring person, popularized under this rubric in the 1950s by the comedian Jerry Lewis. The poet Phyllis McGinley implied that among the plaguiest of all sinners are dull people when she noted that "though we outwit the tithe, make death our friend/Bores we have with us even to the end."

KVETCH, A; TO KVETCH A complainer, to complain. Leo Rosten in *The Joys of Yiddish* assigns the noun at least four meanings and the verb at least five, but this Yiddish word is usually used to mean either "a whiner" or "to gripe ceaselessly." The "kv" sound in the word suggests the unpleasantness of the chronic complainer. In America, the term dates from the nineteenth century, the period of the heaviest Jewish, as well as other ethnic group, immigration. The expression spread in the northeastern United States during the 1960s and has since been heard from the mouths of such unlikely users as the Southern Protestant millworker of the movie *Norma Rae*. It is also used in England, but less commonly. One sort of KVETCH is frequently a YENTA, a Yiddish word usually used to mean a shrew, gossip or rumor monger. The origins of the word are shrouded, but it was a name or title for an old woman. It is now used for gossips of both sexes. YENTA came into more widespread usage in America when the role of Yenta Telebende was introduced. Mr. Jack Rechtzeit, former star of the Yiddish theatre, composer, playwright and president of the Hebrew Actors' Union, tells us that the character of Yenta Telebende was first played by Bessie Jacobs at the Lennox Theatre in Harlem during the 1920s. Subsequently the YENTA appeared as a stock character in the comic Yiddish theatre.

MUMPSIMUS   Stubborn persistence in error; a person who stubbornly persists in error. This erudite term records a joke of 1517 in which an illiterate English priest, corrected by a young colleague for saying "mumpsimus" instead of *sumpsimus* (we have received), replied, "Son, I've been saying *mumpsimus* for thirty years and I'm not going to change my old *mumpsimus* for your new *sumpsimus*." In other words, my mind is made up; don't confuse me with facts. Although MUMPSIMUS is obsolete in its meaning of an error caused by ignorance, those who practice it are still alive, and, therefore, we suggest the revivification of the term as a euphemism for an old fogey and an insistent error monger.

OLD MOODY   Lies. In *The Signs of Crime*, Powis cites OLD MOODY as a common criminal term currently used in Britain to mask what we in the United States call BUNKUM or BUNK. British euphemisms for lying, like the rest of British speech, are highly class conscious. A less vulgar and more acceptable term for insincere talk or deception is FLANNEL. The *Times* of July 21, 1971, reported that "the government wanted the power to put the troops in. The rest was all fairy tale and flannel." Few are those who can avoid outright FLANNEL and the task is certainly not for those given over to DONTOPEDALOGY (a natural propensity or talent for putting one's foot in one's mouth). This mock-Latin euphemism was coined by Prince Philip of England who, though he calls himself a DONTOPEDALOGIST, is rarely a victim of what we in the United States call FOOT-IN-MOUTH DISEASE.

PECKSNIFFERY Hypocrisy. Charles Dickens's character Pecksniff was the unctuous hypocrite in the novel *Martin Chuzzlewit* (1844). However, the *OED* thinks the term may come from the earlier dialectal word "picksniff" which means a paltry, despicable, insignificant and contemptible person. The expressions PECKSNIFFERY and PECKSNIFFISM have been synonymous with hypocrisy in England since 1874 and in the United States since 1888. Other hypocrites of literary origin are *David Copperfield*'s " 'umble servant, Sir," URIAH HEEP (1849–50) and Robert Burns's HOLY WILLIE, the self-righteous religious hypocrite of the poem, "Holy Willie's Prayer" (1784–88).

RIGHT SIDE OF, GET ON THE To seek favor, usually by means of flattery. The right side, with its associations of virtue and honor, has always been the position in which people want to be. The Bible speaks of the virtuous or the redeemed sitting on the right hand of God and, since the Middle Ages, the position of honor has been on the right hand of the host or king. The RIGHT SIDE is the GOOD SIDE; the left or wrong side reeks of the sinister and the unregenerate as well as the illegitimate (see Chapter 7, REPRODUCTIVE SEX, BLANKET). One may GET ON THE GOOD SIDE of someone by MAKING UP TO HIM or her, a more recent expression dating at least from the 1780s. This process may require some EYEWASH (1884), HUMBUG or BLARNEY, intended to interfere with the flatteree's clear vision.

SHILLY-SHALLY, TO To be weak, spineless or indecisive. A reduplicative form, this British and American euphemism for indecision originated in the question, Shall I, shall I? asked by the WISHY-WASHY person. The earliest form of this euphemism was TO STAND or GO SHILLY SHALLY. By 1700, Congreve, in his *Way of The World*, let a character proclaim, "I don't STAND SHILL I, SHALL I, then; if I say't I'll do't."

STRETCHER CASE, A   A liar. This expression for STRETCH-ING THE TRUTH, in use in England since about 1942, is a contemporary version of a number of puns on lying. A STRETCHER CASE refers both to the stretcher used to carry a disabled person and to the act of lying or making a lie (STRETCHING THE TRUTH). To STRETCH has meant to exaggerate or lie since about 1670. DRAWING THE LONG-BOW, again STRETCHING IT, dates from the eighteenth century, and STRAINING HARD or STRAINING are from the late seventeenth century. If one stretches a tale enough, it becomes FARFETCHED, either false or near being so, since about 1607. All of these terms are varieties of FIBS, and FIB, meaning literally a "trivial falsehood," is often used as a euphemism for a lie. *Cotsgrave's Dictionary* of 1611 puts a FIB in the category of a jest or TALE OF A TUB (A TALL TALE). The form FIBBER for a teller of a LITTLE WHITE LIE has been in use since 1568.

TERMINOLOGICAL INEXACTITUDE, A   A lie. This elaborate governmental euphemism has been in use in the United States in the last decade. But its origin is ascribed to Winston Churchill, who, in a 1906 speech to the House of Commons, said: "It could not, in the opinion of His Majesty's government, be classified as slavery in the extreme acceptance of the word, without some risk of terminological inexactitude." Government statements may also be INOPERATIVE, a term made famous in the Nixon era when the President's press secretary, Ron Ziegler, explained to him: "This is the operative statement. The others are inoperative" (1973). A more recent ingenious disguise for the art of lying is the term SELECTIVE FACTS, reported in the *Congressional Record* of September 23, 1980. The precise meaning of the term is biased or incomplete information; the implications, however, include FABRICATION.

WOLF IN SHEEP'S CLOTHING, A   A Hypocrite. The origin of this expression is St. Matthew's (7:15) admonition to "beware of false prophets, which come to you in sheep's clothing, but inwardly they are ravening wolves." It appears in

English in a variant form as early as 1400. By 1460, in the morality play *Wisdom*, we may read of "a wolf in a lamb's skin." The WOLF IN SHEEP'S CLOTHING is but one of the fabled animal hypocrites among which we meet the JAKDAW IN PEACOCK'S FEATHERS (1739) and an ASS IN LION'S SKIN (probably also 1700s). Hypocrites have been known to cry CROCODILE TEARS. The crocodile has been a hypocrite in English since 1400. In fable, the crocodile wept either to lure someone, to devour someone or, best of all, after devouring someone. W. S. Gilbert summed up a long history of distinguishing the real from the feigned in his lyric "Things Are Seldom What They Seem."

> Things are seldom what they seem—
> Skim-milk masquerades as cream—
> High-lows pose as patent leathers—
> Jackdaws strut in peacocks' feathers.

5

Death

Ever since Oedipus solved the riddle of the sphinx, thereby winning the prizes of kingship, incest, guilt and blindness, writers and thinkers have been trying to outdo his analytical feat. While he knew that what walked on four legs in the morning, two in the afternoon, and three in the evening was man in his three ages, we prefer to think of man's ages as seven in number, taking our cue from Shakespeare. First comes "the infant, mewling and puking," then "the whining schoolboy," then "the lover, sighing like a furnace," followed by "the soldier, full of strange oaths." Hard upon his heels strolls the stately "justice . . . full of wise saws." The sixth age is that of the spindleshanked old man who waits the "last scene of all," a senile second childhood in which he is "sans teeth, sans eyes, sans taste, sans everything."

Surely no mortal lives who has not wanted to escape from the painful reality of all these stages, especially the unmentioned stage, death.

Mankind's desire to forget the process of aging that leads inevitably to death is the source of a number of "kind words" that have made the stages and roles of life seem more bearable. No one in America, for example, is old. The elderly are SEASONED, WELL-PRESERVED, ELDER STATESMEN who are praised for being LONGER LIVING. Like the unsuccessful Tithonus of Greek mythology, Americans demand both eternal life and eternal youth, but the latter is our primary concern. Consequently, we attempt to preserve our looks and our figures through language by calling an aged woman a GRANDE DAME and an elderly man a distinguished gentleman. The euphemistic language of age, still sparse, is beginning to increase as more and more of our SENIOR CITIZENS live to enjoy their GOLDEN YEARS.

But aging, like youth and middle age, still fails to inspire much more than relative silence. Death, older and more successful, has bred thousands of attempts at evasion, ranging from intimate names for the fellow with the scythe to elaborate shroudings of his identity. Throughout history death has been described in terms of every new belief, technology and pastime.

In the late Middle Ages, during the period of plague and famine, death was familiar in the image of a grim reaper. In the Renaissance, attempts to humanize death resulted in tomb sculptures that portrayed the dead man as merely napping, and death was known as a sleep. From the early Middle Ages to our own time, death has been seen as a master gamesman whom everyone tried to defeat. The mortal player who lost was MATED (chess), CASHED IN HIS CHIPS (poker), JUMPED THE LAST HURDLE (steeplechasing or fox-hunting), and TOSSED IN HIS ALLEY (marbles).

Yet America can be linguistically proud. At no other time in history has a culture created a more elaborate system of words and customs to disguise death so pleasantly that it seems a consummation devoutly to be wished. What used to be reserved for descriptions of eternal life and heaven is now used to describe embalmment, the funeral, and the burial. It is here—and in Forest Lawn Memorial Park—that we are LOVED ONES, cared for by a kind BEREAVEMENT COUNSELOR, beautified forever by a DERMASURGEON and attired in a SLUMBER ROBE, gently cradled in a SLUMBER BOX and deposited in a FINAL RESTING PLACE where we can forever hear the sound of recorded heavenly harps. Even our pets now go to HAPPY HUNTING GROUNDS.

The motives for euphemizing death are in many ways similar to those for disguising our references to pregnancy and birth. Great superstition surrounded these events, as did great distaste and a sense of social impropriety. Propelled by these feelings, we have attempted to strip death of both its sting and its pride—in fact to kill death by robbing it of its direct and threatening name. The terms change and the euphemisms grow, but the evasion of the word "death" survives.

ABRAHAM'S BOSOM, TO BE IN or TO REST IN To be dead and WITH GOD. This expression comes from Luke 16:22, "And it came to pass that the beggar [Lazarus] died and was carried by the angel into ABRAHAM'S BOSOM." The biblical phrase itself may have come from the ancient custom of the host's permitting a dinner guest to recline against his chest. This is one of the many biblical expressions or paraphrases that have passed into pulpit oratory, hymnology and eulogy. The lexicon encompasses: TO GO TO ONE'S LAST or JUST REWARD, TO BE GONE TO A BETTER PLACE or TO SLEEP ("and he slept with his fathers," says Genesis), and TO BE AT REST or TO HAVE FOUND REST. The dead in biblical terms are also WITH GOD, IN HEAVEN, WITH THE ANGELS, WITH THEIR FATHER. Those who HAVE BEEN LAID TO REST are HOME and FREE. In 1785, the poet Gray used the now familiar expression IS AT PEACE, which is a derivative of the phrase from the Mass for the Dead: *Requiescat in pace* (RIP), as are the phrases he HAS BEEN LAID TO REST and GOD REST HIS SOUL.

BIG JUMP, THE This cowman's expression (Raymond F. Adams, *Western Words*) describes the victim of death as having taken THE BIG JUMP, often WEIGHTED DOWN WITH HIS BOOTS. Closely related to it is the steeplechase expression for dying—TO JUMP THE LAST HURDLE.

BIT, TO DO ONE'S   To serve one's cause or country, often dying in the course of such service. In World War I, this phrase meant to serve one's country in the military or as a civilian and implied making one's contribution or doing one's share. The connotation of MAKING THE ULTIMATE SACRIFICE was a later one. Its meaning has become as specific as that of the other military euphemisms for death: TO FIRE ONE'S LAST SHOT, TO BE PRESENT AT THE LAST ROLL CALL or THE LAST MUSTER. Compare also the more recent aeronautical expression, GROUNDED FOR GOOD.

BLACK OUT, TO   Robert Browning in *Christmas Eve and Easter Morn* (1850) wrote, "If he blacked out in a blot thy brief life's unpleasantness." In its current use, the meaning of "black out" has been both reinforced and amplified by the theatre and photography. In both arts, artificial light enabled a mere mortal to black out an object or person literally. The general metaphor was certainly inherent in much earlier expressions such as Othello's "Put out the light, and then put out the light" and Macbeth's "Out, out, brief candle," in which lives are SNUFFED OUT. Another theatre and cinema expression for "to die" encapsulates its later origins in its technological terminology; it is SWITCH OUT THE LIGHTS.

BOX, TO GO HOME IN A   To die or be killed and laid in one's coffin. In 1854, W. Henry (*Death of a Legend*) referred to a much earlier colloquial expression when he wrote: "Personally, I'll believe he's [Jesse James] dead when the box is shut and covered up." TO GO HOME IN A BOX goes back, in general use, to World War II and was also gangster lingo, as was TO HAVE A FUNERAL IN ONE'S FAMILY.

CHECK OUT, TO   This is an extremely current and common hospital euphemism. In American hospitals, patients who are OUT OF (THEIR) PAIN or have BREATHED THEIR LAST are described as having CHECKED OUT (literally, "left the hospital"), as being NO LONGER WITH US, as having GONE UNDER (the level of consciousness or of measurable vital signs associated with life), or as having GONE OUT.

CHIPS, TO CASH IN (ONE'S) This expression, one of the many American financial terms for death, refers to SETTLING ONE'S ACCOUNTS or closing up a matter—often in poker. By 1891 it was used, figuratively, for dying, and other forms of the euphemism—CASH IN ONE'S CHECKS, PASS IN ONE'S CHECKS—were in use as much as forty years earlier. (See DEBT OF NATURE.)

CREEK, TO BE BLOWN or GONE ACROSS or OVER THE To be dead of unnatural causes. This nineteenth-century American expression is still in use. It originated with the munitions industry, particularly with the Du Pont gunpowder factories along the rivers and creeks of Pennsylvania and Delaware. Often the powder ignited and blew up the workers, literally propelling them across or over the adjacent creek or river. A few of the other expressions for dying an explosive death are: GO BLOOEY (or BLOOIE), GO FLOOEY (or FLOOIE), or POP OFF.

CROAK, TO To die, or kill. In 1877, TO CROAK was American slang for "to kill," but by the 1920s and 1930s—when the word was extremely popular—it was used in both its active and passive senses. One may BE CROAKED, CROAK, or, more theatrically, DO THE CROAK ACT. Among the other numerous underworld expressions for dying and death are: A BACK GATE or BACK DOOR PAROLE (that is, to die while in prison) and A ONE-WAY TICKET or RIDE. The latter expression comes from the Chicago gangster phrase of the 1920s, still in use—to TAKE SOMEONE FOR A ONE-WAY RIDE (that is, to a secluded place for execution). Other more graphic expressions originally derived from gangland use include TAKING A LONG WALK OFF A SHORT PIER and WEARING CEMENT SHOES.

CROSS OVER, TO To die, TO GO TO THE HEREAFTER. In 1889, Tother, in Barrère and Leland's dictionary, explained CROSSING OVER THE RIVER JORDAN as dying, but the expression originated much earlier in the century. It first appeared in Negro spirituals. From the 1840s on, the phrase was a standard one in the rhetoric of the spiritualist movement.

CURTAINS This is one of the many contemporary theatre metaphors for death. Ever since Shakespeare's comparisons of life, death and theatrical productions—especially Macbeth's "life's . . . but a poor player that struts and frets his hour upon the stage, and then is heard no more"—the theatrical lexicon for death has expanded. It includes: DROP THE CURTAIN, THE FINAL CURTAIN, THE CURTAIN CALL, THE LAST CALL, THE LAST BOW, BOW OFF and BOW OUT. THE LAST BOW is traditionally a farewell, and none is more touching than the dying John Keats's farewell to his dearest friend (1821): "Forgive me, I have always made an awkward bow."

CUT OFF, TO BE In 1888, the phrase was used to denote being deprived of telephonic or telegraphic communication. It assumed its figurative meaning in 1891. Many other expressions for death originated in the growing communications industry and include: RING OFF or RING OUT (telephone) and -30- (a telegraphic signal for "the end," hence death).

CUT ONE'S STICK, TO This British expression was used as early as 1825 when it meant TO TAKE ONE'S DEPARTURE, an event for which one either carved a new or picked up an old walking stick. Shortly thereafter it became a figurative reference to THE FINAL DEPARTURE.

DAISIES, TO COUNT or BE UNDER THE To die and be buried. Daisies and other flowers of the field have figured large in a number of botanical images of death and burial. Daisy imagery, like the flower itself, seems to be the commonest and to have originated with the expression, TO TURN ONE'S TOES TO DAISIES (to decay). The famous "Babes in the Woods," in *The Ingoldsby Legends* (1842), urges us to "be kind to those dear little folks/When our toes are turned up to the daisies." By 1866, George Macdonald further sweetened this already saccharine expression, by saying, "I shall very soon hide my name under some daisies." Commoner and more current forms used in America are COUNTING DAISIES and PUSHING UP DAISIES. Rodgers and Hammerstein set the concept to music in the ironic lyric from the musical comedy *Oklahoma!* (1940) "Poor Judd Is Dead": "The daisies in the dell/Will give off a different smell/Because poor Judd is underneath the ground." Other botanical expressions are the traditional biblical GO TO GRASS and the New World HOLD UP THE BERMUDA GRASS.

DEBT OF NATURE, TO PAY THE The term DEBT OF NATURE, meaning the necessity of dying, was first used in 1225 in the *Ancrene Riwle*, a guide for female hermits. In 1315, Shoreham proved the currency of the expression by referring to "his death's debt" and the term appeared in the later part of the century in Barbour's *Bruce* in its Latin form *debitum naturae*. Marlowe used it in the sixteenth century, thus proving that the euphemism was current over at least three centuries. A comparable and current expression is TO PAY ONE'S LAST DEBT. We still speak of imprisoned or executed criminals as having PAID THEIR DEBT TO SOCIETY. Both natural and unnatural death are often referred to in monetary and accounting terms. Financial metaphors for death include: CLOSING UP or SETTLING ONE'S ACCOUNTS and CANCELLING ONE'S ACCOUNTS, and all such euphemisms echo Shakespeare's suggestion in *Henry V, Part I* that "we owe God a death" to balance the cosmic ledger. Perhaps his longest disquisition on life, death and sorrow as debts appears in his Sonnet 30, where he "tells o'er the sad account of forebemoaned moan,/which I new pay as if not paid before." (See also **CHIPS**.)

FINAL SUMMONS, THE In 1586, the Countess of Pembroke translated Psalm 49, 3 as "sure at his [death's] summons, wise and fools appear." In 1676, Glanville asserted in his *Seasonal Reflections* that "the dead shall be raised by a general summons." The imagery of summoning originates in the Book of Revelation's description of the raising of the dead, as does the euphemism, THE FINAL CALL. Another variation, THE CALL OF GOD (to death), appeared in 1886 in *Leslie's Popular Monthly*: "All the doctors in Christendom . . . can't save him. He's called."

FLUNK OUT, TO An 1823 edition of the *Crayon* (the Yale College magazine) written by Josiah Bartlett declares, "We must have at least as many subscribers as there are students in college or flunk out [fail]!" Bartlett was using the expression in its original sense, "to fail out of school." But this, and other general expressions for failure, were also used to describe death, which was considered (presumably) the ultimate failure. They include TO BE ALL WASHED UP or TO BE WASHED OUT. In 1902 the expression WASHOUT was used in Britain to mean a "disappointing failure" or "sell."

GO WEST, TO To die, perish, or disappear. As early as 1515, a Scots poet, Grey, wrote that "women and money will so [go] away/as wind or water are gone west." Shakespeare frequently used the well-known simile that equates the west, the sunset and winter with death. In 1805, Wordsworth, in "Stepping Westward," described that act as "a kind of heavenly destiny." In our own century, E. Corri in his *Thirty Years a Boxing Referee* (1915) greeted his end cheerfully because he would "now be in the company of many dear old friends now 'gone west.' " The expression mirrors the fact that traditionally the east, where the sun rises, has been considered the place of birth and the west has been seen as the region where the sun and man's life set.

GREAT LEVELLER, THE Death personified. Although we do not know when this euphemism for death was coined, we do know that it is a clear reference to a very old saw popular in the Middle Ages: popes, kings, beggars, and thieves alike must die. Rank and position do not protect one from death, when the humble are raised and the proud brought low. In England, the term "leveller" has had a long, significant history that undoubtedly contributed to the origin of the euphemism or, at least, to its popularity. It was the name of a political party of the 1640s that believed in obliterating all differences and privileges acquired by rank or position. In 1647, the *Newsletter* of November 1 reported that the members of the party had "given themselves a new name, viz. Levellers, for they intend to set all things straight and raise a parity and community in the kingdom." The Puritans, the Diggers and the Levellers alike believed that all men were equal (level) in the eyes of God, but the general concept of levelling as equalizing is earlier. In 1659, debauchery was called a leveller because "it takes off all distinctions." By 1758, Samuel Johnson emphasized the idea of death as a leveller when he wrote that "sleep is equally a leveller with death."

GREAT WHIPPER, THE Death personified. This British colloquial term of the 1860s was drawn from fox hunting. The whipper-in is the huntsman's assistant who prevents the hounds from straying by whipping them back into the main body of the pack, in effect, rounding them up. (For comparison see **LAST ROUNDUP**.)

GRIM REAPER, THE Death personified. The *OED* suggests that the first use of the epithet in English is in Longfellow's *The Reaper and the Flowers* (1839). The poem begins:

> There is a Reaper whose name is Death,
> And, with his sickle keen,
> He reaps the bearded grain at a breath,
> And the flowers that grow between.

However, the image of death as a reaping figure with a scythe that cuts down men appears much earlier; it is found on fifteenth-century woodcuts, in religious poetry, and on seventeenth-century tombstones. Andrew Marvell's poem "Damon the Mower" (1681) ends with the line "For, Death, thou art a Mower too." The expression is still alive and well, and, in a 1931 issue of *Notes and Queries*, a eulogist wrote that "one is startled by the inroads that the great reaper has made in the ranks of the Knights since the fifteenth edition. . . ." THE GRIM REAPER is also known as THE GRIM MONARCH and OLD MR. GRIM. His iconography is, of course, similar to that used for FATHER TIME, and other personifications of him include MR. MOSE or OLD MAN MOSE. The *OED* speculates that the name MOSE may be a corruption of the verb "to mose" (to mourn), which was used by Shakespeare.

HEREAFTER, IN THE Dead; in the afterlife. "We hope to have the life that will come here after," said the author of the poem *Alexander and Dindamus* sometime between 1330 and 1370. Hopes of THE WORLD TO COME also impelled Longfellow's *Hiawatha* some five hundred years later. In 1855, Longfellow "sang of . . . life undying . . . in the land of the hereafter." The term is still much favored in pulpit oratory.

HOOKS, TO DROP or POP OFF THE Although its date of origin is unknown, this expression is probably an irreverent and modern allusion to the crucifixion and unnailing (or unhooking) of Christ from the cross. The ancient antecedent of this euphemism was probably the popular medieval and Elizabethan oath ZOOKS—a polite contraction of "God's hooks," which is simply another version of S'NAILS, "God's nails," which caused ZOUNDS, "God's wounds."

IMMORTALS, TO JOIN or BE AMONG THE Bunyan's *Pilgrim's Progress* (1678) avers that "she thought she saw her husband in a place of Bliss among many Immortals." The expression comes from ancient Greece and Rome, where the word "immortals" was used to refer to the gods or, later, to those who were considered deified. One alternative to the solemn pomposity of this expression has been the coinage of the culinary and preserving euphemism TO BE SALTED AWAY. Salted meat, like the immortal spirit, resists decay.

LAST GETAWAY, THE This expression, in its figurative sense, probably dates from the 1930s, when it meant escape, departure or escape from the police, particularly in underworld and hobo lingo. In 1904, Jack London (*The Road*) used the expression in a literal way when he described "a world of 'pinches' and 'get-aways.'"

LAST RATTLER, TO HOP THE In 1915, "rattler" was a term for a fast freight train. By 1951, it was a general term for all trains. Between these two dates, TAKING THE LAST RATTLER had become hobo slang for dying. Although the connection may not be direct, it is interesting to note that death itself is called THE RATTLER, because of the death rattle in the throat of the expiring victim. HOPPING THE LAST RATTLER is but one of the many travel or voyage metaphors for dying and death, among which are numbered: THE LAST SEND-OFF, THE LAST VOYAGE and TAKING A ONE-WAY RIDE or TRIP or BUYING A ONE-WAY TICKET (see **CROAK**, ONE-WAY TICKET).

LAST ROUNDUP, TO GO TO THE   In *Western Words*, Raymond F. Adams notes that LAST ROUNDUP is an authentic cowboy's expression for death. In its literal meaning, as a cattle-drive, "roundup" came into use in 1769 and by 1880 it also meant a meeting or reunion. Other Western terms that are euphemisms for death are TO HANG UP ONE'S HARNESS, HANG UP ONE'S TACKLE, and HANG UP ONE'S HAT. (See also **BIG JUMP**.)

LAY DOWN ONE'S LIFE, TO   To die for one's country or cause. As early as 1330, the poem *Arthur and Merlin* praised a knight because "his life he laid there." TO LAY DOWN ONE'S LIFE was used in 1611, and in 1862 in the *Temple Bar*, which recorded that a man might be "ready to lay down fortune, freedom, and perhaps life itself. . . ." More jocular variations of this now cliche expression are: TO LAY DOWN ONE'S SHOVEL AND HOE and TO LAY DOWN ONE'S KNIFE AND FORK. Since TO PLAY ONE'S KNIFE AND FORK (see Chapter 4, GLUTTONY: FOOD, **TO PLAY A GOOD KNIFE AND FORK**) was a British phrase of the 1840s that meant to eat heartily and so to enjoy life, to lay them down or cease to eat meant to die. Since the 1930s, one has renounced one's earthly pleasures by HANDING IN ONE'S DINNER PAIL (ca. 1930, P. G. Wodehouse) or by engaging in the linguistically (if not historically) related KICKING THE BUCKET.

LONG HOME, TO GO TO ONE'S   This common pulpit expression originates with the King James Bible's (1611) version of Ecclesiastes, 12:5, "the grasshopper shall be a burden, and desire shall fail: because man goeth to his long home, and the mourners go about the streets."

LOSS; LOSE, TO Death; to suffer the death of a friend or relative. This term, in current use in such common phrases as, "We mourn the loss of our friend, Egbert" and "We are so sorry to hear that you have lost your uncle," undoubtedly originated as both a gaming and a business reference. Today they have, in America, the stentorian tone of funeral rhetoric, but as early as ca. 1369, Chaucer's narrator in *The Book of the Duchess* used them to relate chess and death in a linguistically fresh way. The queen, who was "lost," was dead, and the loser was the surviving mourner, her king. In speech as in life, one man's loss is another's gain; the Salvation Army refers to the dead as those who have been PROMOTED TO GLORY. The more conventional pulpit version is HAVING ONE'S NAME INSCRIBED IN THE BOOK OF LIFE. At Jewish services a general mourning prayer is always said "for those whose NAMES ARE INSCRIBED IN THE BOOK OF LIFE."

NEGATIVE PATIENT CARE OUTCOME In November 1981 Pye Chamberlain noted in the *New York Times* that the Reagan administration had coined many new words for taxes, among which he cited INCOME ENHANCEMENT. He noted that these days nothing in life is certain but "negative patient care outcome and income enhancement." Other patient care or condition terms in use, often in hospitals, are DOA (dead on arrival) and HE (or SHE) IS NOT or WON'T BE COMING HOME. Obituaries are equally obfuscatory. Death because of cancer is generally described as AFTER A LONG ILLNESS, while suicide is often euphemized to AFTER A BRIEF ILLNESS.

OLD FLOORER Death personified. The verb "to floor," meaning to knock or press to the floor or ground, to stun or overwhelm, dates from the period of Old English, when it appears as *flor*. We still speak of being floored or stunned. The concept of death as THE FLOORER is first suggested in the thirteenth-century poem "Memorare Novissima Tua."

If man thought
inwardly and oft
how hard is the journey
from bed to floor,
how sad the flight
from floor to grave,
from grave to pain
that never shall end,
I think no sin
would his heart ever win.

PALE HORSE, A Death personified or animalized. This euphemism for death functions by shortening the full description of death on A PALE HORSE or a RIDER ON A PALE HORSE to the horse. Its source is Revelation 6:8.

> And I looked, and behold a pale horse: and his name that sat on him was Death, and Hell followed with him. And the power was given unto them over the fourth part of the earth, to kill with sword, and with hunger, and with death, and with the beasts of the earth.

It was in common use in England from the time of the King James version of the Bible (1611).

PAY DAY The day of death. In 1634 George Chapman referred to the place "where in the Sutler's palace on pay day/We may the precious liquor quaff." Young, in *Night Thoughts* (1742), is even more explicit about "our day of dissolution!—Name it right!; 'Tis our great pay-day." Although PAY DAY is still in use, a later form of the expression comes from the underworld. Wolfert, in his book *Underworld* (1943), refers to a crowd waiting "to be in on the pay-off." THE FINAL PAY-OFF is an even more explicit version of this euphemism.

PAY SAINT PETER A VISIT, TO This twentieth-century American expression, despite its serious allusion to the keeper of the keys of heaven, has the jocular and irreverent tone of such similar phrases as TO PUSH THE CLOUDS AROUND and TO PLAY ONE'S HARP. (See also **ABRAHAM'S BOSOM.**)

PICTURE, TO PASS OUT OF THE To die, to disappear. This figurative expression was first used in a literal sense (as in not in the picture) to mean not present or in evidence in 1919, when we read that "Rustam Pasha collapsed soon after leaving the field into the straight when Blenheim was not in the picture." By 1930, the *Daily Mail* used the phrase OUT OF THE PICTURE. It may well have originated with early cinematography, in which an actor literally walked out of the picture. This art enlarged the number of euphemisms for death, adding such terms as FADE OUT. "Fading out" and "fading in" referred to the gradual blacking out or brightening of a picture. The large cinematographic vocabulary was first recorded in Croy's *How Motion Pictures Are Made* (1918). The metaphoric use of "fade out" to mean death may have arisen from the combination of the cinematic "blackout" and the earlier term FADE AWAY. The title of a 1980 horror film, *Fade to Black*, records the old usage and coins a new one. Related terms are FOLD or FOLD UP (probably from the behavior of the collapsible chair), first used to mean die (in Britain) in 1914, and BLACK OUT (q.v.).

PLUG, TO PULL THE To practice euthanasia. This expression for MERCY KILLING was popularized by the Karen Quinlan case (1975-76), one in which a comatose patient's vital functions were maintained by life support machines. Whether to turn off the machines—and thus perhaps permit her to die—was the agonizing ethical question of PULLING THE PLUG. The expression itself is an earlier one, meaning to withdraw one's support from or expose another person to danger or unpleasantness. It implies the still earlier image of unplugging a bath or barrel and thus permitting THE WATER OF LIFE TO RUN OUT. MERCY KILLING, itself a euphemism, probably derives from the MERCY STROKE, an English translation of the French *coup de grâce*. The *coup de grâce* is the final stroke, that blow which dispatches the prisoner or the victim suffering great pain. It PUTS HIM OUT OF HIS MISERY.

PRE-NEED MEMORIAL ESTATE, A A grave. This euphemism for A PLOT purchased before death is one of the funeral industry's elegant names for a grave. To be buried in one is to BECOME A LANDOWNER (1920s). The "coffin" in which one was buried, once a perfectly acceptable word, was replaced by CASKET in the 1860s and was thereafter described by Hawthorne as "a vile modern phrase which compels a person to shrink from the idea of being buried at all." By the 1930s, Emily Post found CASKET a tasteless and offensive term also and recommended reinstating "coffin." These days, Americans are buried not in a CEMETERY, itself a euphemism for a graveyard, or in a graveyard, but in a MEMORIAL PARK or REMEMBRANCE PARK.

QUIT IT, TO This Afro-American slang term may have originated earlier but was used in the 1950s in the form of the phrase TO QUIT THE SCENE. It seems related to other phrases that imply that life is a job or a business and death is their closing. Among these are: CALL IT QUITS, CALL IT A JOB, CALL IT A DAY, and SHUT UP SHOP. Although the Black expression QUIT IT may not be related to the British, NOTICE TO QUIT, the latter is an older expression (ca. 1820–50) for being aware that one's illness is fatal.

REMAINS, THE The corpse. As a delicate substitution for corpse, THE REMAINS, which entered the English language in 1700 from Dryden's translation of Ovid's *Metamorphosis*, become—when subject to CALCINATION (cremation)—the CREMAINS. According to Jessica Mitford's *American Way of Death* (1963), CREMAINS is one of the many words coined by MORTICIANS (what undertakers have chosen to call themselves in American since 1895) to disguise the ugly realities of dead bodies and what BEREAVEMENT COUNSELORS—alias undertakers—do to beautify them. THE LOVED ONE (corpse) as described in 1948 in Evelyn Waugh's satiric novel of the same name, becomes A BEAUTIFUL MEMORY PICTURE (an embalmed and cosmetized corpse), attired in CLOTHING, DRESS, A GARMENT or A SLUMBER ROBE (a shroud), lying in a REPOSING ROOM (American), SLUMBER ROOM, VIEWING ROOM or REST ROOM in preparation for its FINAL REST. That rest may be INHUMEMENT (burial in earth), ENTOMBMENT, INURNMENT (cremation and the placement of the ashes in an urn) or IMMUREMENT (the placing of ashes in a mausoleum).

SALT RIVER, TO GO UP   In 1832, Francis Trollope, in *Domestic Manners of the Americans,* referred to a menacing remark as "one of those threats which in Georgia dialect would subject a man to 'a rowing up Salt River.' " Being SENT UP and ROWING UP were alternate forms of the expression, one which probably originated in the political arena. *The Century Dictionary* defines SALT RIVER as "an imaginary river up which defeated politicians and political parties are supposed to be sent to oblivion." In its political as well as its metaphysical implications, it may be compared to another euphemistic expression for death: TO JOIN THE GREAT MAJORITY (see **IMMORTALS**).

SHERIFF'S PICTURE FRAME, TO DANGLE IN THE   To be hanged or to die by hanging. This British expression was current from the late eighteenth to the early nineteenth century and is one of the myriad euphemisms for death by hanging. America, particularly its frontier West, was a fertile breeding ground for hanging terms, since hanging justice was the most common manner of executing the law. The long list of terms for this form of punishment includes a number of allusions to being hanged from a tree: TO DECORATE A COTTONWOOD, TO BE A COTTONWOOD BLOSSOM, TO BE HUMAN FRUIT (see the later "composed folks song" about lynching in the South "Strange Fruit," which refers to "hanging from the poplar tree"), LOOKING THROUGH THE COTTONWOOD LEAVES, RIDING UNDER A COTTONWOOD LIMB. Other terms denoting both the process and effects of hanging are HEMP FEVER, DRESSED IN A HEMP FOUR-IN-HAND (with which compare DIE IN A NECKTIE), NECKTIE PARTY, DYING IN A HORSE'S NIGHTCAP (a halter), DYING WITH or HAVING THROAT TROUBLE, DOING A DANCE IN MID-AIR or A TEXAS CAKEWALK and the commonest of all—being STRUNG UP.

SLIP (OFF), TO   This term appears in 1681 and is of nautical origin. It occurs in a number of varied forms; for example, in Smollett's *Peregrine Pickle* (1751) it occurs as SLIP (ONE'S) CABLE in "I told him as how I could slip my cable without his assistance." In America, we still use the term SLIP OFF with no awareness of its nautical allusion, but other older, rarer expressions preserve maritime imagery. They include LAUNCH INTO ETERNITY, SOUL ALOFT, UNDER SAILING ORDERS (meaning dying), CUT ADRIFT, CUT, COIL UP or SLIP ONE'S ROPES, CUT, COIL UP or SLIP ONE'S CABLE, HIT THE ROCKS, GONE UNDER (which may also refer to land burial; see also CHECK OUT) and, of course, GONE TO DAVY JONES'S LOCKER.

STRIKE OUT, TO   This baseball expression has been in use in American since the 1930s. It teeters somewhere between the maudlin and the whimsical. In the 1950s, a medical professor followed the metaphor to its logical conclusion when he told his students that "sometimes, no matter what you do, the Great Umpire up above will call 'strike three.' " Sports images for death come from many arenas, in some of which one could kill one's opponent. From boxing we have: LOSE THE DECISION; TAKE A COUNT (1913); TAKE THE LONG COUNT, THE LAST COUNT, THE FINAL COUNT; BE DOWN FOR GOOD; and BE KAYOED (or KOed, from "knocked out"). From wrestling (and possibly from the realm of finance also) we have BE THROWN FOR A LOSS. American football gives us THE FINAL KICKOFF. Riding, boxing or wrestling may be responsible for BITE THE DUST.

TAPS, IT'S   Death. TAPS is perhaps the most familiar of the many military euphemisms for death. The word, in its literal meaning (i.e., the music played at sundown and at military funerals), first appears in the *Congressional Report* of 1824 where it is defined as being a drum roll. The drum roll or bugle call of taps, usually meaning extinguish the lights, was first regularly practiced during the Civil War. During that time the bugle melody that was to become standard was written by General Daniel Butterfield and/or his bugler.

Their version was composed to shorten and simplify a longer military call. William and Mary Morris suggest that the American word and practice might have come from the sixteenth century British "tatoo." When the British and the Dutch were fighting in the 1630s, men who did not respond to the final tatoo would be sought in Dutch bars, and the barkeeps, seeing the lights of the parties sent out to search for the men, would say "tap toe" or "turn off the taps," meaning shut the bar. Homophonic, but etymologically unrelated, is the expression TAP CITY, originally a gambling term for dying. TAP CITY is where high rolling gamblers were supposed to go after death because to be TAPPED OUT has long been gambling slang for being broke.

TOSS or PASS IN ONE'S ALLEY or MARBLES, TO Since about 1916, Australians have used this expression to refer to death. "Alley," however, as a name for a marble, dates from as early as 1720. Norman Lindsay, in *Saturdee* (1933), has a character announce, "This book says a bloke kicked the bucket [q.v.], an' Bill says it means that a bloke pegged out [ca. 1900 (cribbage) for "died"], so what's it mean?" "Means a bloke passed his alley in." The more proper British would describe dying as GOING FOR YOUR TEA and the saltier Americans might refer to it as GOING BELLY UP, in an analogy to an unfortunate fish.

TRUMPED, TO BE A troump (archaic), trump, or tromp is a playing card that belongs to the highest ranking suit and can therefore "take" any other card of the other three suits. This card is usually the last turned up by the dealer and the determinant of which suit is highest in a given game. In 1529, Bishop Latimer called his first sermon on cards, "Heartes is Trump," and in his second sermon urged parishioners to "cast thy trump unto them both." By 1598, the word had been used as a verb ("to trump"), an equivalent of the Italian *trionfare* (to trump or win at cards). Thus, TO BE TRUMPED or defeated is to lose the game of life. Since life has frequently been considered a gamble, this expression takes its place among many others that compare death and gaming of all sorts. They include: CLEANED OUT OF THE DECK, THROWN UP THE CARDS, BEEN SHUFFLED, CALLED ALL BETS OFF, and, from dicing, SHOT THE WORKS and THROWN SIXES. From roulette, of course, comes RUSSIAN ROULETTE, a popular American euphemism for attempting suicide. (See Chapter 4, DESPAIR: SUICIDE.)

WAY OF ALL FLESH, TO GO THE   The 1609 Douay Bible's more literal translation in III Kings 2:3, "I go the way of all flesh" (elsewhere varied as "I am going the way of all the living") is rendered in the 1611 Anglican version as "I go the way of all the earth" (I Kings 2:2). Samuel Butler undoubtedly gave greatest currency to this expression by entitling his novel (published in 1903) *The Way of All Flesh*, but Dickens had also used it. The King James Bible (1611) contains another allusion to the metaphor and its terms in the sad reminder of mortality: "Behold all flesh is grass."

6

Crime and Punishment

When a felon's not engaged in his employment—
Or maturing his felonious little plans—
His capacity for innocent enjoyment—
Is just as great as any honest man's—

wrote W. S. Gilbert. His sensitive constables continue:

Our feelings we with difficulty smother—
When constabulary duty's to be done—
Ah, take one consideration with another—
A policeman's lot is not a happy one.

Part of the "innocent enjoyment" experienced by both felons and police officers lies in the argot they create both to conceal and to describe what they do and how they do it. The lot of the much beleaguered policeman may be so unhappy that he seeks a moment of oblivion in COOPING (dozing in a patrol car).

Overburdened by the technical terms and complex regulations he must master, he often makes them more memorable and familiar to himself and his group by simplifying and shortening them. Be they SAINTS (highly scrupulous) or MEAT EATERS (graft seekers), all police officers are united in a private language that is often ironic in its implications. For example, a police person does not buy his or her BRACELETS at Tiffany's; instead they come from Smith and Wesson, the armorer who originally manufactured handcuffs.

Criminal argot, which the police also must know and use, is still more varied, for crime is a highly specialized profession. Whether any or all of the criminal languages should be considered euphemistic is both a philosophical and a linguistic question. Some have argued that the language of crime is a euphemistic one, created principally for concealment from the public. Others have asserted that it is a language for the in-group, used primarily for purposes of quick identification with fellow criminals and is thus not truly euphemistic. But we believe that whichever the motive—and both may exist simultaneously—the cants and argots of crime may be euphemistic. For example, prison argot is sometimes used to conceal inmate activity from the guards but may also be spoken to initiate NEW FISH (new prisoners) into their society and bind them together. Ironic prison terms like CAMP ADIRONDACK or COLLEGE were created by prisoners as a joke and as a way of removing some of the stigma from those who spend time INSIDE.

Con men, the aristocrats of the criminal world, live by their wits and their tongues. Since the con artist works by plying his trade against the innocent and unsuspecting, he often almost hypnotizes his victim by fast talk in words that appear to be socially acceptable. But his primary goal is FLIM-FLAM (trickery; the game) which always appeals to the commonest "sin"—that of greed. Con games are often not reported to the police because the MARK (victim) is ashamed both of his greed and of his folly at having been "taken."

As in any trade, each type of crime has its own specialized jargon. A JACKROLLER (a specialist in stealing bankrolls), a DIP (a pickpocket), and a CRIB MAN (a burglar who specializes in apartments) speak different dialects of the same language and probably have as much trouble understanding each other as a Southerner, a New Englander and a West Indian. But they are united by panic when IT LOOKS LIKE RAIN (an arrest is imminent) and are equally susceptible to DOCK ASTHMA (the British term for a respiratory difficulty feigned by prisoners in the dock).

The language of the drug culture is the most mutable and rapidly changing of all. Terms like CALIFORNIA SUNSHINE (LSD), ANGEL DUST (PCP), BLUE HEAVEN (amytal) and CORPORATION COCKTAIL (coal gas bubbled through milk) both conceal and advertise membership in the society of addicts. While drug terms are changed quickly so that narcotics squads cannot keep up with them, the same term may identify several products (as in JOINT for both a marijuana cigarette and PCP) or return to popularity after a long period of disuse (as in DOPE for marijuana). One last special quality of drug language is that it also has a sizable lexicon of terms coined to describe the private sensations of users—a characteristic shared only by drinking terms, which are often indentical with drug terms. (Compare STONED for drunk and extremely HIGH on drugs.) During the 1960s and 1970s many drug users claimed that no one who wasn't STONED could really make out the lyrics of songs sung by the Rolling Stones.

Part of this section is cautionary both for the victim and the criminal. The victim should beware lest an AUTOGRAPH turn out not to be the signature of a famous person but a blank piece of paper which a con artist persuades him to sign and later uses in forgery. The criminal is warned that an innocently nosey person may actually turn out to be a NARK—Romany for "nose" and American for SNITCH and also for "narcotics agent." If they're on to us, we're on to them!

COPS AND ROBBERS

BATTING AVERAGE Policeman's record of arrests. In the

late 1970s a policeman who COLLARED (arrested) many criminals might be lucky enough TO GET THE GOLD SHIELD or GET OUT OF THE BAG (be promoted to detective and thus out of uniform). However, officers caught COOPING (1958), that is, pulling up in a patrol car and sleeping, probably derived from COOP or CHICKEN COOP (also HEAVE) for shelter in New York or HUDDLING in Washington (1960s), might well find themselves IN THE BAG (1970)—demoted, most specifically to a uniformed rank.

BILL or OLD BILL Member of the London or Metropolitan police or of any British police force. To ask, Is he BILL? is to ask if someone is a police officer in England. BILL FROM THE HILL is specifically a Notting Hill police officer and A BILL SHOP is a police station. The American equivalent to this name for A BLUE (policeman, in England) is A BEAR, a description of police of any kind coined by CB radio operators. BEARS became famous because of the 1970s Burt Reynolds movie *Smokey and the Bandit,* but the term (probably derived from the U.S. Forest Service's forest fire prevention posters showing a bear in the uniform of a forest ranger and named "Smokey the Bear") long predates the film and has bred such other terms as BEAR CAGE (police station), BEAR TRAP (radar trap), BEAR IN THE AIR (police in a helicopter), MAMA BEAR or LADY BEAR (policewoman) and FEED THE BEARS (get a speeding ticket). The popular television series "Kojak," starring Telly Savalas, added the name KOJAK to the lexicon of titles for the police. In CB language, A KOJAK WITH A KODAK is a policeman near a radar trap. CB talk has also contributed EVEL KNIEVEL (from the name of the motorcycle stunt rider) for a motorcycle policeman.

BLOW JOB, A Cracking a safe by using explosives. Although A JUG HEAVY, A HEAVY MAN, A HEAVY G, A BOXMAN, or A PETE, PETEMAN, PETER, or PETER G or GEE—all safe-crackers—may get a HARD ON (reach for a pistol), safe-breakers (British) are not usually violent. Unless a safecracker has HOG EYES (skeleton keys), he is forced to use ingenious and violent means on his victim—the safe. He may do a BURN JOB by using a BLY (British burglar's acetylene torch); he may engage in PEELING or STRIPPING (removing the outer surface of a safe to reveal its lock), using a special tool known as a PEELER or CAN OPENER, and he will try to enter the safe and remove THE DUSTER (cashbox) in it. If he is lucky, the safe will be a CRACKER BOX (an easily blown safe). CRACKERS or CRACKSMEN with strong backs may prefer CARRY AWAY JOBS—in which a safe is transported to a location where it may be opened at leisure. But only a rank amateur engages in a CHOPPING JOB (turning a safe upside down and chopping out the bottom or wall). (See also Chapter 7, EXOTIC SEX, **FELLATIO**.)

BOBBY, A A British policeman, especially a member of the (London) Metropolitan police. In London, BOBBIES have been so named for Sir Robert Peel, who was Home Secretary in 1829 when he introduced a bill to reorganize the London police force. Sir Robert also instituted reforms among the Irish constabulary, who honor him by being called PEELERS. The ordinary constable has been known in Australia and New Zealand as A JOHN HOP (rhyming slang for "cop" since 1909) or JOHN. JOHN may come from the French *gendarme.* Australian police are also called BLUEBIRDS, a sanguine name taken from the color of their uniforms since 1939. In South Africa, municipal police are called BLACK JACKS because of their black uniforms, and the Royal Canadian Mounted Police have been called THE MOUNTIES, THE MOUNTED, THE ROYAL MOUNTED, RCMPs and THE SILENT FORCE, a name drawn from the title of a book about them published in 1937.

BOFFIN, A A police fingerprint man. This modern practitioner of CRIMINOTECHNOL (criminological technology techniques used to apprehend criminals) or A TECPERT (U.S. technical expert) has his headquarters in the police crime labs of Britain and takes his name from Mr. Boffin, the Golden Dustman (garbage collector and junk man) of Dickens's novel *Our Mutual Friend.* Aware of the BOFFIN's skills, British criminals have coined the aphorism "Don't piss into the cash register—it runs into money." (Don't leave your fingerprints around—they'll get you in trouble.) Instead, whether in America or England, the print man's evidence is often highly influential in NICKING (placing on report or arresting), PULLING IN or KNOCKING OFF (arresting) what Americans call AN ALLEGED PERPETRATOR. After a criminal is SNEEZED (British, arrested), he enters what has been known as THE THREE DEGREES. The first is arrest, the second, transportation to jail (NICK) or another place of detention, and the third is interrogation, which, in the expression THIRD DEGREE, suggests torture or brutality.

BOOSTER, A A shoplifter. Shoplifting has probably existed for as long as there have been shops with goods to lift, and the word SHOPLIFTER dates from at least as early as 1698—thieves have been called LIFTERS since 1592. ROOTING ON THE BOOST (working as a shoplifter) may require intricate and ingenious equipment. A good HOISTER or SKIN WORKER—a professional who sells what he or she steals—may be equipped with BOOSTER BLOOMERS, BOOSTER BOXES, and BOOSTER or BAD BAGS. The first of these are underpants equipped with pockets in which to stash stolen merchandise. The second is a "gift box" (a gift-wrapped package the sides of which flip up for the insertion of stolen goods). The third is a large shopping bag. A DRAGGER (shoplifter) may also wear a large coat fitted with HANGER HOOKS (mini-hangers sewed to the lining), or may specialize as a CROTCH WALKER, a professional who puts merchandise, even small television sets, between his or her thighs. Participants in this PEOPLE'S CRIME (as shoplifting is called) may be considered PROS, SHADOW PROS (those who steal as an avocation and for friends and families) or mere amateurs or AMMIES.

BRACELETS Handcuffs. In 1929, Little Caesar, in the film of that name, displayed a fine sense of euphemism when he told an arresting policeman, "You can't put no bracelets on me." By 1950, BRACELETS (British and American) had been transformed into the less romantic IRON BRACELETS and S & W BRACELETS (from Smith and Wesson, a manufacturer of them). They are also known more elegantly as CUFFLINKS and more diminutively as THUMBS—THUMB-CUFFS or small handcuffs are used especially when transporting prisoners. BRACELETS, along with the BATON, BILLYCLUB, NIGHTSTICK (so-called because it was originally used for protection while walking A BEAT at night), or ROSEWOOD (so-called because it was made of that wood; now mainly used in Black English)—names for a policeman's stick—are the LAW ENFORCEMENT OFFICIAL's everyday weapons against the common criminal. The most efficacious of these is still the gun, also known as a CROWD PLEASER (U.S., 1970s), a SPEAKER (Black English), and A PIECE (early 1900s). Gangsters favor the more imposing CHICAGO PIANO (a Thompson sub-machine gun; see **TOMMY**), which can easily cause a man to DISAPPEAR (be murdered without a trace).

BRAINS, THE An ironic term for the CID (Criminal Investigation Department of the London police). Specialized functions and ranks, particularly among the British police, have led to a number of slang euphemisms to identify the particular functions of given divisions of BABYLON (an English term of West Indian origin also used in hippy communes for the police or other "repressive" government agencies). Even an ordinary British constable strolls through his MANOR (its American equivalent is A BEAT and both mean the territory he is to patrol). In both the United Kingdom and Canada, a detective is known as A BULL; in Australia, from 1877 on, a plainclothes policeman or detective has been A D, DEE and sometimes A DEMON (1889). American motorcycle police have been called BIKES since 1958, and entry-level police officers are called "patrolmen" to note their function in the uniformed service. When an American plainclothes police person is set to "observe" other police officers' behavior, he is called A SHOO-FLY—from the song lyric "Shoo fly! Don't bother me." However, his formal title is A FIELD ASSOCIATE and his function is to report malfeasance to headquarters. When he sweeps the precinct station on a regular basis, he is somewhat jocularly called THE BROOM. If a law enforcement official handles clerical work for the precinct, he is known as A 1-24 MAN after the number of the regulation that created his job. (See also BOFFIN.)

BRIEF, A A lawyer; an explanation of law (British prison slang). Before a British prisoner meets THE BARNABY RUDGE (cockney rhyming slang for "judge," from the title of the Dickens novel), he will want to have a conversation with his BRIEF. BRIEF is clearly derived from the practice of writing an account of the case, called a brief. Only then may the prisoner appear before THE GARDEN GATE (rhyming slang for magistrate). When he does, he may hope to hear CHAMBER MUSIC, that is, an off-the-record meeting of his lawyer and the prosecuting attorney to arrange for him to COP A PLEA (plead guilty to a lesser offense than the one committed and thereby reduce a sentence). If his lawyer is A PENITENTIARY AGENT (a double-crossing or ineffectual lawyer), however, the music may be discordant indeed.

CRIB MAN, A A burglar who specializes in apartment houses. Although a CRIB JOB is the criminal community's euphemism for any easily accomplished crime, a CRIB MAN'S expertise is in burglarizing—robbing without force or threat—apartment buildings. He may be A DAY MAN or NIGHT MAN, and he will often use what is called A SET-UP, A CASE MAN or A FINGER MAN or WOMAN. These are names for the confederate who finds victims, gets information, and works as a lookout or CASES THE JOINT for the skilled professional. A burglar hopes that the premises he enters are without INFRARED INTRUSION DETECTORS, INTERIOR INTRUSION ANNUNCIATORS or INTRUDER DETECTORS—burglar alarms.

CRIME CARTEL, THE Organized crime, particularly that of the Mafia (see also **FAMILY** and **JUST MEMBER**). Also known as SYNDICATED CRIME and CONFEDERATED CRIME, this body of criminals and their activities have, according to the 1967 estimates of the President's Commission on Organized Crime, cost the country nine billion dollars per year.

No doubt inflation has considerably elevated the government's expenditures for the Mafia's FORAYS, EXPEDITIONS, JOBS and HITS (illegal and violent activities). The picture is further complicated by the fact that the Mafia, a word of much disputed origins, has so many local and regional names. In Chicago it is THE SYNDICATE or THE OUTFIT; in many Western states, THE PEOPLE; and, in upstate New York, THE ARM. Whether members of the COSA NOSTRA (see **FAMILY**) or of other crime families such as Chicano, Cuban, Jewish or Irish ORGANIZATIONS, their most useful men are STAND UP GUYS. These are men who live and, if necessary, die by the rules, putting the organization's welfare ahead of their own. They are the CRIMINAL CARTEL's equivalents of what men in prison call A RIGHT GUY (see THE BIG HOUSE AND SMALLER COOLERS, **REAL MAN**). The continued welfare of all of these organizations is dependent, in part, on a large circle of SOCIAL ASSOCIATES, that is, nonmembers who voluntarily deal with and assist members of a syndicated crime group.

DIP, A   A pickpocket. The language of pickpocketry is both rich and conservative. A DIP has been thieves' slang for a pickpocket since 1859, and the verb form, TO DIP, or to pick pockets, is even earlier (1817). Those who engage in the trade have been considered LIGHT-FINGERED since at least 1547. Also known as A WIRE (from the apparatus he or she may use) and A SAUSAGE ROLL (British rhyming slang for "Pole" since the 1960s when Polish pickpockets in London established new and more sophisticated techniques), A DIVER (pickpocket, 1674) uses a series of euphemistically named procedures and accomplices. He may have A STALL or STALLS (accomplices who distract victims) or be part of A WHIZ (organized gang of pickpockets). He may give his MARK (victim) A FAN (a brush or feel to locate the place where money is kept, U.S., 1958). When A DIP JOSTLES (picks pockets; A JOSTLE is also a pickpocket), he will look in the PRAT (rear pants pocket), the BREECH (side pants pocket) and the BRIDGE (left or right front pocket) to make sure that he has not met A CANNON (a non-mark who keeps nothing in his pockets and is thus inaccessible to theft). He may use the maneuver called FRAMING (as in a picture frame)—that is, placing his victim between two STALLS—and he will always look for a good TIP (crowd). (See also **MOLL BUZZER**.)

DOCK ASTHMA Gasps of surprise feigned by prisoners in a British dock (court enclosure for the prisoner). When an alleged offender's AKA (also known as), MONIKER or ALIAS—all terms for false names—are openly disclosed in court, the defendant may suffer from this classical trial ailment.

ELIZA SMILES It's a good time for a robbery. Between 1870 and 1910, the time during which Eliza was a generic name for a maid and a thieves' accomplice (note George Bernard Shaw's *Pygmalion* and Eliza Doolittle), ELIZA was considered a patron though not a saint of robbers. If she SMILES, it's a good day for A BAG JOB, that is, a burglary (American, 1950s; most recently one designed to steal secret documents, as in the Watergate incident), for A FAN JOB (American, 1958; a burglary through a transom) or for contributing to a little INVENTORY LEAKAGE or SHRINKAGE (theft; pilfering as from a department store) and possibly even a little BOOSTING (pilfering, especially by shoplifting; U.S., 1958). (See also **CRIB MAN**.)

FAMILY, A A Mafia group, not necessarily related by blood, who work together on Mafia business. FAMILY is one of the cosier American Mafia terms for an operational unit of what Mafia members have preferred to call the COSA NOSTRA. COSA NOSTRA, literally "our thing," was a name coined by Joseph Valachi in 1962 to replace the word "Mafia," which had become offensive to some of its members. The Mafia or COSA NOSTRA, as you will, is also known as THE SYNDICATE (see **CRIME CARTEL**). Originally, SYNDICATED CRIME was not specific to the Mafia and was a more general name popularized by the newspapers in about 1925 for crime run on the model of big business. The original BOSS of THE SYNDICATE was Charles "Lucky" Luciano. Well known for its intricate organization, today's typical FAMILY consists of such specialized workers as BUTTON MEN (hit men sent TO HIT or kill offenders against THE ORGANIZATION), a COUNSELOR (more familiarly known as a CONSIGLIORE, who serves as the lawyer or mouthpiece) and ordinary SOLDIERS (lower-echelon gorillas). Among the technological contributions with which THE SYNDICATE has been credited is the CRUSH OUT, a practice in which the identity of dead victims is obliterated by putting them in cars that are then run through automobile crushing machines. (See also JUST MEMBER.)

FLAKE, A   An arrest made to satisfy public opinion or to meet a quota. A FLAKE is another euphemism for the already euphemistic American police slang term, an ACCOMMODATION COLLAR (1971). Both terms imply that an arrest or COLLAR is made to lessen political or social pressure on the police or simply to make a quota. A COURTESY ARREST is one that is made when a gambler agrees to be arrested on a minor charge or with a legal loophole in order to protect the policeman who is ON CONTRACT, taking a bribe (see **PAD**). In catching a PERP (PERPETRATOR), a policeman may occasionally be guilty of FLAKING (planting evidence) or INVENTING A VERBAL. This last expression is British police slang for creating a false oral confession, and A VERBAL (1970) is any oral confession used in evidence at a person's trial.

GREEN HORNET, A   A Toronto, Canada motorcycle traffic policeman. Since 1965, Toronto traffic controllers have been called GREEN HORNETS. Reminiscent of the character in the "Green Hornet" comic strip and later radio program, popular in the 1940s, they wear green uniforms and ride motorcycles. Canadian police have also been known to use GHOST CARS, since 1962 unmarked police cars used by plainclothesmen. In Britain a police prowl car is known as a PANDA CAR, from its black and white markings. The American equivalent is a patrol car, and prisoners are transported in barred vehicles affectionately known as PADDY WAGONS (possibly from the fact that many New York policemen were Irish or

PADDIES, that is, Patricks) or BLACK MARIAS, the London equivalent.

HAVE SOMEONE RIGHT, TO To buy PROTECTION from an official (British). Buying PROTECTION from the law or from other people in different arenas of power is but one form of SANCTIFICATION—blackmailing for political favors or to obtain evidence. Another is giving someone A NUT, or PROTECTION MONEY paid to police officers or sheriffs for not interfering with illegal business. In less elegant terms, a tip or bribe is known as a BACK HANDER. Bribery itself is called OIL, GREASE, and PALM OIL, all considered quite effective in making the wheels of justice or injustice grind more smoothly.

HAWKSHAW, A A detective. A HAWKSHAW, from the comic strip "Hawkshaw, the Detective," is only one of a number of interesting names for law enforcement officers and their affiliates. American gangster movies of the 1930s popularized such names for detective as RUBBER HEEL, SNOWSHOE and GUMSHOE (from the gum-soled shoes worn to permit stealthy movements) and D, DEE, BULL or BUSY. Policemen have been labelled JOHN HOPS, rhyming slang for cops, and JOHN LAWS, while county police have been jocularly called COUNTY MOUNTIES and take their prisoners to the COUNTY HOTEL (jail). With the advent of female law enforcement officers such terms as MIN for policewoman and the humorous DICKLESS TRACY (a pun on the comic strip "Dick Tracy") have been added to the vocabulary. When a criminal HITS THE PIT (is jailed), he will encounter CORRECTIONAL OFFICERS (guards) as well as BTs, that is, BUILDING TENDERS or prison maintenance men. Although he may never meet the SUPERINTENDENT (the new euphemism for the prison warden), any inmate will certainly encounter EYES (prison guards) and may well see the warden's deputy, known behind his back as A WHITECAP or DOG CATCHER.

HORN, TO GO ROUND THE To transfer an arrested suspect so rapidly from one police station to another that his attorney cannot serve a writ of *habeas corpus*. Whether the arrested suspect has been accused of RUBBING OUT (1848), X-ING OUT, WHACKING OUT (Mafia use, 1982) or making his victim GO COOL—all terms for murder—or merely of being a DIGITS DEALER (numbers racketeer), police who engage in sending them ROUND THE HORN may be accused of CUB, conduct unbecoming an officer.

IDENTITY PARADE, An A police line-up (British). This more euphemistic term for the British "identification parade" is a common sequel to THROWING ROCKS or THROWING A BRICK, committing a crime. Once the prisoner has been chosen from THE GALLERY—short for ROGUES' GALLERY, a book of mug shots—it is clear that he already has AN ELEVEN-FIFTY (a British inmate's police or prison file) or its American equivalent, A JACKET. Of course, he may sometimes be victimized by DIRTY DISHES (evidence planted to incriminate others) and then left to HOLD THE BAG (take punishment). Such unfortunates are said to be JOBBED (convicted on false charges) or to be the victims of a HUMMER (arrest on false charges).

JUST MEMBER, A A member at the lowest level in a Mafia FAMILY (q.v.). The complex and feudal structure of a BORGATA (family) of the NATIONAL CRIMINAL CARTEL (see **CRIME CARTEL**), what Joseph Valachi in 1962 called the COSA NOSTRA, is a source of fascination to scholars of the KAKISTOCRACY. The KAKISTOCRACY (from the Greek for "rule by the worst" and also known as "control by mob aristocrats or higher-ups called KAKISTOS") is led in every Mafia FAMILY by THE BOSS, equivalent to a president. He passes on his orders to his vice-president, the UNDER BOSS who is known to the in-group as the SOTTOCAPO. Attempting to avoid direct contact between the upper and lower echelons, ORGANIZED CRIME leaders have, in their wisdom, created a third rank known as the CAPOREGIME or CAPODECINA (captain of the regiment, or *decine*, taken from the organizational structure of the Roman army). These CAPOS, also known as LIEUTENANTS, lead the ordinary SOLDIERS, known as BUTTON MEN, PEOPLE, MEN or JUST

MEMBERS. No matter what one's rank, any person considered a FRIEND OF OURS, AMICA NOSTRA, AMICO NOSTRO or AMICO NOS (dialectal) must first BE MADE, that is, initiated into THE ORGANIZATION. Every five years, the bosses of the FAMILIES, who form a group known collectively as THE COMMISSION, meet to make major strategic and organizational decisions for what they call OUR OUTFIT or OUR ORGANIZATION (the Mafia). The BOSS OF ALL BOSSES is known as THE GODFATHER, but there has been none since the death of Carlo Gambino, known as Don Carlo, in 1976.

KG, A A known gambler. This recent American police abbreviation is among the many terms concerned with betting and bookmaking. When the police receive A COMMUNICATION (a public complaint, particularly on a violation of the gambling or morals law; a tip) or A CRUDE (an informant's message; a tip) they may attempt to raid HARD CORE LOCATIONS. These are candy stores, bars and other small businesses where illegal gambling operations are regularly conducted. If the police are successful in raiding them, they will obtain samples of WORK (the written records of the members or bets that have been placed with bookmakers), thus cutting down on the bookmakers' VIGORISH (margin of profit built into the betting odds). In any event, they will file A VF 128—the form used to report the results of gambling and morals investigations.

LOOKS LIKE RAIN, IT An arrest in imminent. This dour remark in American twentieth-century tramp slang arises from the justifiably pessimistic view likely to be held by a variety of such rapscallions as SUNDOWNERS (an American cowboy term for men travelling west to avoid the police), BOTTLE BABIES (derelicts, Bowery bums, 1958) and HEAVY FEET (speeders, 1958; see FLIMFLAMS; FELONIES AND MISDEMEANORS, JEHU), all of whom might adopt SUMMER NAMES, the American Western expression for ALIASES (see **DOCK ASTHMA**).

MAN, THE A policeman. Since the 1960s, Black English speakers have been using the term THE MAN to mean not only an establishment figure or the boss but also the police. Another term, probably of Black English origin too, is FUZZ, which was widely utilized (and still is) first to identify the police in America and later to refer to them in England. Other Afro-American terms for law enforcement officers are: SKY (referring to a policeman's blue uniform), NAB (because he NABS or catches his quarry), SNITCHER (from TO SNITCH, meaning to inform; see **NARK** and **PCI**), and SNATCHER. Most graphically, the American policeman is referred to in Black English as THE MAN WITH THE HEADACHE STICK (nightstick).

MAVERICK, TO To acquire something illegally. From the name of Samuel Augustus Maverick (1803–70) comes this term for illegal acquisition. Maverick was a Texan whose ranch holdings were so vast that he did not brand his cattle, so that many were stolen. Thus, "a maverick" came to mean a stray cow, and TO MAVERICK meant to steal. If one receives stolen goods, he is called A BUYER and A FENCE (British, *Canting Crew*, 1700). Among the other more ingenious names for forms of illegal activity related to theft are the American PAPER HANGER for a passer of bad checks, JUICE DEALER for a loan shark and JUICE MAN for a collector of the illegal loan. Both are from TO JUICE (to pressure or squeeze someone at least since the 1970s). A MOONER has been the name for a pathological lawbreaker since 1958 on the assumption that his morality is affected by the light of the full moon. Last but not least are THE COBBLER and SCRATCHMAN. The former, of more recent origin, is the more versatile since he may be a passport forger, a general forger or a distributor of counterfeit currency and stocks, while the latter is an older and more general term for a forger.

MOLL BUZZER, A A pickpocket who confines himself to women's purses or pockets. A MOLL BUZZER is a specialized DIP (q.v.) and specialization seems to be the mark of pickpockets. A CANNON, for example, is the name not only for a victim but also for any Caucasian pickpocket who works on men, and A SHOT is the name for his Black brother. Also known as MECHANICS, PICKS, FORKS, FIVE FINGERS, FRISKERS and HOOKS (because a pickpocket literally HOOKS a pocket by catching its lining with two fingers and pulling it up), pickpockets use various techniques in numerous settings. They may WORK THE WELL (the steps of a bus) or THE HOLE (the subway or underground). They may even KISS THE DOG, that is, DIP face-to-face with their victims. This maneuver is carried out by an expert called A SPITTER, A PICK who finds an elegantly dressed MARK (see FLIM-FLAMS, FELONIES AND MISDEMEANORS, **ADDICT**), pretends to sneeze on his clothing and then removes his wallet while apologetically wiping off his shirt or jacket. Many pickpocketing games require auxiliaries known as STALLS (see **DIP**), STICKS, BUMPERS (because they bump into the victim), and NUDGERS. The last is the person who pushes a victim into a crowded elevator. One may STALL by PUTTING ONE'S HUMP UP (using one's hips to push or distract a victim) or by using A STIFF (a prop such as a newspaper or bag held to block the MARK'S view of what is going on). In all, ROOTING ON THE CANNON (working as a pickpocket) is a complex, intricate and profitable enterprise.

NARK, A An informer, particularly a copper's NARK, a police informer. Although the expression, "copper's nark" (British, 1894) is hardly euphemistic, NARK alone is. It has been used since 1865 in Britain, and later in America, to refer to what is now more politely called an INFORMANT. An informer is also called a NOSE or NOSER and NOSE TROUBLE is prying curiosity. Indeed, the *OED* suggests that the origin of the word NARK may lie in the Romany or Gypsy word for nose, *nak*. In England, a nosey person who gives information to the police is known in cockney rhyming slang as a BUBBLE AND SQUEAK because he speaks out against other offenders, while in the United States he is A CANARY because he SINGS (informs). Although a smart NARK knows how and when to, as the British say, BE LIKE DAD (and KEEP MUM, a 1783 euphemism still current for keep quiet), his American cousin too is no fool and can play D AND D (the euphemism dating from the 1960s for withholding information from the police by acting deaf and dumb).

PAD, THE   A list of people from whom the police can collect bribes. This expression, which is still current, is apparently drawn from the pad or tablet upon which a list of prospective graft payers is written. TO PAD is to accept graft and ON THE PAD is the same as being ON THE TAKE, receiving illegal or illicit money. MEAT EATERS (policemen who aggressively seek graft) can make vast gains from CONTRACTS (police cuts from illicit bookmaking) or PROTECTION (a form of extortion that businesses pay to police for turning a blind eye on infractions of the law or giving special attention to the safety of their premises), and COOPTATION (extortion, buying off the police). Whereas a dishonest policeman may be pleased to be ON THE PAD, his more scrupulous colleague, called A SAINT, prefers to COVER THE SHEET or GET ON THE SHEET (make his arrest quota, 1962). A YELLOW SHEET (1958) or RAP SHEET is current American police slang for a criminal's record of arrests.

PAPERS IN, TO PUT ONE'S   To retire from the police force. Since 1958 in America, retiring policemen and women have PUT THEIR PAPERS IN. By the time they do so, they hope they have been MADE (see **JUST MEMBER**). TO GET MADE is to be promoted in rank or to get a preferred police assignment. This may be achieved by a series of QUANTITY ARRESTS (the arrest of lower-level criminals), a number of QUALITY ARRESTS (those of higher-echelon criminals), through A CONTRACT (a favor a policeman does for another policeman) or through A HOOK. A HOOK is a person with sufficient power to influence police decisions and especially to get good assignments for police officers, while THE HOOK is the process by which this is accomplished.

PAT DOWN, TO   To search. The ALLEGED PERPETRATOR of a crime, as a suspected criminal is often pretentiously called, is usually PATTED DOWN, that is, FRISKED or searched. When the premises in which he/she lives are searched, London police call the procedure SPINNING DRUMS. British police hope that a person arrested will GOOF, that is, give himself away to the police. American law officers often threaten AN OFFENDER with FELONY AUGMENTATION (1981), which is THROWING THE BOOK AT someone (sentencing a person to extreme or maximum punishment, about 1930). In England, a DETAINEE is an offender who is subject to PREVENTIVE DETENTION (1948)—that is, imprisonment without bail to prevent his fleeing or committing another crime before he is brought to trial. The United States has no-knock laws (1970), euphemistically called QUICK ENTRY LAWS, which permit warrantless and unannounced searches.

PCI, A A potential criminal informant. This term is a somewhat flattering abbreviation for a possible "stoolie"—one who may GRASS (British for "rat"). He is also known as A CAT or A MOUSE, probably because he "rats." A police INFORMANT may pass information by DROPPING A DIME (making a phone call to the police) or he may simply SING LIKE A NIGHTINGALE. When he does, the police hope that this RINGTAIL (squealer) is not conveying A RINGER (false information). (See also **NARK**.)

SEAT, A A regular assignment to an American patrol car. Every American police officer who has A SEAT must first have his SHIELD, POTSY or TIN (badge). The badge, which is generally shield-shaped and was formerly made of tin, has, in New York at least, a shape reminiscent of the bent tin can top used in the children's game of "potsy." While he has the convenience of WHEELS (a synecdoche for a car) a patrolman may never have the opportunity to be responsible for AN OVERHEARD, an arrest made by a plainclothesman on the basis of overhearing illegal bets being placed.

SECOND STOREY MAN Burglar who enters a residence through its upstairs windows. The American epithet SECOND STOREY (or STORY) MAN, for a specialist in breaking and entering, is only one of a number of graphic names for a burglar. Another and older name for a burglar or safecracker is A YEGG or YEGGMAN, in use in the United States since 1903 and considered by some to be derived from the last name of an infamous practioner of the art of CRACKMANSHIP (see **BLOW JOB**). A long and prosperous history of theft is recorded in a series of eponyms. A ROBIN HOOD for an outlaw or bandit comes, of course, from the legendary English hero of the fourteenth century and A DICK TURPIN from the name of the bold highwayman and horse thief hanged at York in 1739. Less well known is A JEREMY DIDDLER (a swindler)—now usually abbreviated to DIDDLER—derived from the name of a character in J. Kenney's play *Raising the Wind* (1803). (See also THE BIG HOUSE AND SMALLER COOLERS, **BUSH RANGER**.) TO DIDDLE means to swindle (1806) and much DIDDLING is performed by A BUNCO or BUNKO MAN (U.S., 1883), derived from "bunko," a swindling card game. Synonyms for BUNKO MAN include CON MAN or CON ARTIST, both from *The Confidence Man*, the title of Herman Melville's novel of 1854. CON MEN and BUNCO MEN specialize in subtle games like THE DRAG or PIGEON DROP (See FLIMFLAMS, FELONIES AND MISDEMEANORS, **PIGEON DROP**) and, in general, in any good STING (ca. 1910, an American expression for a con game in which much money is involved). They are greater craftsmen than the ordinary thieves or safecrackers who attempt such vulgar enterprises as BREAKING or BUSTING A JUG (U.S., 1958, robbing a bank).

SHUT EYES, A A SEX OFFENDER. This general term is joined by even vaguer phrases referring to both sexual assault and rape. The list includes the American PERSONAL VIOLENCE and the British MOLEST, INTERFERE WITH and INTERFERENCE. Known also as ASSAULT and ABUSE, sex crimes, like those who commit them, have become considerably more specialized. In Britain, JUMPING is an expression for an unexpected attack and for sexual intercourse, whereas a JUNIOR JUMPER is a Black English expression for a rapist under sixteen who may also commit R AND R, not rest and recreation but rape and robbery. A SHORT EYES, an American euphemism for a child molester, may find himself engaged in a process called DEVIANCE DISAVOWAL. This is a

three-pronged legal argument in which the alleged MALE-
FACTOR (felon or criminal, in use since at least as early as
1440) denies that he ever MOLESTED a child or that he knew
what he was doing when he did, or maintains that he was
drunk or powerless to control his behavior. In New Jersey,
some SEX OFFENDERS may be entered into ROARE—
REEDUCATION OF ATTITUDES AND REPRESSED EMOTIONS, a
treatment program designed to reveal the trauma underlying
or responsible for their crime (1969).

SMALLPOX, TO HAVE   To be wanted on a warrant and thus
avoided by fellow criminals who fear the contagion of guilt.
While HAVING SMALLPOX is not as serious as DYING OF THE
MEASLES—murder made to appear like death from natural
causes—or having GONE COOL (gangster lingo for the
murder of A fellow gangster), all carry the threat of A RAP—
arrest or indictment—and of subsequently being SENT DOWN
(sent to prison, British; also used for expulsion from a
university). In America, anyone caught DOING what the
English call A MOODY (acting suspiciously) is entitled to A
MIRANDA—warning a person of his rights before arrest and
police questioning—derived from the Miranda decision of
the United States Supreme Court.

TOMMY or THOMPSON, A   A sub-machine gun. Named
after Colonel John Thompson of the U.S. Army, the TOMMY
GUN is a familiar member of the arsenal of weapons known
to law enforcement officials as FIRES and criminals as HARD-
WARE, RODS and HEATERS. Among the more interesting
names for a pistol are: A BETSY (reason unknown), A FORTY-
SOME-ODD (on the basis of its caliber), AN EQUALIZER (all
men are equal in its sites), A PEASHOOTER (a handgun of less
than magnum caliber), A SNUG (a small gun that fits snugly
in the hand) and the infamous American SATURDAY NIGHT
SPECIAL (a cheap handgun). Names for larger firearms include A TYPEWRITER for a machine gun (on the basis of its
rat-tat-tat, typewriter-like sound; and one who operates A
TYPEWRITER is A TYPIST), A CHOPPER (also used for a machine gun or its operator) and A TASER (Thomas A. Swift

Electric Rifle, named after Tom Swift, the fictional hero). All are DWs (deadly weapons), and it is no accident that a WEEPER is another name for a pistol, since what British police call being TOOLED UP (carrying arms while committing a crime) and American police call DDW (displaying a deadly weapon) or CCW (carrying a concealed weapon or WEEPER) will get the offender a longer term in prison.

UNDERGROUND ECONOMY, THE People who do not report all or any of their income to the Internal Revenue Service. The 1980s have been called the great era of THE UNDERGROUND ECONOMY, the population of which includes street merchants and criminals of all varieties such as drug pushers, con men and disciples of the Reverend Sun Myung Moon. Being part of THE UNDERGROUND ECONOMY is one of the more highy publicized and quasi-respectable forms of theft. More conventional thieves include LOID MEN (burglars who use celluloid to open locked doors), KIRKBASHERS or KIRKBUZZERS (British terms for petty thieves who steal from churches and take their tithes from collection plates), and READERS (sneak thieves who trail delivery people to read the addresses on their packages, then race to the address given to receive the parcel). However, more conventional thieves, even those who GLEEP A CAGE (motorcycle gang slang for "steal an auto"; a stolen car is known as A SHORT) need A FENCE, A NEIGHBORHOOD CONNECTION or A SHADE—all receivers of and dealers in stolen goods—and may use A SHIFTER, a handler of stolen goods. Even with such elaborate channels and assistance thieves' booty sometimes becomes mere WAIFS—goods stolen but waived (or abandoned) by the thief in his haste to flee.

WASH, TO BE AT THE To pick pockets and steal in the washrooms of populated public places. British TEA LEAFING (rhyming slang for "thieving") has its own colorful language. A TEA LEAF has meant a thief since the nineteenth century, and a bank has been called AN ARTHUR or A J. ARTHUR RANK since the time of the great movie producer (1940s). The Australians speak of SWAGGING—SWAG has meant booty in

English thieves' cant since 1812. The English and the Australians share several expressions for inquiring if merchandise is NICKED or stolen (British, 1869). The British will ask, "Did it fall (drop) off a lorry?" and, since 1950, the Australians substitute the term "truck" for "lorry." Both may inquire if the merchandise was FOUND BEFORE IT WAS LOST. If IT FELL OFF THE BACK OF A LORRY (1974), Americans might describe it in CB English as A FIVE FINGER DISCOUNT (stolen merchandise).

FLIMFLAMS, FELONIES AND MISDEMEANORS

ADDICT, AN A chosen MARK of a con game who permits himself to be repeatedly conned. The essential ingredients of any con game are simply a con man, a scheme and a victim. Con men wax prolix in their names for APPLES or PIGEONS (MARKS), on whom they can repeatedly PUT THE TOUCH (take money from) or, if they are lucky, THE COMEBACK or THE BIG BLOCK (the second TOUCH). Victims are variously BATES, MR. BATES, JOHN BATES, EGGS, SAVAGES and WINCHELLS. A MARK may CHILL (lose interest in a game), particularly if he cannot be RIBBED (convinced he'll get something for nothing) or isn't properly RIPPED (prepared and/or filled with expectations). However, con men hope that they can COOK A MARK—that is, calm him down after he has been fleeced—lest he threaten to become a COME-THROUGH (one who, after being TAKEN, refuses to be BLOWN OFF or gently dismissed) and therefore attempt to pursue con men and BRING THEM TO JUSTICE.

AUTOGRAPH, THE A con in which the victim is led to sign a blank piece of paper that is later turned into a check by con men. THE AUTOGRAPH is one of several con games involving falsifying checks. KITING CHECKS is another and ancient practice. In KITING, one increases the amount of a customer's check or checks, and, by quickly transferring the funds from one bank to another, makes it appear to a naive outsider that there are large amounts of money in a number of banks.

Much smaller are the amounts of money gained by A FAST CHANGE ARTIST. In this SHORT or petty CON, a person confuses a bank teller, storekeeper or even a private individual by presenting him with a large bill and repeatedly and rapidly asking that it be changed in different ways. Thus, he receives more in change than he has given. In this, as in various other cons, large bills, called COARSE ONES, may be used to impress the MARK (see **ADDICT**).

BAIT AND SWITCH False advertising of a product followed by pressure on the customer to buy another, more expensive product. Also called DISPARAGEMENT, BAIT AND SWITCH is a popular technique among SHADY retailers. The BAIT is an advertisement for quality merchandise sold at an extremely low price. The SWITCH is the unavailability of that product or its disparagement in favor of a far more expensive one when the customer enters the store. Con games are so ingenious and con men so clever that only a highly trained and skilled police detective can MAKE A MAN ON HIS MERITS (pick up a GRIFTER by his appearance and mannerisms).

BUCKET SHOP, A The headquarters for the illegal sale of worthless, fraudulent or extremely speculative stocks and bonds. A BUCKET SHOP almost always has a TELEPHONE BOILER ROOM. Here CON ARTISTS, posing as legitimate stockbrokers, use telephones, which may truly be in a boiler room, to make BIG PITCHES (sales talks) to persuade their victims to buy worthless securities.

CADGE, TO To beg or borrow. In the fifteenth century, British itinerant peddlars were known as CADGERS, and by the eighteenth century begging and sponging were called CADGING. To CADGE meant to steal by 1812, but this meaning is obsolete and has been replaced by that of borrowing, as in the American BUMMING or the British CADGING a cigarette. By the twentieth century, PINCHING (robbing, 1673) and BAGGING (stealing, ca. 1700) were familiar English euphemisms. British public school language abounds with euphemisms for stealing because, according to Morris

Marples (*Public School Slang*, 1940) "among boys the distinction between stealing and borrowing is at times somewhat ill-defined, especially at boarding schools, where anyone may APPROPRIATE someone else's book or football jersey without feeling particularly dishonest." Marples explains that the words of the 1940s were BAG (to steal and reserve or engage, as in BAGGING a seat) and PINCH, which he traces to the fourteenth century. Others include SNAFFLE (1725), PRIG (thieves' cant, 1591), and SNITCH (originally American, 1904). Today, British thieves MAKE, American thieves LIFT or RIP OFF (1960s) and Black English speakers TAKE (A VICTIM) TO THE CLEANERS (rob, strip or take serious advantage of). British victims of swindling are said to BUY A PUP.

CONFUSION, A A street fight. In *The Signs of Crime*, a British book on crime, David Powis cites this rather charming West Indian name for a street fight. When an English offender takes part in a street fight, he is described as AT THE MICK or MICK'S (causing trouble) or, in older parlance, MIXING IT UP. An American variant is the RUMBLE (1946), a fight between rival teenage gangs. A RUMBLE may unfortunately involve ROUGHING UP opponents (beating them) or what is generally called ROUGH STUFF (beating, torture, even manslaughter).

CROSS FIRE Conversation in con argot used to distract a victim. One of the commonest tricks used by con men to make sure they GET THE BEST OF IT (win the con) or make it A CINCH or A SURE THING is for THE INSIDE MAN and THE OUTSIDE MAN or ROPER to converse in terms that are incomprehensible and confusing to their MARK. THE INSIDE MAN is the con who stays near THE BIG STORE in THE BIG CON or operates THE SHORT CON. (See **FLY GEE.**) THE OUTSIDE MAN finds the MARK, brings him to THE STORE and helps to TAKE him. In order to prevent anything from CURDLING (going wrong) while CUTTING INTO (SETTING UP) a MARK, INSIDE and OUTSIDE MEN may CUT IN—that is, start a distracting conversation with each other or with the MARK. The best con men and their cleverest games are known as CARRIE WATSONS (of the highest order), a name taken from the fancy old Carrie Watson House in Chicago.

CUSTOMER'S MAN, A   A bookmaker's RUNNER. Borrowing from Wall Street, America's bookmakers describe the RUNNER who gathers bets and calls the WIRE ROOM A CUSTOMER'S MAN. In illegal betting, a WIRE ROOM is one filled with SHEET WRITERS (telephone personnel who accept and record bets). RUNNERS are part of A SALES TEAM, which consists of MOBILE RUNNERS, A STATIONARY RUNNER in a RETAIL OUTLET (where bets may be placed) and COLLECTORS (those who collect the payments). Since today's betting is done mostly by telephone, those who run WIRE ROOMS have become accomplished in such illegal techniques as BACKSTRAPPING and CHEESEBOXING. According to Kornbloom's glossary (*The Moral Hazards*, 1976), BACKSTRAPPING is a procedure bookmakers use to relay bettors' calls to remote areas. All of the money gained by RUNNERS and A WIRE ROOM goes through the hands of CONTROLLERS or DISTRICT MANAGERS, terms again borrowed from Wall Street for higher-ups who supervise the RUNNERS. These funds end up in a POLICY BANK (the headquarters for a numbers and gambling racket) run by the top official, called THE BANKER or CENTRAL OPERATOR.

EASY MONEY   Stolen or illegally gained funds. Originally an American expression (1896), EASY MONEY is now used in both Britain and America in the same sense as EASY VIRTUE (thoroughgoing sexual dishonesty, generally in a woman). An Australian woman of EASY VIRTUE has been A GINGERER since 1945 only if she GINGERED (robbed and stripped) her JOHN (see Chapter 7, PROFESSIONAL SEX, **TRICK**). The lexicon of thievery is highly specialized because of the ingenious variety of ways TO BUZZ (steal, U.S. since 1925) and items to take. One may accomplish one's ends by BRACING a victim (accosting and begging money, U.S., 1939). The available items may be BULL'S WOOL (stolen clothes) or A POKE (pocketbook or wallet, U.S., 1958).

FLY GEE, A   A person who understands con games or believes that he or she does. The confidence game is so complex that A FLY GEE often fails to recognize A C-GEE, a confidence man, and seldom knows when a real professional is what the British call AT IT (DOING A FIDDLE or pulling a con). Confidence games are divided into two major types, THE BIG CON and THE SHORT CON. THE BIG CON is an operation that depends upon more funds than those playing it have on their persons. Therefore BIG CON players frequently employ A SEND (a person who leaves the game to bring back more money with which to play). To assure the availability of funds and a variety of both games and professionals who direct them, BIG CON men frequently operate out of BIG STORES, now elaborate gambling clubs or phoney brokerage houses in which con games are played on suckers. In *The Big Con*, David W. Maurer describes THE BIG STORE, which began in the 1860s when the entrepreneurial gambler, Ben Marks, took advantage of the railroad traffic on the Union Pacific to open a "dollar store" where goods were sold for a dollar but various con games played there cost customers a good deal more. Maurer said that "merchandise never changed hands" but money did. From these humble beginnings arose many kinds of STORES named, according to the games played there, THE FIGHT STORE, THE FOOT-RACE STORE, THE WRESTLE STORE (since MARKS were conned into betting on fixed contests in these sports) and THE WIRE STORE. THE WIRE STORE involved a telegraphed bet on a horse race supposed to reach the betting office after the winner was known but before the bets were paid. It was often housed in a telegraph office, and the con man who ran it was known as THE MANAGER, a term that is now generic for any C-GEE in charge of a BIG STORE. Since the development of THE BIG CON depended upon the invention of THE BIG STORE, there were no BIG CONS until the twentieth century, only SHORT CONS, those played on a street, in a train etc. with only the money the players had and without the aid of A SEND. Today, SHORT CONS also sometimes use STORES, but they are impermanent, mobile affairs that handle smaller sums of money. Both BIG and SHORT CONS use accomplices known as SHILLS or SHILLABERS. (Shill is a doublet of skill and comes from the West Saxon *sciel,* meaning "sonorous" or "quick in movement." SHILLABER is probably a con lengthening of SHILL.) These are assistants who play the game in order to let victims or MARKS (see **ADDICT**) see them win. HANDLERS are accomplices in a SHORT CON game who indicate to SHILLS how they should bet. In both types of cons, private hand, eye or tongue signals are known as the OFFICE. THE OFFICE is an "equal opportunity employment" situation and some of the SHILLS who use it may be women or girls, called TWISTS, from Australian rhyming slang for girl, TWIST AND TWIRL.

JACKROLL, TO To rob, especially of money or a bankroll. JACKROLLING, a term used in Canada more than one hundred years ago, is one of the many forms of what is now called MUGGING. The term MUGGING, from "mug" (face), is derived from the nineteenth-century thieves' practice of locking an arm around a victim's chin and throat as he attacked him from behind. Chicagoans speak of MUGGING as being TAKEN OFF, and TO PUT THE ARM ON is still an expression for "to rob." Washingtonians call the same practice of being CLIPPED (robbed) being YOKED. Nowadays, muggers wear sneakers or running shoes so frequently that their footwear has come to be known as FELONY SHOES. They are experts in COPPING A HEEL and LIGHTING A RAG (running away).

JEHU, A A fast and reckless driver. This British eponym comes to the language of vehicular crime from the Bible (II Kings 9: 20): "and the driving is like the driving of Jehu the son of Nimshi; for he driveth furiously." Such modern charioteers are likely to be PICKED UP by American police on A 100-200, the signal for "police needed at [a special site on the road]." The American DWIs or DUIs (those driving while intoxicated or under the influence) may be reported by CB operators as 10-55s (also a police code for drunken driving) and accused of being HARVEY WALLBANGERS (from the alcoholic drink, so named because it makes you bang into the wall). They are often among the HORATIOS of this world (hornblowers, from the novel, *Horatio Hornblower*). A BREATHALYSER TEST (British English, 1967, for a sobriety test) will show whether or not they have been ROLLING THROUGH THE RYE, driving while intoxicated.

MURPHY (GAME), A   A well-known confidence game. Actually, there are two forms of MURPHY GAMES in America today. In one version, an envelope filled with money is quickly switched by the con artist for another filled with newspaper scraps. The expression THE MURPHY dates from the 1960s, but the practice of this form of the game is supposedly named after an earlier Irish perpetrator of it. Not dissimilar is a British criminal practice called CORNERING. TO CORNER is either to sell cheap goods to tradesmen or the public while pretending that they are expensive stolen goods, or to sell stolen goods to tradesmen and then retrieve them by pretending to be police officers reclaiming them. The other and far more popular American version of THE MURPHY involves the promise of sexual services. A procurer invites a potential client to store or deposit his valuables so that a prostitute cannot steal them. Instead, he steals them. This version of the game supposedly dates from the period when the MADAMS of BORDELLOS (see Chapter 7, PROFESSIONAL SEX, **MAMA-SAN**), called MRS. MURPHYS, used male assistants to collect cash from clients so that they and their prostitutes could not be arrested. Another sexual con is THE ENGINEER'S DAUGHTER, in which a "seduction" of a "young girl" is broken up by a con man pretending to be her father, the engineer, who has actually engineered the seduction and collects the damages.

PECULATION   Embezzlement, particularly that committed by a person in a position of trust. One of the more elegant indirections for criminal behavior, PECULATION has meant swindling in England since 1658, and those who commit it have been called PECULATORS since 1956. More colloquially, Americans speak of such offenders as being CAUGHT WITH A

FINGER IN THE TILL. Other oblique expressions for criminal behavior include: being ON THE EARHOLE (engaged in swindling), CREAMING (stealing from an employer in such a subtle manner that one is "merely" SKIMMING THE CREAM OFF) as contrasted to WEEDING (looting from an employer at the scene of a crime already committed), and EXPROPRIATING property or money. The last expression meant to seize property legally in 1611 and for long thereafter but now indicates theft. Just as the equally oblique form TO MAKE implies sexuality, so the indefinite TO DO implies criminal behavior. TO DO SOMEONE (an expression more British than American) is to cheat him or, sometimes, to kill him. TO DO A JOB is to commit a crime. TO DO FOR is the British way of saying to kill or destroy, whereas TO DO IN is the American expression. A DO-OVER is one expression the British have for an assault. When the aggressor hits a person in the face he may say that he DID HIM ONE and an assaultee is said to have BEEN DONE UP (assaulted).

PENETRATE, TO To break and enter. During the 1970s, this CIA and underworld euphemism for committing a burglary gained currency, particularly in the Watergate incident. Experienced and polished burglars of that period were more likely to be concerned with such subtleties as what the British call DRINK (blackmail payment) or SAUSAGE AND MASH (a cash bribe) than with vulgar violence of A JAMES or JEMMY (a burglar's crowbar since 1885).

PIGEON or POCKETBOOK DROP, THE One of the most popular con games, in which money is supposedly found and the MARK or PIGEON who "finds" it is persuaded to give up his own funds in order to be given a share of the "found" money. THE PIGEON DROP is one of the favorite forms of FLIMFLAM, con games in general. It involves an offer to share profits another person has found on the condition that the MARK will give up some of his or her own money as a sign of trust, to a "lawyer." The fake attorney is actually a con man who "happens" to be acquainted with the first con man, who is a co-discoverer of the lost money. After he or she has surrendered money as security, the MARK (see **ADDICT**) receives in return what turns out to be a wad of torn-up newspaper, and the "attorney" and the stranger mysteriously vanish. Almost equally popular is THE HANDKERCHIEF SWITCH, known as THE SPANISH HANDKERCHIEF SWITCH when it is used in the Puerto Rican community. After a long and sometimes heartbreaking WORKUP (preparation of the MARK), an offer is made by a seeming simpleton, who is actually a smart con man, to give the victim a dollar for every dollar he or she takes out of the bank. When the victim agrees, often out of greed, he offers his own money and receives in exchange money wrapped in a handkerchief. In reality, the money is A MICHIGAN ROLL (see **SLIDE**) or wad of paper. Among other colorful cons are THE ROCKS (a diamond swindle in which paste stones are substituted for real ones), THE DOUBLE TRAYS (in which loaded dice are substituted for legitimate ones), and THE DUCATS (a game in which marked business cards are used for gambling purposes).

SCALE, TO To practice petty fraud, particularly to use public transportation without paying. SCALING, the Australian expression for riding buses or trains without paying, is only one of a number of indirect names for relatively minor crimes. SCALE itself comes from the older and more serious practice (1576) of chipping or splitting off scales from coins for fraudulent purposes. Australian criminals are also partial to a RORT (1930), any small swindle, racket or DODGE, and RORTER has meant a professional swindler, card sharper or petty confidence man in Australia since after World War II. More serious behavior may involve a STAND-OVER (the extortion of money since 1939) and a STANDOVER MAN is an Australian criminal who will use force or the threat of violence to intimidate his victim.

SLIDE, TO To slip bills out of a stack. SLIDING is a variation of WEEDING or taking out several bills when handling either a stack of money or a wallet. Those TURNED OUT (initiated) into con games may also make easy money by using A

MICHIGAN ROLL—a stack of fake money with a few real bills on top. SLIPPING out bills has its analogue in cards—dealing from the bottom of the deck, the speciality of a card expert known as A SUBWAY DEALER.

TRIPS AND TRIPPERS

ARTILLERY Equipment for injecting drugs, also known as A HEAD KIT because HEADS or drug addicts use it to prepare for and take injections or FIRES. ARTILLERY is an essential part of the arsenal of A STATION-WORKER, an addict who injects drugs into his or her arms and legs. Unless he has THE BUSINESS (injection, and/or cooking equipment), A HIPPY (British for drug user) cannot give himself A JIMMY (Canadian), BINGO or BANG—all terms for narcotics injections.

BABY One of the many names for marijuana or *cannabis*. The names for marijuana, America's most popular soft drug, are endless and ever changing. Users of harder drugs have called it BABY because, in their eyes, it is for novices to the drug world. Because it is an herb, marijuana has been known since the 1920s as TEA and was later called BUSH, BLUE SAGE, INDIAN HAY, LOVE WEED, TEXAS TEA, VIPER'S WEED, HAY and, of course, GRASS. It is even called DAGGA, from the South African name for marijuana, *dagba*, and HERB. Another whole set of names for this drug are based on its initial, "M," and its name, marijuana, which is Spanish for Mary Jane. Hence, it is called MARY, MARY JANE, MARY ANNE, MARY WARNER, MUGGLER, and even 13-M for the thirteenth letter of the alphabet. Another popular name for it, more mysterious in its origins, is BOO or BO-BO. In the 1950s this word meant excellent, remarkable or satisfying, and perhaps became a name for the drug as a result of users uttering this comment on its high quality. These terms may have originated even earlier, in the 1930s, as a corruption of an African word, JABOOBY, meaning fear, and the use of an African term is perhaps confirmed by the British name for marijuana, AFRICAN WOODBINE. Also known as DEW, SNAP, SPLAY and GAGE or GAUGE, marijuana is now most popularly referred to as POT, DOPE and REEFER. The last was an earlier term for a marijuana cigarette (see **RAINY DAY WOMAN**). Those who smoke *cannabis* are sometimes called GRASSHOPPERS, HAY BURNERS and TEA MEN. Those who eat it may enjoy it in the form of an ALICE B. TOKLAS or a TOKLAS, a fudge brownie laced with this secret ingredient. Wistfully, marijuana has been called THE OPIUM OF THE POOR.

BLACK AND WHITE MINSTRELS Amphetamines. This British term is probably derived from the colors of the capsules and the association of black and white with the word "minstrels" ever since the 1960s, when a TV series called "The Black and White Minstrel Show" was popular. Most commonly known as SPEED, amphetamines, especially methedrine, are so named because they speed up a user's reactions and produce an UP or HIGH. Thus they are also known as UPPERS, THRUSTERS and LEAPERS or LEEPERS. Another common name for amphetamines in America is TRUCK DRIVERS, from the fact that truck drivers take them in order to stay awake during long hauls. The varying colors of the tablets, often used as DIET PILLS, are responsible for such other names as FRENCH BLUE or DOUBLE BLUE (also terms used for barbiturates). Metamphetamine—a related drug—is known as CRIS, CRISTINA, CRYSTAL and ANGEL DUST (more commonly known as a name for PCP). Both amphetamines and LSD are commonly known as A but those who take a childlike pleasure in these PEP PILLS have called them JELLYBEANS, and more sentimental users call them HEARTS, particularly when they are AMPED (high on amphetamines). (See also **OVERAMPED.**) Equally sentimental about their habits are those who take DOWNERS (see **BLOWN AWAY**), the most popular of which is still Valium. Those who are on Valium call their five milligram pills MELLO YELLOS and their ten milligram blue tablets TRUE BLUES.

BLOWN AWAY or OUT HIGH and HAPPY on narcotics. In the language of drug addiction, BLOWING has three general meanings. It can mean to sniff drugs, as in TO BLOW CHARLIE or SNOW (SNIFF cocaine) or BLOW HORSE (SNIFF heroin). It can mean to smoke a drug, as in to BLOW HAY (smoke opium) and, last, it can mean the elation otherwise known as A THRILL, A KICK or A CHARGE (1950s) that addicts who are WIGGED OUT, WIPED OUT or ZONKED OUT (very HIGH on drugs) feel. (See also Chapter 4, GLUTTONY: DRINK.) Generally speaking, CONTROLLED SUBSTANCES (drugs) are divided into two classes: UPPERS (a 1970s term for euphoriants such as amphetamines), and DOWNERS (depressants such as barbiturates). Those who are COASTING, HAVING A BUZZ, FLYING, JOY RIDING or SLEIGH RIDING are having an UP experience. DOWNERS, however, can cause an addict to become comatose (TO NOD) and being STONED or TRIPPING OUT is reported by some as an experience characterized more by exhilaration than by grogginess. TO BE BROUGHT DOWN (British) is an experience combining initial elation followed by sudden deflation. For every addict, however, TAKING THE CURE or KICKING THE HABIT (breaking an addiction) is painful and, therefore, addicts are reluctant TO CHILL (submit to arrest) or to become MR. FISH (give themselves up for THE CURE). Whether addicts go COLD TURKEY (rapid and forced abstinence) or taper off, they will still suffer BOGUE (a drug withdrawal without sickness). Those who MAIN-LINE (inject drugs directly into the bloodstream) and are thus STRUNG OUT (a 1950s term for heavy addiction to a hard drug) find the experience of SWEATING IT OUT and DOING WITHOUT so torturous that they are often known to KICK BACK, or return to THE HABIT.

BOY Heroin. Since the 1920s, heroin has been called BOY presumably because of the relation between giving oneself A BANG or BANG IN THE ARM (a shot) and the male role in intercourse. For men, it is supposed to be a sexual shot in the arm (see **GIRL**). Hence many of the names for it, such as HIM, HERO OF THE UNDERWORLD and the punning HARRY

---

or BIG HARRY, are specifically male. It is also frequently called THE BIG H, DOJEE, HORSE or CABALLO (Spanish for horse), WITCHHAZEL, ANGEL, TRAGIC MAGIC, NOISE or SMACK—the last term from the nickname for the jazz band leader, composer and heroin user James Fletcher Henderson (1898–1952). The most familar way to take SMACK is first to COOK it (heat and prepare it), then DO UP (distend a vein) and POP it (take it by injection; also to have sexual intercourse; and recently, as BE POPPED, to be arrested), using a POINT or SPIKE (a hypodermic needle). British rhyming slang labels taking H by injection LAMB or LAMB CHOP to rhyme with POP. However, there are both other forms and other methods of taking ANTIFREEZE, as heroine is also called. Powdered forms that may be SNIFFED or taken orally include the British CHINESE (heroin adulterated or CUT with a white powder), JACK (British, a heroin tablet), FLEA POWDER (diluted heroin) or SALT, and GOLDFINGER (synthetic heroin; from Ian Fleming's James Bond novel of that name, 1950s). Since the 1970s, any addict on this form of HARD STUFF (hard drugs) has been known as A SKAG JONES.

CANDY MAN, THE A drug pusher. ADs (as drug addicts call themselves, reversing the initials) have given their PUSHERS many names (see **NIXON**). One's CONNECTION, as A PUSHER may be called, is known as THE MAN, perhaps a shortening of the older REEFER MAN, a marijuana seller since 1920. HOUSE CONNECTIONS are drug DEALERS who work out of private houses or apartments and are thus unlikely to be easily BUSTED (arrested). BINGLERS or BINGLES and JUGGLERS are ordinary sellers and pushers of narcotics, while TRAFFICKERS and BROKERS are more elegant names for higher-echelon PUSHERS. A PUSHER who attempts to make non-users into regular addicts is known, ironically, as A MISSIONARY. Be they humble or exalted, however, all CONNECTIONS seek to avoid BIG JOHNS, GAZERS, UNCLES or UNCLE SAMS, DOPEBULLS and WHISKERS—all names for narcotics agents or members of the police who specialize in drug detection.

CARD, TO GET A To receive narcotics that have been

placed between the sides of a split and resealed postcard. MULES (narcotics smugglers) have devised ingenious ways to supply USERS with their drugs. Among these are THE CARDS mentioned above, especially useful for prison inmates, and the equally ingenious WRITING—a letter written on absorbent paper that has been saturated with a solution of drugs. When one gets A GIFT (obtains narcotics) or A CARRY (the British expression for a load of drugs), he must be sure to protect it from TAKE OFF ARTISTS (addicts who steal from other addicts to support their own HABITS) and to avoid being BURNED (having his drug "borrowed" and not returned). He will STASH his F-13 (drugs) in a safe place.

GIRL Cocaine. Users believe that "things go better with coke," and because cocaine is purported to be an aphrodisiac for women, it is frequently identified by such female names as HER, GIRL, CONNIE, CORINNE, COOKIE and such euphoric titles as WINGS, HAPPY DUST, JOY FLAKES or POWDER, HEAVEN DUST and, most opulently, GOLD DUST. Its white, powdery nature has led addicts and PUSHERS to call it by such snowy terms as OLD LADY WHITE, REINDEER DUST, WHITE CROSS, SNOWBIRD, SNOWBALL and, of course, SNOW. Those who prepare to inject it are said to HOOK UP REINDEER and those who take NOSE CANDY or SNORT DUST (sniff cocaine) are known as SLEIGHRIDERS, ARTIC EXPLORERS or people FROM MOUNT SHASTA (a snow-covered California mountain). BIG BLOKE—rhyming slang for COKE—also known as LEAF, CECIL, WHITE MOSQUITOS and just plain C (an initial sometimes used for heroin) has a long and fascinating history. It comes from the coca plant, was once an ingredient of the other kind of coke (Coca-Cola), and came to the West from Cochin China in 1874, whence its name. It was originally used as a local anesthetic, and its chemical formula is $C_{17}H_{21}No_4$. Both because of the initial "C" and because an ounce of cocaine (or heroin) is so expensive, it is known to some as CADILLAC.

GONG Opium. The opium habit is an ancient one, and

Thomas De Quincey coined the expression "opium-eater" in the *Confessions of an English Opium-Eater*, which he wrote in 1822. Opium had, of course, long been used as a painkiller and, mixed with alcohol as laudanum, was one of the nineteenth century's most popular medicines. Perhaps for this reason it is euphemistically called GOM or GOD'S OWN MEDICINE (see **WHITE NURSE**). Its use as a soporific and its association with dreams has led to its being known as DREAM WAX, DREAM BEADS (pellets), DREAMS, MIDNIGHT OIL (also because one burns it) and POPPY (also associated with its source). Some of the other names for opium or O come from its oriental origins. It is known as YEN-SHEE, and A YEN meaning a CRUSH ON or THING FOR someone comes from this (see Chapter 7, STRAIGHT SEX, **YEN FOR**); it is called GONG, while a smoker is called A GONGBEATER, and his substance is known as GEE, GOW and GHOW. In order to use TWANG (as the Australians have called it since 1898), one must heat it. Thus it has been called THE LAMP HABIT, and those who use it are known as CAMPFIRE BOYS. Opium residue (and opium itself) is called BLACK STUFF, GREASE, MUD and TAR. One may smoke O in a pipe known as A SAXOPHONE, DREAMSTICK, JOYSTICK, and the act of smoking is known as A LAY DOWN or LIE DOWN because reclining supposedly prevents or alleviates the nausea and vomiting that may be side effects of a drug that produces an otherwise pleasant PIPE DREAM.

HEAVEN AND HELL PCP or phencyclidine. According to users of P-STUFF (PCP), it does plunge one from the heights to the depths, and ANGEL DUST is another particularly appropriate name for it since BUSY BEE, CRYSTAL, ELEPHANT TRANQUILIZER and SUPER JOINT, as it is also known, can often be fatal. Equally hellish is RED DEVIL (Seconal, a powerful sleeping pill), DEVIL'S TESTICLE (mandrake, also known as SATAN'S APPLE) and DEVIL'S TRUMPET (jimson weed). Purportedly at the other end of the mood scale are the drugs that give one HEAVENLY PEACE (see **BLACK AND WHITE MINSTRELS** and **BLOWN AWAY** for UPPERS, etc.).

These include BLUE HEAVEN (amytal, a barbiturate), BLUE VELVET (paregoric taken by injection or, in Britain, paregoric combined with antihistamines) and HEAVENLY BLUES (morning glory seeds). All of these, in addition to making the user HAPPY, also offer him or her SERENITY, TRANQUILITY and PEACE, which is also the name of a synthetic hallucinogenic drug more familiarly known as STP. Methadone, originally used to detoxify heroin addicts, has produced addicts of its own. In its various forms the drug is known as DOLLS and DOLLIES. Also of recent popularity are quaaludes, known as LUDES. But, to some, LUDING OUT, getting high on quaaludes, may be far less attractive than going for COLD AND HOT or C and H, a mixture of cocaine and heroin. In their inimitable elegance, the British have contributed the CORPORATION COCKTAIL—coal gas bubbled through milk—to the pharmacopoeia of THE VALLEY OF THE DOLLS, the name for the world of addiction taken from the book of that title by Jacqueline Suzanne. A somewhat anticlimactic conclusion to such exotic euphemisms is the American FRUIT SALAD, a mixture of drugs that teenagers, experimenting at FRUIT SALAD PARTIES, assemble from their parents' medicine chests.

ICE CREAMER, AN An occasional user of drugs. One who has an ICE CREAM HABIT uses drugs on an irregular basis and does not devote his or her entire income to their purchase. Such a habit is also known as JOY POPPING or a SATURDAY NIGHT HABIT, although JOY POPPER is the name given to a heroin addict who believes, perhaps naively, that he is in control of his JONES or HABIT. The names for types of addicts are numerous, but, in general, those on drugs may be divided into people with A BELLY HABIT (taking drugs orally), A MOUTH HABIT (smoking drugs), A NEEDLE HABIT (injecting drugs), and A NOSE HABIT (sniffing drugs through the nose or SNORTING). HABIT, itself a euphemism, was first used to describe the taking of addictive drugs in the 1840s, and users have since been said to BELONG to a given drug. A VIPER, for example, is one of the older terms for a chronic marijuana taker who BELONGS to MJ (marijuana). References to VIPERS are enshrined in such 1920s American songs as "The Viper's Rag," "The Viper's Dream" and "Youse a Viper." More recent terms include A CUT DOWN, a teenage user of alcohol and/or drugs who steals to support the HABIT, and A JUNIOR CUT DOWN or MIDGET, a pre-pubescent dope addict who does the same. The traveling HEAD, who obtains his drugs from doctors in small towns, is ironically titled an RFD, the American postal abbreviation for "rural free delivery," while the doctor who is willing to sell them illegally is called A RIGHT ROCKER or ICE TONG DOCTOR. In order to get sympathy and, therefore, drugs from a physician, some addicts will simulate the CART-WHEEL, the CIRCUS, the FIGURE EIGHT, the TWISTER or the WING DING (all names for the contortions and spasms associated with withdrawal).

LUCY IN THE SKY WITH DIAMONDS LSD or lysergic acid. Made most famous by John Lennon and Paul Mc-Cartney's song of 1967, this picturesque name describes the hallucinogenic sensations and images experienced by users of this most popular form of INSTANT ZEN during the 1960s. Also known as YELLOW, ORANGE, CALIFORNIA and HAWAIIAN SUNSHINE (because of the colors of the tablets), BLUE CHEER or BLUE FLAGS (if the tablets are blue) are taken by members of the EXPLORERS' CLUB. This name was commonly applied to ACID USERS or ACID HEADS because, under the aegis of such prophets of "psychic drug research" as Timothy Leary, CUBE HEADS (habitual users of LSD who were so called because they often took the drug by saturating a sugar cube with a solution of it) thought the drug would allow them to explore the unconscious. While ON A RIDE, DURING A SESSION or EXPERIENCE (an LSD TRIP), those tak-ing PEACE or BIG D (LSD) have found it necessary to have CO-PILOTS or GUIDES (experienced LSD users who are "sober" at the time) on their FLIGHT or TRIP. Such assistants BABY SAT with them, that is, helped them through the ex-perience until REENTRY (COMING DOWN OFF A HIGH or

BACK FROM A TRIP). Despite the fact that LSD users call the drug COFFEE (because it is sometimes taken with cubes of sugar) or CANDY, high quality LSD is actually more accurately known as OWSLEY ACID or OWSLEY'S. It was named after Augustus Owsley, who illegally manufactured this drug on which people BLOW THEIR MINDS (get HIGH on a hallucinogenic).

NIXON, A   A low quality, low potency drug passed off as a powerful, pure drug. Richard M. Nixon has added his name not only to political history but also to the chronicle of drug terms. Just as some American voters would not "buy a used car from *that* man," so experienced addicts will not buy their GOODS, MERCHANDISE, or CEMENT from AN OPERATOR (PUSHER) known to sell NIXONS. When A BUYER wants TO SCORE (obtain a supply of drugs) or MAKE A BUY (a term also used to indicate the purchase of drugs by police or narcotics agents to trap an alleged DEALER), he will check the GRAPEVINE TROLLEY (secret channel) to make sure that he gets a good DECK (the amount of narcotics needed for one dose). THE CANDY MAN, in turn, has the right to sell to an addict, that is, TO SAIL or TO TURN, or to refuse to sell to him, giving him what is called THE GO-BY. Both parties may choose to KEEP THE MEET (an appointment for drug sales, also used by the police) or to BLOW THE MEET.

OVERAMPED   Overdosed, especially with amphetamines. OVERAMPED is both a pun on the overuse of amphetamines and a metaphor suggesting the "charge" an overdosed addict gets when he OVERJOLTS. While amphetamines are among the newer substances in the pharmacopoeia of addiction, HASH or HEMP (hashish) is one of the oldest. Dried for smoking and chewing in Arabia, Egypt and Turkey since 1598, HASH was praised in *Purchas His Pilgrimage* (1613)—the book that was the basis for Coleridge's opium poem, "Kubla Khan"—as causing "laughing, dalliance, and mak[ing] one as it were drunken." Addiction itself has been known as DOPING since the nineteenth century, when the *American Newspaper* condemned it for "stupefying" men when they took tobacco "prepared in a peculiar way." These comments were written in 1889, and by 1896 the *New York Sun* defined the term "dopey" or "dopy" as "heavy or stupefied as from drugs," particularly the POPPY (opium). DOPE seems to have been originally the name for opium, especially for the viscous substance produced by heating it (see GONG), but by 1909 it was applied to all kinds of narcotics. Over the years the word DOPE has been used to indicate specific drugs—depending on their popularity at the time; it is now used particularly to refer to marijuana.

RAINY DAY WOMAN, A A marijuana cigarette. Marijuana cigarettes, one of the most popular forms of the drug, have many names. In older parlance they were REEFERS, DREAM STICKS, TEA STICKS, JOY STICKS (hence, J-STICKS and J-SMOKES), GIGGLE STICKS or GIGGLE SMOKES, ROCKETS, TWISTS, DUBBYS, DUBES, and GYVES. Among their more interesting species are MEZZROLE or MIGHTY MEZZ, a potent marijuana cigarette named after Mezz Mezzrow, a jazz musician notorious for both smoking and selling them. Milder cigarettes, SPLIFFS, may be made by mixing marijuana and regular tobacco. Then they are known as COCKTAILS, STRAIGHTS, SLIMS and, somewhat pejoratively, SQUARES since they are not "hip." Large marijuana cigarettes are called THUMBS, and partially smoked or shared cigarettes are known as BURNIES. The butt of A REEFER is popularly called A ROACH and is held in AN AIRPLANE or ROACH CLIP. A brew made from the seeds and stalks of marijuana after it has been MANICURED (cleansed of them) is known as POT LIQUOR. When a user wants to BLOW A STICK (have a smoke), he may well go to A BALLROOM, PARACHUTE (1940s), BALLOON ROOM or A SPOT (1980s), that is, an illegal HEAD SHOP (a store for selling drug paraphernalia) or apartment where fellow users gather to smoke. He hopes that he will not end up getting the opposite of such famous high quality blends as ACAPULCO GOLD and have to suffer with LIPTON TEA (a poor quality of the drug; see also **NIXON**).

WHITE NURSE Morphine. Also known as RED CROSS, MISS

EMMA, MEDICINE and GOD'S OWN MEDICINE (see GONG), morphine, certainly the most popular nineteenth-century analgesic, was already familiar as an addictive drug by 1892, when the morphine HABIT had become well known. Like LSD (see LUCY IN THE SKY WITH DIAMONDS), IXEY (morphine) is now also known as CUBE JUICE. By World War II morphine addicts were having SLUMBER PARTIES (group indulgences in the drug) at which they sometimes took mixtures of barbiturates and morphine and occasionally obtained A PURPLE HEART (a Nembutal capsule mixed with morphine). Codeine, a milder relative of morphine, originally used for the same purposes, is innocently known as SCHOOLBOY.

THE BIG HOUSE AND SMALLER COOLERS

BUSH RANGER, A An escaped convict; an outlaw who lives by robbery. A BUSH RANGER is an Australian name, first for an escaped prisoner (1801) and second for an outlaw who lives in the bush and steals from those he encounters (1806). Among the numerous other names for an escaped prisoner is A RABBIT FOOT—since one planning an escape has ITCHY FEET or RABBIT FEVER. He has taken what prison officials universally call UNAUTHORIZED DEPARTURE and what fellow inmates call COPPING A MOKE. Thus he is officially termed A PAL (prisoner at large). A BUSH RANGER of the second variety is a cousin to the American JESSIE JAMES, the name of the Western bank robber, horse thief and outlaw who lived from 1847 to 1882 and is closely related to a British MOSS TROOPER (1701, now obsolete), a bandit or raider named after a group of outlaws who pillaged the Scottish border in the mid-seventeenth century. All are capable of carrying out effective STICK-UPS (U.S., 1905) and HOLD-UPS (U.S., 1887). The American term HOLD-UP comes from the thief's demand that his victims hold up their hands or be shot. Australian robbers tell their victims to stick up their hands. However, a convict on the run is so busy ON THE BRICKS or ON THE

GROUND, having GONE OVER THE HILL, or OVER THE WALL, HITTING THE FENCE or TAKING TO THE TALL TIMBERS, TALL TREES or THE TULES (tall reeds that grow in the American Southwest)—that is, escaping—that he has no time for robbery. What he hopes for is to make THE E LIST (escape list, British), or MAKE A CLEAN GET (AWAY).

CHUM, A NEW   A newly arrived prison inmate. In Australia, since 1812, CHUM has been the name for a convict. The word is also used in Britain of a criminal and is sometimes made into the diminutive CHUMMIE. Australian prisoners are divided into NEW and OLD CHUMS (see **FISH** for the American equivalents) depending upon the length of confinement, but they are all CANARIES (convicts, from their yellow clothing since 1827). At his entry to prison an English prisoner is elegantly greeted by a RECEPTION BOARD (a group of department managers who check the inmates in). Any CANARY who is DOING BIRD—time in prison (U.S.: see also **NICKLE TO A DIME**) does well to become friendly with THE BARON (British for a powerful inmate who lends and/or sells goods and services), particularly if he is going to be an LTI (long-term inmate). The American slang equivalent of serving a long sentence is MAKING LITTLE ONES OUT OF BIG ONES, from breaking rocks as prison work. American, Australian and British prisoners who are DOING TIME (American) refer to themselves as being CANNED (imprisoned; from being in THE CAN or TIN CAN, prison in American slang), ON THE CORN (from the hominy prison diet of Australian convicts, 1949) or as DOING THEIR PORRIDGE (a British 1970s variant of IN STIR or in jail).

CROSS BAR HOTEL, A   A prison. This general American euphemism is joined by more familiar ones such as THE BIG HOUSE and THE BIG PASTURE (penitentiary), THE COOP, THE COOLER (prison); their rural cousins (CORRECTIONAL FACILITIES in the country), RANCHES, FARMS and CAMPS; and the more diminutive PLAYHOUSE (a prison with a small population). In America, prisons are also known as QUADS or QUODS (not because of their academic pretentions but because of their yards), as CAMPUSES and as COLLEGES. But few American terms can match the British euphemism for the ironmongery department of a prison, known since 1945 as HIS/HER MAJESTY'S SCHOOL FOR HEAVY NEEDLEWORK.

CWR Counseling, warning, and releasing pre-delinquents without formally charging them. This American practice of DIVERTING YOUTHFUL OFFENDERS (releasing delinquents without formal procedure) is sometimes employed against those found either BOPPING (gang fighting systematically, and often with weapons) or "brawling," less destructive and organized group fighting. A convicted JD (juvenile delinquent) is likely to be sent to A CORRECTIONAL CENTER, YOUTH GUIDANCE CENTER or YOUTH CENTER. Among the types of centers are AN INDUSTRIAL SCHOOL or A FORESTRY CAMP—for boys (see also **FILLET OF VEAL**). However, CWR is usually the sole "punishment" meted out to juvenile delinquents who have run away or are on alcohol and who would not be considered criminals if they were adults. JDS guilty of such behavior qualify as STATUS OFFENDERS.

DECOMPRESSION CHAMBER, A A residential center for inmates on their way to release. DECOMPRESSION CHAMBERS are part of what is known in America as the graduated release program. Ex-offenders, for example, may find themselves in half-way houses, more recently dubbed COMMUNITY TREATMENT CENTERS, at least by the federal government. Inmates still imprisoned may find themselves in WORK or WORK/STUDY RELEASE PROGRAMS or CENTERS. The state of Vermont began these practices in 1906, when it permitted prison inmates to leave prison and work outside in the community, returning to imprisonment only in the evening. British COMMUNITY TREATMENT CENTERS are called HOSTELS and their inmates are HOSTELERS. Along with these WORK RELEASE CENTERS, the United States now has RESTITUTION CENTERS (1972). These are small dwelling places for inmates who pay room and board, and even damages to their former victims, while they work in the community. Those who successfully achieve graduated release may be said in prison argot to have DONE A BIT STANDING UP, to have handled their prison sentences and experiences with minimal trauma.

DERWENTER, A An Australian ex-convict. This current Australian euphemism dates from 1853 and the establishment of the convict settlement on the Derwent River in Tasmania. Whether he was A KATH, short for A KATHLEEN MAVOURNEEN (an habitual criminal; also the term for an indefinite jail sentence, 1914) or merely A PIE-EATER or CRUNCHER (a small-time crook in prison slang since the 1950s), he was NOT QUITE THE CLEAN POTATO (of bad repute). KATHLEEN MAVOURNEEN is a term originating from the chorus of an Irish popular song: "It may be for years, it may be forever." A PIE-EATER or PIE-CRUNCHER is so called because he lives on meat pies, small-time food, instead of proper meals. NOT QUITE THE CLEAN POTATO is a negative form of the British expression THE POTATO (1882), meaning the real or correct thing since 1877. None of the above is likely to have forgotten HOMINY (prison food, 1895), the HOMINY BUS (the jail tram, 1953) or the HOMINY GAZETTE (jail rumors).

FILLET OF VEAL Prison. As early as 1887, this euphemism has been an English rhyming slang term for "steel" (bars). Its less elegant analogue is the British BUCKET AND PAIL (jail) where inmates spend their time in A FLOWERY DELL (cell). The language for American prisons is infinitely rich; an example is the Black English SLAMMER (1930s, jail; now general but questionably euphemistic) in which prisoners spent time ON ICE (in prison, especially solitary confinement) sometimes doing A BIG BIT or extremely long and unjust prison term. With the prison reforms of the 1960s and 1970s, STATE FARMS (prisons), STATE TRAINING SCHOOLS (reformatories) and CORRECTIONAL FACILITIES in general have begun to sound positively inviting. A CAMP, for example, is a minimum-security institution that operates around a work program. YOUTHFUL OFFENDERS (convicted juvenile delinquents) may attend TRAINING SCHOOLS (institutions for long-term commitment and reform). GREENSBURG PREP, however, is not a juvenile facility but a model state prison pre-release center near Greensburg, Pennsylvania (see **DECOMPRESSION CHAMBER**). Inmates of girls' reformatories refer to their domiciles as FINISHING SCHOOLS, GIRLS' SCHOOLS or HEN PENS. The British equivalents of these JUVEYS (Black English slang for reform schools) are BORSTAL INSTITUTIONS (1908), which provide educational opportunities comparable with those afforded by the adult American NEWGATE PROGRAM (post-secondary educational program for inmates, 1960s). Most modern of all, keeping step with college trends, are COED CORRECTIONS or COCORRECTIONAL INSTITUTIONS—sexually integrated prisons.

FISH, A FRESH or NEW   A new prison inmate. The opposite of the Australian euphemism for an experienced convict, an OLD HAND or OLD CHUM (see **CHUM**), A FRESH FISH is one just caught and DROPPED INTO THE BUCKET or TANK (jailed). Having ignored the Eleventh Commandment of prisoners, "Thou shalt not get caught," he now has a PEDIGREE (criminal record) and must learn to avoid some of his fellow inmates and emulate others INSIDE (in prison). He will learn to step aside for an OBC—inmates' abbreviation for an "old brutal convict" who threatens younger, weaker prisoners and often tries to get them to ROBUCK (from a Louisiana prison slang term, ROBOT, to do what he wants) and stay away from A S-A-N MAN, a "stop-at-nothing" man, and AN SD (a shit disturber or troublemaker) or what the English call A COWBOY (a know-it-all). All are in the category of WRONGS (wrong guys; those who do not uphold inmates' values; see also **REAL MAN**). Instead, he will work to be considered ACES HIGH, one trusted by his fellow inmates, and will seek to be A POLITICIAN, an inmate with a good prison job and prison privileges. He would rather be what British prison officials consider A DADDY (a strong personality) than what they classify as A JOE or DIV (a weak one). Whether he is AN APPLE KNOCKER (a farmboy convict) or a city slicker, he will try to find A BACKER (a person who has influence with the prison authorities) and eventually to become A BIG SHOT (a person with authority in a prison).

HAVE IT AWAY, TO To escape from legal custody. A British prisoner who escapes from custody HAS IT AWAY or HAS IT ON HIS TOES, while his American cousin who departs from prison without leave has, since the 1920s, been ON BUSH PATROL (see **BUSH RANGER**). As if in sympathy, Australian criminals at large are ON THE GRASS (1925), which has, since 1941, also meant released from jail. Those who are released the legal way in America HIT THE BRICKS and in England have BEEN TO SEE CAPTAIN BATES (a well-known prison governor). But even AN OLD HAND (Australian ex-con since 1845) remembers his GATE FEVER (restless moodiness and anxiety before release, a condition also known in Britain as being GATE HAPPY) for years.

HUMMINGBIRD, THE The electric chair; also a prison torture. Since the U.S. Supreme Court reestablished the death penalty in 1976, THE HUMMINGBIRD or electric chair, also sardonically known as THE ELECTRIC CURE and THE HAIR CURLER—because it gives one A PERMANENT WAVE— is again in the news. American gangster films have long depicted convicts walking THE LAST MILE to PAY THE SUPREME or EXTREME PENALTY involved in SOCIAL KILLING (the death penalty). To get THE WORKS is, in America, to be sentenced to death, and execution is often by MANUFACTURED LIGHTNING (THE CHAIR).

KITE Prohibited communication, note or letter, passed around or smuggled out of prison by inmates. Sending around or FLYING A KITE may get an inmate A WRITE-UP, that is, a negative disciplinary report or demerit. In England, if a prisoner gets A WRITE-UP, he may go DOWN THE BLOCK (into the punishment cells), find himself CC (confined to cell) or enter THE ROSE GARDEN (solitary confinement cells in the punishment block). In America, he might even find himself part of a LOCKDOWN. From 1973 on, this term has meant a situation in which all inmates are incarcerated in their cells (except for meals) to avoid violence. If a riot or a mass breakout attempt occurs, CERT (the CORRECTONAL EMERGENCY

RESPONSE TEAM) may be called. This is a group of police sent in to quash prison uprisings.

NICKEL TO A DIME, A Five to ten years in prison. Prison inmates have devised a number of colorful if ironic euphemisms to announce the length of their terms in prison. English cockneys are responsible for the rhyming slang expression SORROWFUL TALE (three months in jail), and perhaps American convicted gamblers coined THREE DEUCES JAMMED (three two-year sentences running concurrently) and THREE DEUCES RUNNING WILD (three consecutive two-year sentences). British prisoners may DO A POUND (five years), and American ones may DO A QUARTER (twenty-five years), proving in each case that time is money. Whatever one's BIT or STRETCH (time to be served in prison), whether it be A NEWSPAPER (thirty days in jail), A HALF-A-STRETCH (six months), A CALENDAR (one year), THE CLOCK or THE BOOK (a life sentence) or even just AN OLD LAG (British prison slang for a three-year sentence), an inmate hopes for A LIFEBOAT—the commutation of his sentence or an order for retrial or freedom.

PINK CLINK MOVEMENT, THE Institutional support of the use of pink walls in a prison or cell to calm violent inmates. PINK CLINKS, known more formally as BAKER-MILLER PINK PRISONS, after the corrections officers who first conceived of using color therapy as a tool in calming prisoners, are one of the newer techniques in penology. A modern prison has changed its nomenclature (if not always its practices) so that it no longer talks of a strip-and-search room for incoming prisoners but speaks instead of AN INTAKE ROOM, A RECEPTION CENTER, or A HOLDING AREA. It is surprising that even PINK CLINKS may contain A DADDY TANK (a special cell reserved for lesbians to protect them from attack by their fellow inmates). ABOLITIONISTS, a term in use since the 1960s for those who believe that prisons cannot rehabilitate prisoners effectively and that non-dangerous OFFENDERS should therefore not be incarcerated, must be seriously doubtful about the behavioral modification achieved by interior decoration schemes in prisons.

PINS; PERSONS IN NEED OF SUPERVISION Juvenile delinquents and pre-juvenile delinquents. Young malefactors who commit such offenses as truancy, vagrancy and violation of curfew laws are now subject to YOUTHFUL OFFENDER TREATMENT, a court trial that is neither publicized nor recorded. Those in need of rehabilitation or prevention from further slippage are known as PINS (from the above acronym), MINS (MINORS IN NEED OF SUPERVISION) or CHINS (CHILDREN IN NEED OF SUPERVISION). JUVENILE OFFENDERS who are incarcerated may be put into INTENSIVE-CARE UNITS—locked units especially for violent juveniles. The English equivalents, BORSTAL BOYS and GIRLS, are submitted to BORSTAL TRAINING (time in BORSTALS or reformatories also known as REMAND CENTRES or REMAND HOMES). If MINS, PINS, CHINS or BORSTALS grow up to be HIGH BINDERS (criminals or hoods), the laws protecting juveniles from being responsible for their past records no longer apply, and repeated criminal behavior will cause them to be classified as RECIDIVISTS, defined by the *Pall Mall Gazette* in 1882 as those "who relapse into crime."

PROBLEM CHILDREN Juvenile delinquents. In 1958, children in 700 SCHOOLS—those provided for "known ruffians and indicted hoodlums"—were sometimes called more tactfully JDs, JUVIES or MINORS. The language of euphemism indicates that the problem of YOUTHFUL OFFENDERS is an international one. The English had their TEDS, NEDS (Scotland) and TEDDY BOYS in the 1950s—so called because they adopted the dress of the Edwardian era if not its manners. The Australian cousins of the English boys and girls who BOVVER (fight in the street, in their cherry-red BOVVER BOOTS) are WIDGIES (female toughs) and BODGIES (male). All, young though they are, are known to be capable of what the British Home Office terms GPV (gross personal violence; using a weapon, see CWR).

REAL MAN, A A prisoner who lives up to and by the value system of his fellow inmates. In *The Society of Captives*,

Gresham Sykes describes the ways in which prisoners evaluate each other. A REAL MAN or RIGHT GUY is a prison hero. He can TAKE IT (handle prison discipline effectively) and he PULLS or DOES HIS OWN TIME and "stays cool." Among his less desirable fellow inmates are "rats" (informers) and "gorillas," prisoners who steal from and use force against their fellows. A RIGHT GUY is more desirable than A CENTER MAN or SQUARE JOHN, an inmate who tries to ingratiate himself with the prison staff. A CENTER MAN is so called because he hangs out near the control center of the prison where the staff congregates. Among other undesirables is A MERCHANT, a prisoner who sells cigarettes, candy and materials stolen from the CORRECTIONAL FACILITY (official parlance for prison) instead of sharing them with his friends, and "a ballbuster," an inmate who gives THE SCREWS (guards) a hard time. It is dangerous to be his HOLMES (buddy, partner: from Arthur Conan Doyle's Sherlock). Prison RUMBLES (information conveyed by inmates) suggest avoiding him. Oddly enough, A TOUGH is a highly respected member of the inmate community. Although he may be touchy and often picks fights with his fellow cons, he is to be treated with respect—and fear. He is more valued than A HIPSTER who, although his name sounds less "square," is merely a fake TOUGH—described by his colleagues as ALL WIND AND GUMDROPS.

REMITTANCE MAN, A A man sent by his family to a British colony in order to keep him away from home and out of trouble. Yesterday's bad seed was the REMITTANCE MAN, a young man kept alive by funds remitted by his family. A REMITTANCE MAN (Australian, 1890s) might be sent away from home because he was what Americans would call A BRIGHAM YOUNG (a bigamist, after the famous polygamous Mormon leader), a too vigorous sower of wild oats or what the cockneys term A BABBLING BROOK (rhyming slang for crook). If he did not behave himself in Australia, he might end up in THE TENCH or convict barracks. TENCH is an abbreviation of "penitentiary," literally" a place for penitents."

SCREENS, THE A solitary cell surrounded by fine wire so that nothing can be passed through it. Gently and traditionally known as SECLUSION, A STRETCH (period of time) in SOLITARY is spent in a cell less attractively called by inmates THE BRIG (from the term for a naval prison), THE BANK, KLONDIKE (for isolation in A COOLER; see **CROSS BAR HOTEL**) or, in officialese, THE CONTROL UNIT, which is a solitary confinement unit. Being IN SOLITARY is known as being ON THE SHELF (a phrase that takes its cue from the social world's term for being out of circulation). Such an interval is also ironically called P AND Q (peace and quiet) or TIME OUT (of sight). In less enlightened prisons, A MONTH IN CONGRESS (a term in SOLITARY) may be partially spent TENDING THE BAR—inmate argot for being handcuffed, in a standing position, to the bars of the cell. However, the era of psychological rehabilitation has transformed a stay in solitary confinement to a therapeutic-sounding period in what may be called THE ADJUSTMENT CENTER or THE SEGREGATION UNIT.

WHISPER, A The last few months of a prison sentence. An inmate is GETTING SHORT when his sentence is near its end. If he does not attempt to MAP A GET (plan an escape), use A BRIAR (a file or hacksaw since 1830) or become involved in A CREATIVE CONFLICT (prison riot), he may hope to get TIME OFF or GOOD TIME (time off for good behavior). He will then be eligible for parole. In Australia, such a parolee is called A TICKET OF LEAVER or A TICKET OF LEAVE MAN. In England, he is described as being ON LICENSE or receiving STATUTORY AFTERCARE. In America, a parole is A CR (conditional release). A parolee needs A COMPASH (compassionate parole officer, chaplain or social worker) and hates A RAPPER (a person or fellow inmate who protests an inmate's release to the parole board). If someone abuses parole, he or she will be forced to serve his BOT—the balance of time to be served by a parole violator.

7

Sex: Amateur and Professional

In the Victorian age, a woman was *never* pregnant, she was *enceinte*. Emily Eden, in *The Semi-Detached House* (1859), takes her heroine through seven months of a DELICATE CONDITION and introduces its OUTCOME without once mentioning the word "pregnancy," even after THE LADY-IN-WAITING is TAKEN ILL, a phrase all her neighbors and family perfectly understood meant "in labor." Perhaps this is because pregnancy issues from sex, always a delicate subject. In Western societies, sex has often been surrounded by guilt and shame. Only the initiated—those sufficiently old, trained and experienced— were supposed to know its secrets, for sex itself was considered powerful magic as well as primal knowledge. It was to these qualities the Bible referred when it said that Adam "knew Eve." References to sex were also indirect because they could arouse or titillate men and women by stirring up their four humors. We still refer to the humoral tradition when we speak of a woman or man who is "hot" or "frigid." (See the Introduction.)

Children, whom we sometimes sentimentalize as BLESSED EVENTS, are religiously and socially sanctioned products of a legitimatized sexual union. Although this would suggest that they should not be targets for euphemism, our vocabulary is full of oblique terms for LITTLE ONES. If they are illegitimate, shame and perhaps a desire to protect the child from social disapproval has led to such expressions as BORN ON THE WRONG SIDE OF THE BLANKET.

Still euphemized, but far more openly mentioned than they were years ago are the subjects of homosexuality, prostitution and other unconventional or exotic sexual practices. The bonding political and social force of the Gay Liberation movement has contributed to the abolition of the indirect vocabulary for homosexuality and its practices. It has substituted new, less pejorative terms for "old snarl words." These days, the "straight" sexual world is far more inhibited about hurling epithets like "pansy" or "fruit." But other motives have also prompted these linguistic changes. Both fear of legal and social punishment and the desire to identify fellow members of the group have led homosexuals to coin their own special argot.

Prostitutes too have their own euphemistic language, preferring to think of themselves not as purveyors of furtive sex but as members of THE OLDEST PROFESSION. Both prostitutes and the general public euphemize THE TRADE or THE LIFE for a variety of motives: fear of the law, the desire to make THE BUSINESS seem respectable by removing its stigma, and the new permissiveness that allows GIRLS to advertise. Because prostitution is so ancient and so international, its euphemistic vocabulary is vast. Many of the terms are humorous because they reflect the sense of both embarrassment and irony experienced by some BODY WORKERS and many of their CLIENTS. Thus prostitutes have been called SHADY LADIES, CHICKEN RANCHERS, HELLO, DEARIES (British, from the traditional greeting English PROFESSIONALS proffer a potential customer) and PAVEMENT PRINCESSES (the CB translation of the French term *nymphe du pave*). Some of the terms for prostitutes, like CAMILLE and PHRYNE, are literary and romantic; some, like A SOILED DOVE, are sentimental; still others are borrowings from the worlds of crime, gambling and business. Still further euphemisms allude to other professions; these include FREE-LANCER, MODEL and HOSTESS, and prostitutes who are plying their trade often refer to common societal terminology, as when they call their activities DATING. Their exotic practices are always spoken of as if they had originated in some other and more sinful nation. In America, some of the inventive delights are named for the Greeks, the French, the Dutch, the Germans and the English.

Growing numbers of trysting places, the activities they provide and, finally, the relatively new ads and columns that publicize them have spawned a new advertising category called "carnal classified." There the interested reader may find listings of those who enjoy B/D, TV TRAINING, and SHOWERS in at least two colors. This code language is accessible only to the initiated—and to the fortunate reader of this book.

But whether sex is straight or gay, amateur or professional, it is often obscured by a cloudy but seductive veil of words. A "Saturday Night Live" TV program once gave a "sex test." They concluded that the answer to the question, "Who invented sex?" was "The Dutch." One need only look at the many terms for sex—DUTCH WIVES [not a synonym for "spouses"], DUTCH HUSBANDS, DUTCH WIDOWS—and the fact that the sexual devotee may often find himself or herself "in Dutch." We don't know who invented this eternally popular pursuit, but we *do* know that the inventers of sexual euphemism were, are and will continue to be legion.

STRAIGHT SEX

ACTION Sexual intercourse. At least since the 1960s, Americans have euphemistically described sexual intercourse as ACTION. The term is probably Black English in origin and is much more recent than the related euphemism BUSINESS, found in Chaucer. The Chaucerian BUSY is a euphemism for "engaged in sex," and Shakespeare's Antony is said to have BUSINESS with Cleopatra "which cannot [be done] without him." We are more prone to be specific about our BUSINESS; to Australians LOVEMAKING has been LARKS IN THE NIGHT since the 1930s, while Americans speak of BALLING (since the 1960s). BALLING is probably a compound based on "balls" for testicles, "having a ball" for having a good time and perhaps BALLING THE JACK. A more cynical American expression for "to copulate with" is TO SERVICE.

BART, A   A girl, especially one of loose character. BART is an Australian euphemism that entered the language in about 1882. It probably originated in the British pet name TART, used to describe both a chaste and an unchaste woman. Although the *OED* dates the entrance of "tart" into the vernacular as 1887, Partridge finds it in use as early as the 1860s and we believe that it is an even earlier term, perhaps from the eighteenth century. However, it seems that the specialization of the word to mean only an immoral woman occurred in the late nineteenth or early twentieth century. Farmer's *Dictionary of Slang* (1903) defines a tart both as "a girl" and as "a wanton mistress." Now "tart" is not considered euphemistic and the word BART functions as a euphemism by changing the initial "t" to a "b." In an Australian jingle of 1899 we read:

> And his lady love's his 'donah'
> Or his 'clinah' or his tart
> Or his 'little bit of muslin'
> As it used to be his 'bart.'

Here, none of the terms is prejorative. Like BART, DONAH, from the Spanish *dona* for "woman," is now nearly obsolete and was used in Britain and Australia to mean SWEETHEART. CLINAH or CLINER, still in use, is from the German *Kleine* (meaning "little one").

BUSTLE PINCHING   Attempting to rub against a woman. BUSTLE PINCHING is a British police term for the common practice of a man rubbing his penis against the buttocks of a woman. The term dates from the 1830s—even before the prominence of the bustle as an item of dress. This is because, as early as 1788, A BUSTLE was a euphemistic term for a woman's DERRIÈRE. (See Chapter 1, THE POSTERIOR, HONKIES, DERRIÈRE). Australians, at least from the 1950s, have called the same area A DATE or A DOT. Thus, TO DATE someone means in Australian parlance "to goose" someone.

CASH AND CARRIED Married. This British euphemism is one of the many practical but reluctant ways of saying one is married, here through rhyming slang. The condition of marriage is one that—perhaps because it has traditionally evoked fear or contempt among people, especially young men, who fear loss of freedom—has spawned a variety of evasions. These include: BEEN AND DONE IT or GONE AND DONE IT (note the indefinite "it"), which are nineteenth- to twentieth-century British and American terms, GOTTEN HITCHED (U.S., 1850s) and YOKED—as in a team of oxen—and TIED THE KNOT. Since the 1940s Americans have MERGED, drawing the image from corporate business mergers. More socially touchy, however, is the matter of COMMON-LAW MARRIAGE. For this, the British have used MARRIED BUT NOT CHURCHED since the nineteenth century and the now obsolete MARRIED ON THE CARPET AND THE BANNS UP THE CHIMNEY. Even the term COMMON-LAW MARRIAGE is a euphemism for what has been more directly called "living in sin" and what is presently called A LONG-TERM RELATIONSHIP.

COMPANION, A A lover, usually live-in. In our liberated and transitional society, certain formerly exotic social roles are now considered routine. The change has wrought the necessity of finding acceptable names for one's lover that are convenient to use in social introductions. The attempt has been to make the nature of the activity discreet, but the nature of the possession clear. One offspring of the new freedom has been the euphemism COMPANION or CONSTANT COMPANION. It has partially replaced the designation MY FRIEND, the more casual MY ROOMMATE and THE PERSON I'M WITH or INVOLVED WITH, an introspective circum-

---

locution of the 1960s. Perhaps it's time to return either to such colorful English expressions as BARREL OF TREACLE or the sweet and simple Afro-American SUGAR.

CORNIFICATION   Sexual arousal in its final stages. Originally an eighteenth-century term, CORNIFICATION was a learned euphemism for lust or "horniness." It was coined by upper-class DANDIES (see Chapter 4, PRIDE, **DANDY[ISH]**) or MACARONIES who affected erudition by sprinkling Latinate and French words among English ones, thus speaking a macaronic language (one in which various tongues are mixed with the predominant language). CORNIFICATION was derived from the Latin word for "horn" (cornus). The term fell into disuse during the nineteenth century but was apparently preserved in the conservative dialects of the American Southern mountains. It resurfaced as a semi-jocular term in the American country western song of the late 1960s "The Horn Hangin' Blues," which began: "You may think I'm corny, but I'm cornificatin' over you." The entire concept of being horny (lustful) is a late medieval one that originated in the notion that the man who was cuckolded (sexually betrayed) by his wife had HORNS HUNG ON him. A vast repertoire of infidelity or horn jokes arose from this metaphor and have survived through the ages. See, for example, Christopher Marlowe, *Dr. Faustus* (1604), IV, ii, 77, where Faustus says of an unsuspecting cockold, "He sleeps, my lord, but dreams not of his horns."

CREEPER, A   A cuckold. This Black English euphemism may have come from the British term "creeper," used in 1589 to mean a stealthy, abject or timid person who moves as one branded a cuckold might. By an interesting coincidence the word "creeper" in eighteenth-century England meant a clog or patten for walking on ice. This has the stability, silence and comfort of the modern sneaker. If such is the case, A CREEPER might be considered a sneak. In England, the opposite of A CREEPER is A CRUMPET MAN (a womanizer) who loves his BIT OF CRUMPET or BISCUIT (both terms for a sexually attractive woman, the former since 1903). In Britain, sexual activity is politely called HAVING A BIT. Having an orgasm is BRINGING ONESELF OFF and the fondly amorous talk that can conclude in consummation is CANOODLE (see **HECTOR'S PECKING**).

CRUSH ON, TO HAVE A   To be infatuated with, attracted to. This euphemism originated in the United States as a slang term about 1914. It was institutionalized by the popular song of the twenties, written by the Gershwins (George and Ira), which crooned, "I've got a crush on you, Sweetie Pie." In later usage, ca. 1929, A CRUSH became the person one HAD A THING FOR, or, in British terms, WAS GONE ON.

DISCUSSING UGANDA   Fornicating. This is a current British euphemism for MAKING LOVE (1580, Lyly's *Euphues*). But Britishers say they GET THEIR KNICKERS (panties) IN A TWIST (become sexually aroused or have intercourse) in such LEGOVER SITUATIONS. Australians who achieve sexual intimacy FEATURE WITH their partners—a term popularized by the "Barry McKenzie" comic strip in the 1960s. They equate this with A SCORE BETWEEN THE POSTS, a 1970s Australian phrase of football origin.

DOG SOMEONE AROUND, TO   To treat badly; to follow; to be unfaithful to. This Black English euphemism for cheating is but one in the long American lexicon that disguises infidelity. Some Americans YARD ON (cheat) their wives or husbands and TIP them (cheat on them) by WORKING LATE AT THE OFFICE—the commonest excuse, used to conceal an infidelity.

DOLLYBIRD, A   A slim, young, attractive and usually fashionably dressed girl. Although this British euphemism is a relatively recent coinage, A DOLLY has meant a mistress since the early seventeenth century and was occasionally used to mean a slattern. The British BIRD is a euphemism for a girl or girlfriend. BIRD was revitalized during the 1960s but is of much older origin. By 1300, a *bird* or *burd* was a maiden or a girl and the term came into full flower from two separate earlier words, *bryde* and *burd*. Another euphemistic development from the British era of rock and roll is A BAND

MOLL, that is, a rock and roll GROUPIE or camp follower. "Moll" in this euphemism is also from the seventeenth century. Middleton used it to mean a harlot in 1604. It also meant an unmarried companion of a thief or vagrant, as it still does. The archetype of all such molls was Defoe's Moll Flanders. In 1785, the fine distinctions were blurring when Grose defined a moll as simply a whore. It is the older, more general group of meanings that has survived into the twentieth century.

DON JUAN, A A playboy or philanderer. Gabriel Tellez (1571–1641), writing under the pseudonym of Tirso de Molina, was first responsible for publicizing this name for a indefatigable pursuer of women. Don Juan is the chief character in his play about the life and loves of a legendary Spanish nobleman, *El Burlador de Seville.* Mozart further enhanced the gentleman's reputation, Italianizing his name and using it as the title of his opera *Don Giovanni.* By the second decade of the nineteenth century, when Byron wrote his satiric epic *Don Juan,* the name had already become the universal synonym for A PLAYBOY. The behavioral syndrome exhibited by such PLAYBOYS became known as DON JUANISM, and by 1898, women were honored as DON JUANESSES. DON JUAN is but one of the many eponyms for A WOLF, FAST WORKER, MAKE-OUT ARTIST or OPERATOR. Among the other proper names for FREE-LANCERS, we find LOTHARIO—from Nicholas Rowe's play, *The Fair Penitent* (1703)— and ROMEO—from Shakespeare's *Romeo and Juliet* (1597). A CASANOVA, second only to A DON JUAN as a lecher, is derived from the name of an actual gentleman— Giovanni Jacobo Casanova de Seingalt (1725–98)—who chronicled his amours and intrigues in twelve volumes of memoirs.

ELIGIBLE MAN or WOMAN, AN An unmarried person, a bachelor or spinster. The old term "bachelor" carried with it opprobrium on the one hand and the prospect of happy hunting on the other. To ensure that fair game rules were followed, bachelors (originally candidates for knighthood and other degrees) and their allies coined a bevy of euphemisms: ELIGIBLE, AVAILABLE and UNATTACHED are frequently used to describe the SINGLE MAN. These same terms are now applied to the SINGLE WOMAN as well. SINGLE is America's most popular generic term for the unmarried of both sexes, and during the 1960s the term SWINGLES was coined to indicate that certain SINGLES liked TO SWING (see EXOTIC SEX, **SWING BOTH WAYS,** SWING). The terms "old maid" and "spinster," nowadays almost always opprobrious (although the latter originally simply indicated the work a single woman did), have virtually disappeared from polite usage. With the advent of women's rights and women's careerism, "such persons" are no longer primarily perceived as LADIES-IN-WAITING (see also REPRODUCTIVE SEX, **EXPECTING**) or as ODD WOMEN—a term coined in England in the 1880s and used in George Gissing's novel of the same name (1894) to denote women who, though not peculiar or homosexual, were unmarried and thus not paired.

FRATERNIZE, TO   To have intercourse. It was during World War II that Allied soldiers were first ordered by their commanding officers not TO FRATERNIZE or FRAT with the local inhabitants. This presumably meant "avoid mingling," but came to mean "avoid commingling" A man of this period who HAD GONE TOO FAR did so with a woman who WENT ALL THE WAY or WENT THE LIMIT (that is, was willing to have sexual intercourse, 1950s). In Vietnam, soldiers who LIVED WITH Vietnamese women called the arrangement BUNGALOWING, a politer term than the older, vulgar "shacking up with."

FREE LOVE   Sexual relations without or outside marriage. This British and American expression was made famous in the 1890s by Edward Carpenter, one of the early British sexologists. However, as early as 1859 in America, those who believed in sexual relationships without the restraint of marriage or other legal obligations were known as FREE LOVERS and their practice as FREE LOVING and FREE LOVISM. Americans have also described a long-term pre-marital relationship as A TRIAL MARRIAGE. This expression was coined by Judge Benjamin Lindsey in 1925. In a book called *The Revolt of Modern Youth,* he described it as "an informal agreement on the part of a man and woman to live together until they change their minds." The Canadian version of A TRIAL or COMMON-LAW MARRIAGE is A COUNTRY ALLIANCE or COUNTRY MARRIAGE (1935). Historically, this was a long-term relationship between a Caucasian and an Indian woman—originally forbidden by the trading companies, but considered legal in the twentieth century. Thus, MARRIED COUNTRY STYLE (1953) has come to be used in the more general sense of couples LIVING TOGETHER in unwedded bliss.

FRENCH LETTER, A   A prophylactic or condom. Rawson points out that Casanova (1725–98), one of the first to use condoms, called them *redingotes d'Angleterre* (ENGLISH OVERCOATS) and that the French have called them *capotes anglaises* (ENGLISH CLOAKS). English-speaking people have returned the favor by calling them FRENCH LETTERS. Some old words for them are ARMOR—perhaps reflected in the brand name Trojans—and PURSES. A FRENCH LETTER is also known as a FRENCHY in both the United States and Australia and as a FROG (the pejorative word for a Frenchman). In England they are often more neutrally called A JOHN, and in America, after a popular brand, A TROJAN. Diaphragms, female contraceptives, are known in England as SEX CAPS or CAPS and in America, jocularly, as RUBBER COOKIES. The now quite popular IUD (itself an acronym for "intrauterine device") is called A PUSSY BUTTERFLY because of its shape. A male prophylactic is often known simply as A PRO, an obvious shortening, or as A RUBBER, from the material from which it was originally made. All of these devices are used to give PROTECTION (contraception) to their users, and the practice of using them is euphemistically known as TAKING PRECAUTIONS (avoiding pregnancy or venereal disease).

GETTING ANY (LATELY)?   Have you had any (or enough) sexual relations recently? Eric Partridge believes that this expression is Australian (ca. 1930) in origin, and Wilkes, in his *Australian Colloquialisms*, asserts that it is armed services slang from World War II. Whichever is the case, it is current in the United States and has been so at least since the 1940s. Stock Australian macho answers are: CLIMBING TREES TO GET AWAY FROM IT, GOT TO SWIM UNDERWATER TO DODGE IT, and SO BUSY I'VE HAD TO PUT A MAN ON TO HELP.

GOSPEL, TO LEAVE BEFORE THE   To perform *coitus interruptus*. Irish Americans have been announcing that they LEFT BEFORE THE GOSPEL, in an obvious analogy to the part of the mass, since the early twentieth century. Australians GET OFF AT REDFERN (1956), the stop right before the central station in Sydney. This latter expression is probably derived from the English phrase GETTING OUT AT GATESHEAD. Since the nineteenth century the people of Newcastle-upon-Tyne have used this alliterative and physiologically analogous phrase.

GRIND   Coital movement; also the woman's role in sexual intercourse. This originally Black English term has many spin-offs. A GRINDER is a man in the act of coitus. Dillard says that A COFFEE GRINDER (meaning the same) is a term that came from Sierra Leone, where the word *grayno* means "to eat." Perhaps the most famous use of the phrases and their associations occurs in the Bessie Smith lyric "Grind my coffee with a deep deep grind." Another Black English term from the world of domestic life is TO COOK (to have intercourse). What the male cooks is THE CABBAGE (vagina). (See Chapter 1, FEMALE GENITALS, **MUFFIN**, CABBAGE.)

HECTOR'S PECKING   Necking, hugging, kissing and fondling. HECTOR'S PECKING is cockney and Australian rhyming slang for NECKING, originally an American expression, which has been in use since at least 1910. Flexner suggests that PETTING, which Americans now think of as more serious than NECKING, was originally a milder euphemism for hugging, kissing and exploring. Both terms are extremely popular but have been supplemented by other colorful expressions such as BOONDOCKING (from the Tagalog word *bundok*, meaning "mountain" or "wild place"). TO BOONDOCK implied a couple's going to an isolated place TO NECK. By the 1960s, BOONDOCKING was replaced by SUBMARINE WATCHING, which originally meant simply holding hands and staring into space and was popularized by the American disk jockey Murray the K (1960s). Another American parallel is GOING ON BUSH PATROL, which implies the seclusion provided by a clump of bushes or a park. BUSH PATROL also means sexual intercourse. NECKING and PETTING are also called CANOEING since, before cars, canoes were associated with romance and to CANOODLE meant to kiss and cuddle as early as 1859. All of the above expressions would be described in England as DIRTY WORK AT THE CROSSROADS (minor intimacies, though the phrase is more commonly understood as underhanded dealings) and, in the United States, as MAKING OUT.

HEN, A   A young woman, especially an attractive one. The American term HEN is a variant of the more familiar CHICK, in wide use since the 1940s and sometimes with modifiers such as SLICK CHICK or, in the 1950s, with the advent of hipsters, HIP CHICK. A HIP CHICK KNOWS, that is, is sexually aware or experienced. Since World War II the expression SHE KNOWS, using that verb in the biblical sense, has meant that a woman has CARNAL KNOWLEDGE. These are but other ways of saying that a woman is not SAVING IT (1950s). To the euphemistic gynecological question about her virginity, CAN YOU INSERT A TAMPAX? the woman who KNOWS would answer, "Yes." A virgin has been SAVING IT FOR THE WORMS in Canada since the 1940s, and when the euphemism is posed as a question (ARE YOU SAVING IT FOR THE WORMS?), it is intended to seduce a girl. This expression is very close to the seventeenth-century lines by Andrew Marvell in his poem "To His Coy Mistress." Here he asserts that if the lady does not "make [their sun] run" or "stand still" (for which Herrick's phrase is "gather ye rosebuds while ye may"), or, in rural terms, MAKE HAY WHILE THE SUN

SHINES (all phrases meaning to have sexual relations before it is too late), then only "worms shall try/that long preserved virginity."

HIT ON, TO To proposition, to attempt to seduce. In contemporary America, A HEAVY HITTER is a man who constantly SCORES (succeeds in seducing a woman). The word SCORE in the sense of "to have sexual relations with" has been adopted from baseball, as has HITTER or HEAVY HITTER. But SCORE has also been used to mean to have an orgasm or, in America, TO COME, TO COME OFF or TO GO OFF. If one person asks another, "Is your rhubarb up?" or "How's your rhubarb?" (American, since 1830), he or she means "Do you want to make it?" (see **MAKE SOMEONE**).

HOT FOR, TO BE To lust after. Lust as heat is a legacy from the theory of the humors (see the Introduction), and, as early as 1387, Chaucer's Wife of Bath points to the obvious connections among the zodiacal sign of one's birth, the heat of one's body and temperament, the heating effects of liquor and the warming qualities of lust. Chaucer's post-pubescent squire (*Prologue*) is described as "loving so hotly that he slept no more than does the nightingale" at night. The term HOT has been used ever since Chaucer to describe the passions of both sexes. Even the distinguished lexicographer Dr. Johnson used the word when he said, "Her desires were too hot for delay." In more recent parlance, such a lady or DISH has been called A HOT TAMALE and A HOT BABY (ca. 1900). Men have described themselves as HOT AND BOTHERED, while both sexes have been called HOT STUFF, HOT LIPS, HOT AS A FIRECRACKER (Canadian since ca. 1920) and HOT TO TROT when they have admitted to HAVING THE HOTS. To HAVE THE HOTS is TO BE ROOTY—sexually aroused or passionate—(from *rutty*, a term for animals' mating when in heat).

IT Sex appeal. IT was the mysterious THING most notoriously exuded in the 1920s by the Hollywood star Clara Bow, also known as "the It Girl." This delicious and effective piece of advertising ingenuity exploited the common older and indirect reference to "sex appeal," which was already known as A THING and was later more graphically abbreviated to SA. Males are better known for SAM (sex appeal and magnetism). A recent greeting card that culminates in an indecently lustful sentiment attempts to woo the recipient by listing a series of current euphemisms for "sexually appealing"; the items that we find most convincing are: PROVOCATIVE, ALLURING, ATTRACTIVE, COMPELLING, THROBBING, CAPTIVATING, ENTHRALLING, MAGNETIC, THRILLING, FASCINATING, OVERWHELMING, PIQUANT and ARTFUL. A well-known author of current Gothic romances notes that the standard contemporary phrase for the feeling a hero experiences in the presence of a woman who has IT is a THROBBING URGENCY. When he restrains himself, it is because of the reverence he feels before this TEMPLE OF VIRGINITY.

LICKERISH Sexuality or sexual attractiveness. The SWEET TOOTH (see Chapter 4, GLUTTONY: FOOD, **SWEET TOOTH**) for the DELIGHTS OF THE FLESH, or, as a sensational book of the fifties called it, CANDY, has been described as LICKERISH since at least as early as the fourteenth century. Chaucer's Wife of Bath, that inexhaustible source of the lore of lust, made its origins (and its consequences) clear when she said, "a likerous [liquorous] mouth must have a likerous tail." This pun, well-taken by all her husbands and lovers, is explained in an earlier line when she says that she "must think on Venus after wine." In short, a woman when she drinks is lecherous—liquor at one end begets lust at the other.

MAKE EYES AT, TO To ogle; to stare at and flirt. In 1852, Thackeray wrote of a woman who "used to make eyes at the Duke of Marlborough." In America, this expression was used in about 1918 as TO THROW EYES AT. It comes from the still earlier TO TAKE EYES AT (1842). Many Americans are familiar with Eddie Cantor's rendition of the song "Ma, She's [He's] Makin' Eyes at Me." TO EYE, meaning to ogle, has spawned a large family of relatives. TO CUT ONE'S EYE AT

(U.S., 1827) meant to cast a glance, but came to have the specifically flirtatious meaning used more than two centuries earlier by Edmund Spenser when he wrote (*The Faerie Queene*, 1596) "his roving eye did on the lady glance." This may be compared with the WANDERING EYE of the constant flirt who LOOKS SWEET ON whoever's near (compare LICKERISH). In Australia and later in America, an attractive girl has been considered AN EYEFUL since the early twentieth century. American VISIONS OF DELIGHT are well aware that the GLAD EYE is quicker than the GLAD HAND. But old-fashioned lovers still long for the man or woman who will sing and mean "I only have eyes for you" (Cole Porter).

MAKE SOMEONE, TO To have sexual intercourse with someone. Originally an American euphemism used by men of female conquests, TO MAKE was current in the United States at the turn of the century. It has been used in Canada since 1918 and seems to have spawned the expression ON THE MAKE (which, in earlier usage, also means ambitious). A sign of more liberated thinking is the fact that women now also use the term in reference to the conquest of men. In Australia since 1925 and Britain since 1943, the expression ON THE MAKE has meant engaged in winning affection. A variant form, used in discussing sex, is MAKING IT. IT here refers to coitus. A partial equivalent of MAKING IT is DOING IT, which Cole Porter knew when he wrote "Let's do it! Let's fall in love." An unmarried man or woman who DOES (IT) may be having an AFFAIR—an illicit sexual relationship, the name for which is derived from the older French form *à faire* (to do or make).

MATINÉE, A Sex in the afternoon. Rawson says that a variant of this American euphemism for a working girl's or man's QUICKIE is LUNCH. At least since the 1920s illicit sexual relations in America have been known as LIAISONS, but the term was used for OUTSIDE SEXUAL CONTACTS as early as the eighteenth century in the French novel *Les Liaisons Dangereuses*. In England, an extra-marital AFFAIR, known as A LOVE AFFAIR since 1591 or A FLING (1920s; see MAKE SOMEONE), has been called HAVING A BIT or HAVING A THING ON THE SIDE. From the French, Americans have adopted the casual expression CINQ À SEPT for a visit from "five to seven" in the evening, usually to one's lover. If both partners in an American marriage agree to have separate but equal MEANINGFUL RELATIONSHIPS (1960s), the arrangement is known as AN OPEN MARRIAGE. In both America and England, such AN INDULGENCE has been known as AN INDISCRETION or INFIDELITY (where marriage is involved) and A DELICATE SITUATION. If either partner in the affair is older, he or she may seek this kind of FULFILLMENT by enjoying A ROMAN SPRING (a love affair in later life).

NAUGHTY BUT NICE, IT'S A description of sex. This saucy American expression for copulation entered the language in the 1890s from a popular song sung by Minnie Schult. By 1900, it had reached Great Britain, where it has remained more popular than in the United States. A similar musical allusion to sex is the expression IT TAKES TWO TO TANGO, from an American song of the 1930's, which had spread to Australia by 1935. But before the TANGO is the seduction, which, in Australia, is known as RACING or RACING OFF (1960s) and is preferably conducted by those who are SHOOK ON (attracted to or infatuated with) the seducee. SHOOK ON (1882) is now used about infatuation with anything as well as anyone. Such feelings would lead a South African to VIRY (court, kiss, and/or caress) and LOVE the object of his affections.

NIGHT BASEBALL Necking, petting or sexual intercourse. Watching or playing NIGHT BASEBALL is a current American expression for having sexual intercourse or merely engaging in romantic interludes. If NIGHT BASEBALL is a fairly recent phenomenon (from ca. 1950), it has its ancient predecessors. Sexual intercourse has been known as NIGHT PHYSICK and NIGHT WORK since the sixteenth century, although the former has been obsolete since the mid-nineteenth century. NIGHT BASEBALL is but one example of the coinage of a sporting metaphor for sex. RIDING is another (see **TOWN BIKE**). As early as 1520, a woman called Mayde Emlyn (obviously no maiden) was described as follows: "And because she loved riding/at the stews [brothels] was her abiding." Sexual activity has been disguised by literally hundreds of terms, many based on the motion entailed. Among them are: BUMP BONES, FRISK, JIGGLE, KNOCK, SHAKE, and TUMBLE.

PDA; PUBLIC DISPLAY OF AFFECTION—Kissing, Cuddling, Necking or Petting in public. Dating from at least as early as the 1950s, this American euphemism, now adopted by the preppy set, would never be visible in a case of URL— preppy for "unrequited love." PDA is part of an intense romantic relationship known to preppies as H^2 and derived from HOT AND HEAVY (1940s). The relationship might be consummated by PARALLEL PARKING (sexual intercourse). Only after the male partner had REELED IN THE BISCUIT (lured a girl to bed) could he HIDE THE SALAM (short for "salami") or FIRE HER UP—both preppy expressions for the act of sexual intercourse.

PHAT CHICK, A An attractive woman, A FOX. These two terms for an appealing girl are part of a rich Black English vocabulary describing sexually appetizing females. The list includes A HAMMER, A FLAVOR and A MINK. Flexner notes that high-class BEAVER (female pubic hair or the female sexual organs in general) is MINK.

PICK-UP, A A flirtation or dalliance with a stranger; the stranger involved. As late as the turn of the century Gilbert and Sullivan could portray two castaways who lived side by side on a desert island without speaking because they had not been formally introduced. This little plot is some indication of how late formality in social, and certainly in amorous, encounters survived among the middle and upper classes. The vestiges of these attitudes are preserved in the censorious meaning associated with the phrase PICK-UP. It is now considered euphemistic if it masks actual sexual consummation. The phrase itself is old and indicative of class.

Before 1689, "to pick up with" was Standard English for the act of making an acquaintance with someone whom one had met casually; by 1689, "to pick up" was to take into one's company (or ship or carriage) someone or something one had met or overtaken. Also in 1689, we find the startlingly early first use of the term in its opprobrious sexual sense. A character in a Vanbrugh play asks a comrade: "So—now, Mr. Constable, shall you and I go pick up a whore together?" At present, A PICK-UP refers both to the encounter and to the person thus met. In America people looking for A PICK-UP are currently said to be CRUISING, whether in an automobile or on foot.

POUNDCAKE, A   A beautiful or desirable woman. This American euphemism is a compound of two others—TO POUND (to have sexual intercourse) and CAKE (a Black English euphemism for the female genitalia). It is one of the many American euphemistic expressions that compares sex to food. CHEESECAKE is another, this time referring to erotic posters or photographs of women popular with American GIs in World War II. An analogy to CHEESECAKE is the recent BEEFCAKE—meaning an attractive display of the male body and exported from England to America.

PRE-ORGASMIC WOMAN, A   A frigid woman. This American euphemism comes to us from psychology. It is as indirect a way of saying "frigid" as the OED's definition of an orgasm—"excitement or violent action in an organ or part, accompanied with turgescence, specifically venereal excitement in coition" (ca. 1930s).

ROCK, TO   To have sexual intercourse, to act the "female" or passive part in coitus. This Black English term for sexual intercourse is closely related to ROCKING CHAIR, the Black English name for the same activity. The counterpart of the Afro-American TO ROCK is TO ROLL, meaning to play the active or "male" role in sexual intercourse. These words may have been responsible for the musical term "rock and roll." However, the origins of the terms are obscure and may be West African. In Black English, ROLLING means both "working" and "fatigued." Another Black English expression meaning to have an orgasm, to arouse sexual passion and/or to achieve a romantic mood is TO HAVE ONE'S LOVE COME DOWN. Achieving orgasm is known to Black English speakers as HAVING ONE'S ASHES (semen) HAULED (compare with PROFESSIONAL SEX, **ASHES HAULED** or EMPTYING ONE'S TRASH. This expression is probably derived from rhyming slang for "ash" (which may be a corruption of "ass"), but it also suggests the ancient and medieval concept of semen as poison if not regularly vented. The Standard English expression for the commonest sexual position is not ROCK or ROLL but the MISSIONARY POSITION (man on top).

SET ONE'S CAP FOR or AT, TO To try to gain someone's hand or heart, usually said of a woman. As early as 1387, Chaucer's Manciple, the steward for a group of lawyers, "set all their [the lawyers'] caps" by outsmarting them; however, this expression was first used colloquially to mean TO SET ONE'S SIGHTS AT or FOR a love-object in the eighteenth century, when "all was fair in love and war." By 1848, a character in Thackeray's *Vanity Fair* warns a guileless man, "That girl is setting her cap at you." The expression has a French equivalent in the phrase *mettre le cap sur* (to head for [someone]), which Eric Partridge thinks comes from nautical jargon. The suitor who TAKES A FANCY TO (conceives an attraction for) someone hopes TO BE TAKING (attractive) or HAVE TAKING WAYS. In the eighteenth century (Richardson, *Sir Charles Grandison),* a person whose eye or attention was caught was said TO BE TAKEN. Now, in American English, we still say, when we are attracted to someone, that we are TAKEN WITH that person.

SLEEP WITH, TO To have intercourse with. TO SLEEP WITH is one of the oldest euphemisms for the act of coition and dates from the year 900. This expression works by substituting the whole experience for its most important part, the actual coitus, just as other sexual terms such as HAVING RELATIONS do. (See the Introduction.) RELATIONS is a general term, and the word "sexual," which would make it more specific, is left to one's imagination. In the same way, the general term RELATIONSHIP and its peers—FRIENDSHIP and CLOSE PERSONAL FRIENDSHIP (1960s and 1970s)—are often used to mean sexual AFFAIRS. Two other ways of abstracting sex out of existence are to describe its successful orgasmic outcome as GRATIFICATION and coitus itself as DATING or, in Irish-American circles, as KEEPIN' COMPANY.

SUGAR DADDY, A A male sweetheart with money, especially a wealthy older man who spends freely on a young woman in return for her sexual favors. In use in the United States at least since 1920, this term was imported to England by the talkies (films). It was coined from the term SUGAR AND HONEY, both rhyming slang for money, and later a euphemism for sex or affection. The terms for this male sexual GOLD MINE or GENEROUS KEEPER (of a kept woman) are numerous, including CANDYLEG, BIG GAME, OYSTER (the source of pearls), SUGAR BOWL and, most blatantly, MONEY-HONEY. Still another offshoot, HONEY-MAN, is a term for "gigolo." Black English has been extremely rich in euphemisms for lovers—though not always rich ones. Among these are A JELLYROLL, A BISCUIT ROLLER, A MULE (a male lover) and A SKINNER (both a man and a penis). Black English expressions for female lovers include such domestic terms as CORNBREAD (a woman not up to high standards of quality) and the antonym HOME COOKING (an attractive girl or woman).

TONGUE SUSHI, A LITTLE Tongue kissing. This preppy expression is one of the newer American euphemisms for two old favorites, FRENCH KISSING and SOUL KISSING. FRENCH KISSING, probably the oldest, does come from France and is *un baiser tres appuye* (literally, "a heavily applied kiss") in French. It became an American colloquialism in the early 1920s, perhaps as a result of American exposure to the French in World War I. SOUL KISSING probably became a favorite Americanism in the 1930s. We wonder if Cole Porter's popular song "Body and Soul" had anything to do with the currency of this expression. (See also EXOTIC SEX,

---

FRENCH WAY for other Gallic practices.)

TOWN or OFFICE BIKE, THE A promiscuous woman. This originally Australian euphemism for a woman who liberally bestows her favors upon all who seek them probably comes from the concept that "a ride" was an apt analogy for sexual intercourse. The term RIDE has been in use in Australia since 1945 and was in use in America (1800) and England far earlier. The best known American equivalent to THE TOWN BIKE is THE TOWN PUMP, clearly also based on an analogy, this time between pumping and the act of intercourse.

TUMESCENCE Erection. The *OED* refuses to define in any particularity this euphemism for erection. Literally, it means "swelling." Its antonym is DETUMESCENCE, "limpness." Havelock Ellis, the British sexologist, used TUMESCENCE in its specifically sexual sense in 1901.

VAMP, TO; A VAMP To flirt, to attempt to seduce; a flirt. This word was used both as a verb (TO VAMP) and as a noun (A VAMP) in 1918 to describe an adventuress who ensnared and exploited men. In that year, it appears in the mouth of a literary character who brags, "We walked into the vamp's house. We all got lit [see Chapter 4, GLUTTONY:DRINK, **LOW BLUE FLAME**] and had a hell of a time." It has been suggested that the word is derived from "vampire," and its most famous symbol was Theda Bara, the Hollywood star who slunk her treacherous way through the studies and smoking rooms of swooning men. It is no accident that the Bronx-born Theda pretended to be a Hungarian from vampire country. In 1922, Margaret B. Houston (*Witch-Man*) made free with the verb when she wrote, "Look! . . . Cinderella is trying to vamp him." Since that time, the word has been used in such adjectival forms as VAMPISH and VAMPY. It should be noted that A VAMP is distinctly classier than "a tramp"—straight talk for a disreputable woman. The British protect the reputations of their promiscuous women by saying, SHE'S ALL RIGHT (see **WILLING WOMAN**), and Americans, always more action-oriented, described such a woman in 1920s crime slang by asserting, SHE SAILS. Compare our more contemporary SHE GOES DOWN!

WILLING WOMAN, A   A sexually available or promiscuous woman. An old saw proclaims, "As long as I can buy milk, I shall not keep a cow." This aphorism is merely an indirect way of saying that men have always sought and found women who were sexually available without having to marry them. The expression A WILLING WOMAN has even made its way into a college textbook on rhetoric. Amusingly enough, it is used as an example of "climax," the arrangement of words or events so that the last is the most significant. "A sweet girl, a fine girl, a tender girl is Mary, and a willing." A WILLING WOMAN, especially one who is young, unmarried and discreet about her activities, since World War II has been called A CHARITY GIRL, because, like Mary above, SHE GIVES IT AWAY FOR FREE or FOR NOTHING. A less delicate identification is "broad," meaning, in 1926, a promiscuous woman considered unworthy of respect. "Broad" may have been derived from the older "bawd." By 1932, Damon Runyon indicated that it had come to describe all women. Runyon reports: "He refers to Miss Perry as a broad, meaning no harm whatever, for this is the way many of the boys speak of the dolls." Oscar Hammerstein took his cue from Runyon's interpretation of the word when he assumed in *South Pacific* (1950s) that a perfectly respectable dream girl could be a HONEY BUN. "Honey bun" was "a hundred and one pounds of fun . . . [and] broad where a broad should be broad." The Black English equivalent of A WILLING WOMAN or BROAD (in the narrower sense) is A RED HOT MAMA, for which see the torch song of the same name. In later use, A MAMA has been a girl or woman who belongs to an entire motorcycle gang.

YEN FOR, TO HAVE A   To desire sexually. This expression originated in the United States and was adopted by the British in 1931. Eric Partridge believes that the word "yen" is simply a "thin" form of the word "yearn." More fancifully,

Wentworth and Flexner (*Dictionary of American Slang*) think the word comes from the Chinese expression for "opium" or "opium addict," *yen-shee*. TO HAVE A YEN FOR someone is not much different from TO HANKER FOR or HAVE A HANKERING AFTER someone. HANKER, a much older word than YEN, was first used in 1601. Mrs. Browning (Elizabeth Barrett) used it in our current sense, noting in *Aurora Leigh* that "Romney dared to hanker for your [Aurora's] love." "To have an itch for" was used in its general meaning of a restless desire or hankering as early as 1340. To HAVE AN ITCH, meaning to have a sexual urge, has been used colloquially since the seventeenth century. Until about 1900, a man would say that he HAD AN ITCH IN THE BELLY when he wanted to indicate that he was sexually aroused. The ITCH has now spread both physically and chronologically, and both sexes, when married, may ITCH—especially after seven years.

GAY SEX

CAMP, TO To behave or conduct oneself according to homosexual mores. This British and American euphemism has had a long history. As an adjective meaning "acting or gesturing in an exaggerated manner," "camp" was current by 1906. The meaning of "homosexual" came in in 1920, probably from theatrical language. In the 1930s, it was used in theatre argot to mean effeminate and, by 1945, CAMP was used in a general sense to mean characteristic of homosexuals, as in "camp words" and "camp greetings" (compare with IRON HOOF, POOVY). Now the word is used both as a noun, as in HIGH CAMP (which can mean homosexual, clichè or kitsch) and as a verb, CAMP AROUND, meaning to act in an affected manner in general or in a homosexual manner in particular.

CHICKEN, A A male homosexual, particularly a young one. This twentieth-century euphemism for a homosexual boy may be derived from the earlier meanings of "chicken" as a young and tender fowl or a chicken-hearted person (one who is cowardly or a sissy). CHICKENS are pursued or preyed upon by CHICKEN HAWKS (older male homosexuals). Other terms denoting the age of the participants are: CATAMITE (a corrupt form of Ganymede, Jupiter's cupbearer, in English for a young boy since 1593), KID, LAMB, FAUNET, FAUNLET (on an analogy to nymphet), SEX-BOY, BIRDIE (all for a young boy), and BIRD TAKER and AUNTIE for an older man. More general terms are A MAN'S MAN, A THIRD SEXER, A TWILIGHT PERSONALITY, A WHAT-IS-IT, ONE OF THOSE, AN EYE-DOCTOR, A CANNIBAL, A PUNK (American Midwest), A BUGLER (another musical reference to FELLATIO; see **MALE IDENTIFIED,** FLUTE), A JOCK, A JOCKER or JOCKEY, A TRAPEZE ARTIST, A TUSK, A WOLF, A RING-TAIL (because he RIMS the partner's TAIL), A GUNSEL or A SOD. "Sod" is an abbreviated form of "sodomite" (1380 in English) from the biblical city of Sodom. The term is also used as an affectionate casual greeting among British men: "How are you, you old sod?" All of the above figures are said to belong to THE TWILIGHT WORLD or THE THIRD SEX.

COME OUT, TO   To admit one's homosexuality publicly. This originally American expression from about the 1960s was imported to Britain. It refers to COMING OUT OF THE CLOSET, and male homosexuals who concealed their preferences have been called CLOSET QUEENS (late 1950s). The expression COME OUT marks a change in social attitudes toward homosexuality. The greater acceptance of varied SEXUAL PREFERENCES or of A PARTICULAR TASTE (in French *le goût particulier*) was noted by Faubion Bowers in a *Saturday Review* article of 1972: "Today's homosexual can be open ('come out') or covers ('closet'), practicing [active] or inhibited, voluntary or compulsive, conscious or unaware, active or passive, manly ('stud') or womanly ('fem')."

CROSS (adj.)   In the 1890s, CROSS began to be used to mean dishonest, particularly in America. It now means homosexual in Britain on an analogy with the questionably euphemistic British term BENT (1945)—not STRAIGHT, that is, not heterosexual. Traditionally terms for homosexuals—male and female—have been derisive, and the male names include such scornful terms as "bugger" (also a British legal term for a male homosexual); "queen" (1890s in Britain, later imported to America, but based on the much earlier *quean* or whore) and "screaming queen"; "fairy" (1920s); "fag" (American) and "faggot"; and "fruit" and "pansy" (British and American). Sometimes expressions are invented to soften pejorative names, as in FEY (British, 1920), a politer form than "fairy," and the jocular British rhyming slang KING LEAR for "queer."

GAY GAY is the most popular British and American euphemism for homosexual. Rawson suggests that it may have originated from the term GEYCAT for a homosexual boy (ca. 1935), but asserts that it came into use as "the simple gay" in the 1950s. Partridge cites an earlier Australian form of the term, GAYBOY for a homosexual (ca. 1925). The term GAY has had a long and somewhat shady history, meaning frivolously showy and affected since the 1380s, and addicted to social pleasures, dissipation and an immoral life since 1637. At one point in its history—around 1825—GAY referred specifically to a woman who lived by prostitution and often operated out of A GAYHOUSE (1740) or BROTHEL. The straightforward term "homosexual" was used by Havelock Ellis, the British sexologist, in 1897, although he claimed "no responsibility for this barbarously hybrid word." Instead, he preferred the now British term SEXUALLY INVERTED and, in 1896, noted that SEXUAL INVERSION best described the proclivities of AN INVERT (a homosexual).

IRON HOOF, A A male homosexual. IRON HOOF, British rhyming slang for POOF, is an expression that is sometimes shortened to IRON. The terms POOF, POOFTER or POOFTA are among the commonest British, Australian and New Zealand euphemisms for a GAY or effeminate man. Partridge believes that POOF was originally PUFF (an 1870s British term for a sodomist) and, between 1900 and 1910, was changed to POUF or POUFTER. By 1941, it was spelled POOF or POOFTER.

The adjective POOVY (originally New Zealand) has come to mean of or like a homosexual. Another British expression for a male homosexual is A CLOCKWORK ORANGE (see Anthony Burgess's novel of the same name, 1962) and, in Britain, an overtly effeminate man is said to be QUEER AS A CLOCKWORK ORANGE. QUEER, itself a somewhat vulgar euphemism for homosexual, has meant of questionable character since 1315 and came to have its specialized meaning only within the last hundred years.

LAVENDER CONVENTION, A A gathering of male homosexuals or male homosexual prostitutes. This American expression is one of a number coined for events and activities in the GAY WORLD. Best known among these is A DRAG PARTY—one to which a male or female homosexual will come IN DRAG (in the dress of the opposite sex). Less well known is THE BIRD CIRCUIT—a circuit of GAY BARS across the country and the touring of these bars—and the activity of PLAYING CHECKERS (looking for a partner by changing seats in a movie theatre, especially in A MALE MOVIE HOUSE). A GAY pick-up place is sometimes called A MEAT RACK (questionably euphemistic). At A MEAT RACK one homosexual may ask another: "What number and what color?" that is, "What sexual practices do you prefer?" (See EXOTIC SEX, **FELLATIO** and **S AND M**, etc.) He may even become part of A SISTER ACT (two male lovers who share the same tastes). MALE BROTHELS have also spawned euphemisms; a brothel has been called A CAMP (from CAMPING AROUND or acting GAY; see **CAMP**) or A PEG HOUSE (a reference to the penis). Often such places are forced to pay GAYOLA (a U.S. expression for undercover payments made to police for not interfering, 1966). If homosexuals decide to settle down or MARRY, one of the pair may speak of him- or herself as A WIFE.

MALE IDENTIFIED or ORIENTED Homosexual (male). Since the 1970s in the United States, a MALE ORIENTED or IDENTIFIED man has been a practitioner of homosexuality. This phrase has replaced earlier names for homosexuals, including: AN OSCAR or AN OSCAR WILDE, the name current after the trial of Oscar Wilde for sodomy in 1895, AN ANGELINA, A PRUSSIAN, also PRUSHIN and PRESHAN (based on the supposed proclivity of the "manly Prussian army" for homosexuality, Britain, 1870s), A MOLLY (1750), A LAVENDER BOY and A NANCY, MISS NANCY, NANCE or NANCY BOY. The name NANCY has given rise to the British rhyming slang expression A TICKLE YOUR FANCY (after World War II). It is still often used, as is MARY, to mean a male homosexual who prefers the passive role in sexual relations. Other names for homosexuals that are at least not overtly pejorative include such American terms as: AN ANGEL, A BABY, A BIRDIE, A FRUIT (questionably euphemistic) or FLUTE (both a pun on fruit and an allusion to FELLATIO), A NOLA, A CRUISER (because a homosexual may CRUISE or look for a potential partner), A SALESMAN, A MASON, AN UNDERCOVER MAN, A POGEY, POGY, POGGIE (from that fact that "pogey"—food or sweets—may be used to tempt someone into a homosexual relationship). In British rhyming slang a homosexual male is GINGER (BEER), for QUEER.

NAMELESS CRIME, THE Sodomy. Committing sodomy has always been taboo and legally punishable in both British and American law; thus it has been known as THE SECRET SIN, and THE LOVE THAT DARE NOT SPEAK ITS NAME (a term made famous by Oscar Wilde in his testimony during his trial in 1895 but which comes from his earlier [1894] poem "Two Loves"). In the United States today, it is sometimes referred to simply as a STATUTORY OFFENSE. More colorful American expressions for committing sodomy are: GO HOLLYWOOD, KISS or KISS OFF, KNEEL AT THE ALTAR, RIDE THE DECK, YODEL, SNAG or BURGLE (from "bugger"). Only the last of these terms is locatable. The non-euphemistic "bugger," in English by 1558, is derived from the Bulgars, who were supposed to commit abominable sexual practices, which the Albigensian heretics copied from them.

SKIPPY, A A homosexual or effeminate man. SKIPPY is one of a number of euphemisms, in this case American, that do not clearly discriminate between effeminacy and homosexuality. Others include the Black English term MOTHER, the American expression CAKE EATER (a term that, according to Safire, is based on the preference of "real men" for pies over cakes), and the American expressions LIMP-WRISTED and SISSIFIED (1905). Other American euphemisms disguise homosexuality by generalizing it, as in the use of the word MALE for "homosexual" (see, for example, such uses as MALE MOVIES), WINK or WINK-WINK (referring to generally effeminate behavior or to THE SECOND EYE or anus), BROWN HATTER (British for a male homosexual and also a reference to RIMMING [licking the anus] and anal intercourse), LEFT-HANDED (see EXOTIC SEX, **AMBIDEXTROUS**), LIGHT-FOOTED (American since the 1950s) and the Australian SHIRT LIFTER (1966). More specialized in-group terms include WILLIE (a gay male who wears make-up), the affectionate use of HOMO and PLATER (British for a male homosexual who, as Powis says, "is prepared only for oral sexual encounters"), and SISTER, a Black GAY person.

THREE-LETTER MAN Male homosexual or an effeminate man. The British and American "three-letter man" was first used in the 1930s by students to allude to an athlete who proved his masculinity by winning his team letters. In the case of the euphemism, the three letters are FAG. A FOUR-LETTER MAN is "a shit," "a fuck," and "a homo(sexual)." It was used by Ernest Hemingway in his story "The Short Happy Life of Francis Macomber" (1936).

TRIBADISM Female homosexuality. TRIBADISM, one of the more esoteric euphemisms for lesbianism, is mysterious in its origins. It entered the English language in the sixteenth century either from French or from German, and Ben Jonson in 1601 speaks of "Light Venus with thy tribade trine invent[ing] new sports." Among less esoteric euphemisms for lesbians are such terms as SERGEANT or TOP SERGEANT, from the 1940s (a term alluding to the supposed "bossiness" of female homosexuals), such shortenings of "lesbian" as

LESBO (1939), LES (1950s) and LESBIE (1955), and FINGER ARTIST. The Black English term JASPER and the more elegant SAPPHIC are two others. As a term pertaining to the poet Sappho, presumably the original lesbian since she inhabited the isle of Lesbos, this has been used since 1501. In the sense of lesbian, the expression was in use by the nineteenth century (see Swinburne's unfinished novel *Lesbia Brandon*, written in the 1860s). While many terms for female homosexuality are strikingly pejorative (for example, "bull," "bull dike," "butch" and "harpie"), the person who wishes not to insult a GAY woman may call her FEMALE INDENTIFIED or FEMALE ORIENTED (1960s and 1970s).

EXOTIC SEX

AMBIDEXTROUS Sexually attracted to both men and women. AMBIDEXTROUS is an American euphemism for "bisexual." A less euphemistic variation is the pun, AMBISEXTROUS, and another common variant is AMBIVALENT. Also maintaining the image of AMBIDEXTROUSNESS are such expressions as SWITCH-HITTER—from baseball, specifically referring to a player who can bat with either hand—and DOUBLE-GAITED, from horse racing. Americans jocularly disguise their aversion to bisexuality by using the term AC/DC (ca. 1940), a reference to alternating and direct electrical current.

COMBO, A A white man co-habiting with an aboriginal woman. In Australia, COMBO has been used to describe miscegenation since 1896, reflecting a long history of racist attitudes. An aboriginal woman has been called A LUBRA since 1834. A quadroon or any woman of "mixed blood" is, in Australia, A CREMIE (1887). By 1941, anyone who had succeeded sexually, whatever the race of the partner, was said to have CRACKED IT—as in cracking a safe, from which the expression comes.

DOMINATRIX, A A directress or domineering woman who gives orders to the participant(s) in sado-masochistic activities. Those Americans who engage in such practices (see **S AND M**) are either dominant, INTO DOMINATION, or submissive, INTO SUBMISSION. The submissive member of the couple is sometimes known as "a slave" whereas the DOMINATRIX may be called "Mistress" (Anna, Sonya, etc.). She may be educated in or teach her pupils D/T (DOMINANCE TRAINING). Among the courses she may give are B/D (BONDAGE AND DISCIPLINE), C/P (CORPORAL PUNISHMENT), GOLDEN or BROWN SHOWERS (urinating or defacating on one's partner), TV TRAINING (transvestism) and NICE AND NASTY (alternating tender and brutal behavior). The student-teacher relations in this private study group's enactment of ANOTHER WAY TO LOVE are certainly INTIMATE. The vast number of code terms for these unusual practices is one indication that Americans still disapprove of KINKY SEX.

ECDYSIAST, A A strip teaser. This famous American coinage was created by H. L. Mencken in 1940 at the request of the well-known stripper Georgia Sothern. Miss Sothern, who would later be called AN EXOTIC DANCER (1960s), wished to clean up her image. Thus Mencken, utilizing the scientific term *ecdysis* (molting), equated losing one's feathers to plucking them off voluntarily. The last item to be shed are AN ARTISTE'S PASTIES (small breast shields glued on to the nipples) and G-STRING (scanty loincloth).

EIGHT-PAGER, AN An eight-page or longer pornographic magazine, often in comic-book style. One expression used in evading the ears of American censors, AN EIGHT-PAGER is also known as A TWO-BY-FOUR. These pornographic classics contain such immortal articles as "It's About Time You Did," the account of a young couple's first sexual encounter. A more compact version, with more visual impact but less narrative interest, is the FRENCH POSTCARD, an erotic photograph or drawing in postcard size that takes its name from the "dirty pictures" Americans have liked their friends to bring home from France ever since World War II.

EROTOLOGIST, AN A specialist in pornography. The term

EROTOLOGIST (British, 1960s) is one of the many used to veil SEXUALLY EXPLICIT materials and those interested in them. Students of EROTOLOGY (pornography) may frequent ADULT BOOKSTORES or MOVIES (places where pornographic literature or films are available). They may buy NUDIES, SKIN MAGAZINES and TIJUANA BIBLES (so-called because Tijuana, Mexico was, in less liberated times, a town in which pornographic literature could be openly purchased). They may watch SKIN FLICKS and FLESH FLICKS, which are X-RATED pornographic movies or ERODUCTIONS (pornographic films produced in Japan, U.S. term, 1969), or see PEEP SHOWS (with live performers). Some ADULT BOOKSTORES have ONE-ON-ONE BOOTHS for private PEEP SHOWS or PERFORMANCES as opposed to EXHIBITIONS or EXIBEESHES, public performances of sexual acts either live or on film (American, 1965). A place that features many or all of these activities is not merely A BOOKSTORE (U.S.) or SEX SHOP (British), but AN EMPORIUM (U.S.). It may also sell MARITAL AIDS or DEVICES (vibrators, sexual prostheses etc.), also known as ADULT NOVELTIES, CORDLESS MASSAGERS and, less euphemistically, SEX AIDS.

FELLATIO Oral stimulation of the penis. This term, somewhat standard and even clinical in American and British English, is difficult to locate in the *OED*, appearing only in the 1972 *Supplement*. Derived from the Latin *fellare*, "to suck," an older form of this term was FELLATION. CUNNILINGUS (from *cunnus*, "vulva," and *lingere*, "to lick") is the antonym of FELLATIO and means oral stimulation of the female genitals. FELLATIO is also known as A PLATE OF HAM or GAM (English rhyming slang) and A HEAD or BLOW JOB in America. A woman eager to perform such a practice is known as A SMOKER (early twentieth century) or a performer of PENILINGISM. When FELLATIO and CUNNILINGUS are practiced simultaneously, the act is known as 69. In America, a woman or a man engaged in oral sex GIVES HEAD (1970s). A young woman who is sexually available has been called A HEAD since 1941. A prostitute who refuses to GIVE

HEAD (perform FELLATIO) is known to her fellow BODY WORKERS as A VEGETARIAN.

FRENCH WAY or CULTURE   CUNNILINGUS or FELLATIO. This euphemism, often confused with the relatively chaste FRENCH KISS (see STRAIGHT SEX, **TONGUE SUSHI**), is said to have originated with the United States armed forces in France during World War I. Convinced that Gallic lovers preferred oral sex, Americans have named a bouquet of oral practices after them. The "Carnal Classified" of *Screw* magazine lists such practices as FRENCH CULTURE (the appropriate paraphernalia for which is high spiked heels, black silk stockings and a garter belt) and FRENCH LESSONS (an educational experience comprised of a male prostitute instructor and a female pupil who is learning how to perform FELLATIO). Ads in the magazine often read, "We speak French, English and Greek." Willing participants may also have sexual intercourse THE GREEK WAY or study GREEK CULTURE—both terms for heterosexual anal intercourse. These terms, now not pejorative, probably originate from the idea that "a Greekling" (1636) was a degenerate, contemptible practitioner of anal sex. Would-be wits have speculated that the Greek national anthem is "I'm Walking Behind You," a universal American joke based on a song of the 1950s. If not satisfied with FRENCH or GREEK, readers of *Screw* are invited to enjoy THE ROMAN WAY or ROMAN CULTURE, merely a simple orgy. ENGLISH GUIDANCE, the ENGLISH ARTS or ENGLISH CULTURE—whipping, especially with a riding crop or cane—was called LA MALADIE ANGLAISE (THE ENGLISH DISEASE) as early as the late eighteenth century. In its honor, Algernon Charles Swinburne wrote an infamous epic called *The Flogging Block*. It is worth noting that perverse sexuality is always practiced by a nationality other than one's own. Do the French equivalents of "Carnal Classified" list any practices as *a l'americaine*? Yes!

LEATHER   Of or pertaining to both heterosexual and homosexual sadists and masochists. INTO LEATHER is an American expression for those who favor S AND M (q. v.) and wear leather jackets and/or boots and wrist bands. Those who are INTO LEATHER will seek establishments where DISCIPLINE is available. They may enjoy RUBBER (being beaten or beating someone else with a hose), WATER SPORTS (showers or high colonic enemas), SHOWERS (see DOMINATRIX, GOLDEN SHOWERS), TV TRAINING (transvestite training), DIAPERING (just what it sounds like), SUSPENSION HOISTS (also self-evident), INFIBULATON (piercing of nipples or genitalia) or WRESTLING. All of the foregoing may be generically classified as R/S (ROUGH STUFF) or HEAVY LEATHER.

MASSAGE PARLOR, A A store-front or second-story establishment that offers its customers massages but is often a front for A BROTHEL. In America, MASSAGE PARLORS bear such names as The Dating Room, The Delicate Touch and Lucky Lady. The more elegant, expensive version is A LEISURE SPA, one of the most famous of which is called Spartacus. Both kinds of establishments contain more than one CHAMBER OF PLEASURE, manned or womaned by A HOSTESS (a prostitute), where a customer may obtain A BODY RUB (a euphemism for both a massage and sexual services). The larger the number of rooms, the greater the number of HOSTESSES and the more expensive the equipment and furniture, the classier the establishment. The 1970s term for MASSAGE PARLORS, coined after the New York City police crackdown on street prostitutes, is A RAP CLUB or RAP PARLOR (rap is talk). Whatever the name, the institution is always A COVER—a place that ostensibly offers conversation and companionship but actually employs women to provide a variety of sexual services.

ONANISM Masturbation. ONANISM is a British and American euphemism for masturbation that is also used, albeit less frequently, to disguise COITUS INTERRUPTUS. It is so named from the story of Onan in Genesis 38:9, in which he "spilled [his seed] on the ground." Although it has been considered a sin from time immemorial, the expression ONANISM did not enter English until 1727–41. At that time it appeared in Chambers' *Cyclopedia* as "onania, onanism." It is defined there as "abuse, self-abuse . . . a phrase used by some late writers for the crime of self-pollution." SELF-POLLUTION was a term much used, in Latin, during the Middle Ages. In Australian argot, one who masturbates regularly or FLIPS HIMSELF OFF is in the same Victorian danger as were Dr. Acton's patients (see **SELF-ABUSE**) of becoming A FLIPWRECK.

PLAY WITH ONESELF, TO To masturbate. Terms for the act of masturbation are legion and include such everyday euphemisms as TO TOUCH UP (British and Canadian), TO WONK OFF (mostly British and questionably euphemistic), WHACK OFF (American and barely euphemistic), BEAT THE DUMMY (American and not as euphemistic as the also American BEAT OFF). Both British and American mothers may tell a male child not TO PLAY WITH HIMSELF.

S AND M, S&M Sadism and masochism. This principally American euphemism, also known as SADIE-MAISIE, is a thin disguise for an ancient and somewhat universal practice. The two terms that comprise it, "sadism" and "masochism," are eponymous. "Sadism," as most people know, was derived from the name of the Marquis de Sade (1740–1814), famous for his love of cruelty. The term was not, however, used in English until 1888. "Masochism" takes its name from Leopold von Sacher-Masoch (1836–95), an Austrian novelist who described the phenomenon. The compound term "sado-masochism" first appeared in 1915.

SELF-ABUSE Masturbation. Both an American and a British euphemism for SELF-GRATIFICATION or RELIEVING ONESELF, SELF-ABUSE is but one of the many evasions of the word "masturbation." The practice has also been called THE SOLITARY or SECRET SIN and THE SECRET INDULGENCE. A study of the attitudes toward masturbation provides a history of social and sexual customs in miniature. The term "masturbation" originated in English in 1766 when A. Hume wrote his volume *Onanism: or a Treatise upon the Disorders Produced by Masturbation*. Among the disorders supposed to result from this perverse and degenerate practice were insanity, deafness, blindness, hairy palms, generalized debilitation and a withering away of the member concerned. The term "masturbate" (from the Latin *masturbari*, which is thought to have been derived from another Latin term, *masdo*, the VIRILE MEMBER) did not gain currency until 1857, when it was used by Dr. Acton, an eminent sexologist of the era. However, literary critics have pointed to an earlier use of the term in Swift's *Gulliver's Travels* (1728) when the author puns, "My master, Mr Bates" and later refers to his "poor Master Bates."

SWING BOTH WAYS, TO To be sexually attracted to both men and women. One who SWINGS BOTH WAYS (TO SWING is to participate in adventurous sex) is generally considered bisexual, and it was no less a light than Samuel Taylor Coleridge who first used the term "bisexual" in his *Aids to Reflection*. He noted "the very old tradition of the homo . . . androgynous, that is the original man was a bisexual." BI, a shortening of "bisexual," is explicit but still somewhat euphemistic and has been common in England and American since the 1960s. Far older is the shortening MORPH (for "hermaphrodite"), in use in England since 1890. In America today, a bisexual is also known as A HE-SHE and is also called KI-KI (1970s).

SWING CLUB Gathering place for devotees of group sex. The rules for membership in this American association are that each attendee must be accompanied by a member of the opposite sex. Since a male who wishes entrance into this non-exclusive club must bring a woman or FEMALE COMPANION (sometimes a professional prostitute), he is known as a SWING CLUB ESCORT. ON-PREMISE SWING CLUBS are private clubs with facilities for either twosomes or group sex. These clubs have such exotic names as Night Moves and Midnight Interlude. Among the exotic forms of CULTURAL EXCHANGE (swapping of sexual partners and inviting in a third person, etc.) are LES TROIS (sex among three participants, also called A THREESOME), A DAISY CHAIN (simultaneous sexual activity throughout a chain of participants) and A PARTY (two girls on one customer). PARTIES may feature such games as SUGAR AND SPICE (two prostitutes, one of whom is white and the other black, for THREESOMES), VANILLA, CHOCOLATE and PECAN (an interracial threesome), VANILLA AND CHOCOLATE (one white and one black female prostitute working in tandem on a single customer or SWING CLUB member). Among the most appetizing dishes served at such an establishment is A WHITE MEAT TURKEY ON PUMPERNICKEL (sandwich), two black female prostitutes providing services for a white male customer.

SWINGER'S PEN PAL, A   A writer of pornographic letters who may also be willing to trade pornographic photographs with his correspondent. This contemporary American euphemism for some of the more exotic forms of sexual activity is joined by others such as PERSONALIZED PHONE CALLS and CASSETTES. Both these forms of communication are comprised of erotic talk appropriate for accompanying masturbation and they are sold as a service. Some porno clients are turned on by VA (verbal abuse), which can also be obtained commercially.

VERT, A   A sexual pervert. One of many British euphemisms for a person who engages in unconventional sexual practices, VERT (probably a shortening of "pervert") is a general term whereas others, such as TOMMY BUSTER (rapist), RIPPER (vicious attacker), SHEEPHERDER (sodomite) and DANGLER (exhibitionist), are more colorfully specific. British sexual deviants are known as NANCES and what they practice is, according to the British Home Office, USI (unlawful sexual intercourse). A male voyeur, often of upper- or middle-class background, who sometimes acts as a prostitute's slave purely for the reward of looking on, is a TIN SOLDIER.

PROFESSIONAL SEX

ALPHONSE, A   A ponce or pimp. Ponce, the commonest cockney expression for a pimp, is a shortening of the longer

French name "Alphonse," which suggests that only smooth foreigners practice this profession. Several English names that serve as rhyming slang for "ponce" imply a particularly British tradition: CHARLIE (RONCE) and JOE RONCE. Yet another rhyming term for "ponce" is CANDLE SCONCE, which may refer to what has been called "the smooth and greasy nature of the procurer." Another salesman IN THE TRADE is the BOTTLE MERCHANT, a promoter engaged in prostitution or in drumming up trade for male prostitutes. The term "bottle" is a reference to a male prostitute, taken from BOTTLE AND GLASS, which is rhyming slang for "arse" and an allusion to anal intercourse.

ASHES HAULED, TO GET ONE'S To visit a brothel. This American euphemism is one of a number of expressions that disguise illicit sexual activity. A prostitute's CLIENT or JOHN may also SEE A MAN ABOUT A DOG or A DOG ABOUT A MAN (the same expression is used for a visit to the bathroom), GO DOWN THE LINE and VISIT THE RED-LIGHT DISTRICT. A SEXUAL QUICKIE with a professional prostitute is known as a HALF-HOUR SHINE, and this act is performed on a SHINE STAND (bed). When any woman, not necessarily a prostitute, has sexual intercourse with a number of males consecutively, she is said to PULL A TRAIN. In Black English the last RIDER (see STRAIGHT SEX, **TOWN BIKE**) is called A CABOOSE. Whatever his destination, A JOHN hopes that he will not be a victim of MURPHYING, that is, sexual trickery, the fooling of a customer into believing that certain services will be performed. (See Chapter 6, FLIMFLAMS, FELONIES AND MISDEMEANORS, **MURPHY.**)

B-GIRL, A A prostitute who works in bars or nightclubs. According to Rawson, there are three theories for the meaning of "B" in this expression. It may stand for "bar," "bad" or "putting the Bee on someone" (pressuring them) to buy a drink—since B-GIRLS do begin their operations by persuading male customers to buy them a drink. Prostitutes who work in this fashion are also known as MIXERS, SITTERS or TAXI DRINKERS.

BATTLE, ON THE Working as a prostitute. Since 1898, an Australian prostitute has been called A BATTLER and her pursuit of the profession has been known as being ON THE BATTLE, since she BATTLED (1944) or struggled for a livelihood at a low-paying job. Sometimes she was exploited by A BLUDGER, a male bully in a brothel (from 1898). The term now means both a man who lives on prostitutes' earnings and one who avoids effort by either living on someone else's money or acquiring goods without paying for them, both known as BLUDGING. A British variant of ON THE BATTLE is ON THE GAME.

BRASS, A A prostitute. A BRASS NAIL, British rhyming slang for "tail" in the north of England, is a regional term for prostitute. The rest of England has shortened the term to BRASS. BRASSES are also called JANES. A JANE SHAW or JANE SHORE, British rhyming slang for "whore," is probably a naval pun that originally referred to Edward IV's mistress. Whatever the particular name she is given, a prostitute is often referred to as NO BETTER THAN SHE SHOULD BE.

CALL GIRL, A A prostitute who works in an apartment or CALL HOUSE to which a prospective customer telephones when he desires a woman's services. This American euphemism dates from 1935 and has been generally known since 1950. A prostitute who lives in an apartment or CALL HOUSE is more likely to be LIBERATED, that is, not "pimped off" but WORKING FOR HERSELF. However, she too is one of THE LADIES OF ACCOMMODATING MORALS or A BAD GIRL or, in Britain, A POLL (obsolescent), A JADED JENNY (for Jenny, see Dante Gabriel Rossetti's poem of 1850) and A HELLO DEARIE (from her typical greeting).

CAP AND BLOW, TO To have a friendly competition (between two pimps). The American euphemism TO BLOW means, in addition to its specifically sexual connotation, to lose a girl to another pimp, a consequence that is always possible when a prostitute does not CHOOSE (voluntarily decide to join a pimp) or when she is FRESH AND SWEET (just out of prison). The courtship process between pimp and prostitute is an elaborate one. Before THE GAME (a pimp's romance, with or without violence to the girl) begins, the pimp will make A RAP (an initial approach) in order TO HIT ON a girl (try to woo her). Once they have joined forces, the pimp may provide such services as RUNNING DOWN THE GAME (informing her about the presence of police, etc. in her area) and, after TAKING HER APPLICATION (making a deal with her), the pimp may even buy her BONDS or THREADS (elaborate clothing). Such relationships have been known to break up violently, particularly when the prostitute disillusions her MAC (see **MR. McGIMP**) by turning out to be a FLATBACKER (a prostitute who doesn't take the client's money).

CHICKEN RANCH, A　A house of prostitution. Unlike the many other expressions for A BROTHEL, this American euphemism derives from a specific place. There was a famous BORDELLO in Gilbert, Texas in which poor local farmers paid for their sexual pleasures with chickens. BROTHEL, itself a euphemism, dates from the fifteenth century and has been called everything from A BEAUTY PARLOR to A ZOO (a term for A HOUSE that includes girls of various nationalities). A BROTHEL has been known as: A BIRD CAGE (since the prostitute is called A BIRD), A CRIB (a place in which one CRIBS or lies down to sleep), A CHAMBER OF COMMERCE (where BUSINESS is conducted), A FANCY HOUSE, A GAY HOUSE, A GOOSEBERRY DEN (where one is goosed or offers one's BERRY), A HOUSE OF JOY, HOUSE OF DELIGHT, INTIMATERIE, MAN TRAP, KIP (A BROTHEL or low ale house since 1766), A PAD (also meaning an apartment or home), A PLACE, A RED LIGHT (HOUSE) or RED LIGHTERIE (a nineteenth-century term after the red light that marked houses of prostitution), A RED SCATTER and A SCATTER. Crasser and more obvious but still euphemistic are the expressions SERVICE STATION (where a customer is SERVICED; see STRAIGHT SEX, **ACTION**), A SHOOTING GALLERY (where one SHOOTS, i.e., ejaculates or SCORES), A SIN SPOT, A SPORTING HOUSE (American, 1894) and a WINDOW TAPPERY (since the woman's window is TAPPED). One of the oldest euphemisms for A HOUSE OF ILL FAME or ILL REPUTE (1726, but "ill" has meant morally depraved since 1300) is a BAWDY HOUSE (1593), an expression still current today. HOUSES OF JOY range in quality from joints to ICE PALACES, elegant BORDELLOS (from Italian, and in English by the fifteenth century) or OLD LADIES' HOMES (establishments that will brook no improper behavior). In 1970, *The Guardian* referred to a licensed BROTHEL as A HOUSE OF TOLERANCE.

COURTESAN, A   A prostitute, particularly one of more elegant station. The word "courtesan" originally indicated a female courtier, but by 1635 it had come to mean a kept mistress or prostitute. COURTESANS have always been considered more elegant than mere HOOKERS or CALL GIRLS (q.q.v.). The commonest plain term for a prostitute is A JANE, while COURTESANS have been called by romantic and literary names. Among the euphemisms for them are: A CYPRIAN (after the favorite people of the goddess Venus), A DEMI-MONDAINE—from *demi monde* (a word created by Alexandre Dumas fils, 1824–75), A DELILAH (after Samson's Philistine friend), AN ASPASIA (from the COURTESAN who was the mistress of Pericles in Athens in the fifth century B.C.), A MAID MARIAN (from Robin Hood's sweetheart in the ballads of the fifteenth century), A DAUGHTER OF EVE, A JEZEBEL (from the wicked Biblical queen, wife of Ahab), A THAIS (from the Alexandrian seductress) and A DULCINEA (from Cervantes's *Don Quixote*).

DUTCH WIDOW, A   A prostitute. This unusual euphemism for a prostitute was created as an analogy to mechanical DUTCH WIVES or DUTCH HUSBANDS—life-sized machines used in masturbation. In England, prostitutes have also been called COVENT GARDEN NUNS, ABBESSES and VESTALS, since Covent Garden was a favorite area for the trade, and FLEET STREET HOURIS or DOVES after the main street in the newspaper publishing district of London. London gives its flavor to yet another term, this one derived from Fulham, a working-class area. FULHAM VIRGINS are prostitutes. These women have been described as FREELANCERS, MADAME VANS or RANS (ca. 1739) or MRS. MURPHYS and, more generally, as SWEETMEATS, SUNDAY GIRLS or SATURDAY-TO-MONDAYS. In American Black English parlance, a PROFESSIONAL is a highly qualified prostitute (in ordinary American speech, any prostitute). Also in Black English A MAIN LADY is the oldest and, in some cases, the original prostitute procured by her pimp, whereas A BOTTOM WOMAN or MOTHER is the most trusted in a PROCURER'S STABLE. She is a mainstay of his FAMILY; the word FAMILY as a euphemism for a group of prostitutes was used as early as 1748 in Richardson's *Clarissa*.

GENTOO, A   A prostitute. This South African word is one of a number of international terms for prostitute. GENTOO may have originated from the name of a wrecked American ship used to transport female servants from the United States. As a result of the shipwreck the girls were forced to live by prostituting themselves, and they later set up GENTOO HOUSES (BROTHELS). On the other hand, it may be derived from the Hindi word for a Telugu-speaking Hindu. Less exotic sounding is MOOSE (prostitute), but the word is from the Japanese *musume*, "girl," distorted by American armed forces in the Korean War. American forces are also responsible for HERSHEY BAR, a World War II euphemism for both PROS and amateurs in Europe who were said to exchange their bodies for chocolate. A FERRY is an Australian term (transported to Britain by 1942) and compares a prostitute to a means of conveyance since she "carries numerous men." A BLUEFOOT, probably of West Indian origin, is a euphemism for a prostitute favored by hippie communes.

HOOKER, A   A prostitute. Now barely euphemistic, this American expression has been associated with a number of sources. The most popular view is that HOOKERS were named after General Joseph Hooker's Union Army brigade during the United States Civil War (1861–65). Legend has it that the women who worked in Washington's BROTHELS came to be known as "Hooker's Division" or "Hooker's Brigade," according to Rawson, in tribute to the general's character.

Rawson points out that the term HOOKER was used for American prostitutes before the Civil War and that it may have been derived from Corlear's Hook, A RED-LIGHT SECTION (see **CHICKEN RANCH**) of New York. An even older citation (1845) comes from Norfolk, Virginia, where it was used to describe an analogy between a prostitute and a fisherman—she lies in wait for her customers and hooks them in. The profession of prostitution has probably spawned more euphemisms for its practitioners than any other. A small sample includes: A FALLEN WOMAN (nineteenth century, originally British), AN UNFORTUNATE (from Thomas Hood's poem "The Bridge of Sighs," 1827: "One more unfortunate weary of breath/Rashly importunate, gone to her death."), A FORGOTTEN WOMAN, A LOST LADY, A SHADY LADY (because her dealings are dishonest or SHADY) and A PROSS, PROSSY or PRO. On the brighter side of the profession, prostitutes have been called LADIES OF PLEASURE, LADIES OF LEISURE, LADIES OF THE EVENING, JOY SISTERS, DAUGHTERS OF JOY and FILLES DE JOIE, a French translation of the last term.

MAMA-SAN The proprietress of a BROTHEL (see **CHICKEN RANCH**). The British and American expression MADAM has been in use since about 1700, when it meant A COURTESAN or prostitute (see **COURTESAN**) as opposed to the KEEPER or BOSS of a group of prostitutes. A MADAM has also been called an AUNT, AUNTIE, HOUSEKEEPER or LANDLADY. MAMA-SAN is a fairly recent addition. It comes from the Korean War and was used by American GIs to indicate the woman in charge (*san* in Japanese) of a brothel.

MR. McGIMP, A A procurer of women for the purposes of prostitution, a pimp. MR. MCGIMP (American rhyming slang for "pimp") is one of the many imaginative names for men in the flesh trade. Cockneys refer to such men as FISH AND SHRIMP. In American rhyming slang they are also called JOHNNY RONCE (for the English term ponce). A pimp may be known as: A BROTHER-IN-LAW if he pimps for more than one woman, A RACK SALESMAN, A FRIEND, A HUSTLER (HUSTLER is now usually applied to prostitutes), A SKIRT MAN or A

SWEET MAN. He may also be called A MAC or MACK, A MACKO MAN (1960), A MACKEREL and A MISSIONARY (since he converts women to a new and richer way of life). Australian procurers are known as SILVER SPOONS, and SPOON is an old established Australian underground term. SWEET MAN has been reduced in Black English to MAN, and both terms have been gradually replaced in popularity by DUDE. FANCY MAN (as a man who lived off the earnings of a prostitute, 1851), once a term for "pimp," is now used primarily for homosexuals, but it was based on clothing worn by the procurer—such items as ST. LOUIS FLATS or CHICAGO FLATS (elegant shoes with elaborate toe designs) and ZOOT SUITS (tight fitting, wide-lapeled jackets with heavily padded shoulders and high-waisted trousers tapered into narrow cuffs, late 1940s).

MRS. WARREN'S PROFESSION Prostitution. A literary addition to the British euphemistic vocabulary, this expression, drawn from George Bernard Shaw's play of the same name (1898), is also used in America. Those who are IN THE TRADE speak of it in their own private language. This includes such expressions as: TO SEE COMPANY, TO SIT FOR COMPANY (to work in a brothel), TO HAVE APARTMENTS TO LET (to engage in prostitution) or TO GET THE RENT (find a customer, British, from the late nineteenth century). To enhance their TRADE, LADIES OF THE EVENING may have TO CRUISE (solicit trade), HUSTLE or RUSTLE (all meaning to walk about or conduct other activities to solicit trade). In Black English, PROSTITUTES who do this will go ON THE STROLL (walk the area of their operations), or SIT AT SHOW WINDOWS (windows in brothels from which the inhabitants may solicit clients).

MYSTERY, A An adolescent female delinquent often working as a prostitute. A teenage girl absent from her home, approved school or Borstal and "floating around the streets" is how Powis describes A MYSTERY, a British underworld and police euphemism with many progeny. One who is MYSTERY MAD or A MYSTERY PUNTER is a man or woman who obsessively looks for A MYSTERY to pick up and briefly live with—A

PUNTER is A PLAYBOY. The word "mystery" has been used to mean something hidden or secret since 1194 and to mean a service, occupation or trade since 1386. Its present meaning includes both the earlier ones and a sly dig at the possibly professional nature of the girl's secret or sly behavior. A MYSTERY is likely to experience more than one NIGHT ON THE TILES, a British term for being ON THE TOWN or ON A SPREE.

PROSTITUTE, A   A woman who sells her sexual favors for a livelihood. This British and American euphemism for a whore was first used in the form PROSTITUTION in 1553. By 1613, it was used to mean A HARLOT (1432–50), itself a euphemism for a whore. Noah Webster did much to popularize the word PROSTITUTE when he substituted it for "whore" in his bowdlerization of the Bible. PROSTITUTE is now considered sufficiently blatant to require disguise in the form of such terms as HOSTESS (a mistress of an inn from 1290, but ambiguous in meaning by the time Shakespeare created his ribald Mistress Quickly). A more contemporary concealing term for PROSTITUTE is MODEL, but it follows upon the heels of venerable predecessors such as A KATE (an attractive prostitute), A MAGDALENE (1697, for a reformed prostitute, after Mary Magdalene the follower of Jesus), A NIGHT-HAWK, NIGHT-BIRD, or OWL (after her nocturnal hunting habits) and A SISTER-OF-MERCY or CHARITY or A NUN (A COURTESAN since 1770). Less pietistic than the term SOILED DOVE (British, nineteenth century) are such phrases as A RED-LIGHTER or LIGHT SISTER, A NYMPHE DU PAVÉ ("nymph of the pavement") or A PAVEMENT PRINCESS (in CB talk), A PAINTED WOMAN or LADY, A PAVEMENT-POUNDER (an amplification of the old STREET-WALKER, 1592), A SIDEWALK SUZIE, A WOMAN ABOUT TOWN, A SPORT or SPORTING WOMAN—after SPORTING HOUSE (brothel, American 1894)—and the rhyming slang for "whore," A FORTY-FOUR.

STREET-WALKER, A   A prostitute who solicits in the streets. That this British and American euphemism dates at least from the sixteenth century is not surprising, since prostitution has been called "the oldest profession." In ancient Greece, it is said, prostitutes had the words "follow me" carved on the soles of their sandals, thus introducing a revolutionary concept in advertising. Since that time, they have been known as FANCY WOMEN (1892) or FANCY GIRLS (1930), LADIES OF THE SCARLET SISTERHOOD and, among the oldest names, SISTERS OF THE BANK (1550). They have also been called LOVE-PEDDLERS, LOOSE LOVE LADIES, SADIE THOMPSONS (from Somerset Maugham's *Rain*) and, more blatantly, WHOOPIE WENCHES, THRILL DAMES, TARTS (now questionably euphemistic) and TARTLETS. Some of the more humorous disguises for prostitutes are: WEEKEND WARRIORS (for teenage girls who STREET-WALK on weekends), OVERNIGHT BAGS, BACHELORS' WIVES, HIP PEDDLERS, GIRLS AT EASE (perhaps from LADIES OF LEISURE), BROADS (now used generically, if rudely, for any woman) and BROADWAY BROADS (New York City, and of Damon Runyan fame).

TRICK A prostitute's client; the sexual act itself; the prostitute herself. One possible origin of this multifaceted American euphemism is a voodoo term for achieving sexual control, brought to America by Blacks. As early as "Bawdy House Blues," an old jazz song of the twenties, a prostitute complains, "I got an all night trick again;/I'm busy grindin' so ya can't come in." A TRICK, in the sense of A CUSTOMER or CLIENT, is properly called A JOHN (probably for John Doe, everyman). A CHAMPAGNE TRICK is a rich, well-paying customer (1973), while A FREAK TRICK is one who engages in sexual perversions. A child who is born from such a union is A TRICK BABY. To TURN A TRICK is to obtain and service a CLIENT—in other words, to transact BUSINESS—and TO SCORE in the language of prostitution means to find a paying customer. Thus a client is also called a SCORE. According to prostitute superstition, the first TRICK of the evening determines a woman's luck. Thus, TO BREAK LUCK or BREAK LUCK WITH HIM is to succeed in transacting business with one's first customer.

APRON HIGH, TO WEAR THE; BELLY HIGH, TO WEAR or HAVE THE   To be visibly pregnant. Although the precise date of this American euphemism is uncertain, it was current in the South in the nineteenth century. The Southern mountain ballad "Careless Love" records its currency in the words:

> Once I wore my apron low;
> Now I wear my apron high.
> Love, oh love, oh careless love!
> See what love has done to me.

The English and their American cousins also spoke of a pregnant woman as WEARING THE BUSTLE WRONG. Since the word "bustle" for a padded rear appendage was not in use before 1830, the expression certainly dates from no earlier than this period. Clearly no pregnant woman achieved the beau ideal of the time, which was to have "a waist like a wasp, a magnificent bustle."

BAY WINDOW or BELLY, WITH A   Pregnant. Since 1879, a protuberant stomach or abdomen, especially a man's, has been known in the United States as A BAY WINDOW (see Chapter 2, **TUMMY**, BAY WINDOW). However, the term is also used to describe a BIG-BELLIED woman—one FAR GONE in pregnancy—as it has been since 1718 when the English essayist Addison chose this adjective to describe a woman who had ONE ON THE WAY, was IN A BAD WAY or BAD SHAPE or is AWKWARD. Interestingly, the oldest term for pregnancy is still the most delicate: WITH CHILD has been in use in English since at least 1175.

BLANKET, TO BE BORN ON THE WRONG SIDE OF THE   To be illegitimate. Ever since 1771, when Tobias Smollet's Humphrey Clinker declared "I didn't come on the wrong side of the blanket, girl," the English and subsequently the Americans have used the phrase to describe illegitimate children politely. Other variants are TO BE BORN ON THE WRONG SIDE

OF THE COVERS, TO COME THROUGH THE SIDE DOOR and TO BE BORN IN THE VESTRY (as opposed to the church itself). Robert Browning, in his play *The Blot in the 'Scutcheon* (1843), used the expression A BLOT ON THE SCUTCHEON to allude to bastardy and to the traditional heraldic symbol of it, a bend sinister (or band slanting downward to the left). The bend sinister had been in common use since the late fifteenth century, while the late sixteenth century began to coin a number of euphemisms for "bastard." They included: A BEGGAR'S BY-BLOW, A BY-CHOP (Ben Jonson) A BY-SCAPE and A BY-SLIP. Of these, BY-BLOW (1595), a term for a person who comes into the world by A SIDE-STROKE, has continued to flourish.

BULL—IT'S NOT THE BULL THEY'RE AFRAID OF, IT'S THE CALF Women aren't afraid of sex, they're afraid of getting pregnant. With its many cattle stations and its frontier hardihood, outback Australia is the natural parent of this breeding allusion. Australian women and their lovers who are afraid of the calf would clearly not consider its birth A BLESSED EVENT, HEVENT or SHEVENT, but A BLASTED EVENT (all American, twentieth century). America, with its arch consumerism, has another euphemism for calving—PRODUCING, as in "Has she produced yet?" (1980). The product is called THE LITTLE DIVIDEND (see also IN-FANTICIPATING) or THE LITTLE DEDUCTION and, in Afro-American slang, THE EXPENSE.

CLUB, TO JOIN THE To be or become pregnant. Used more frequently in England than America, this expression for pregnancy refers to membership in THE PUDDING or PUDDEN CLUB, a rakish late seventeenth-century mythical organization. The word "pudden" is a double pun, referring both to semen (PUDDEN) and the female pudendum. Until the late 1940s TO PUT IN THE PUDDEN CLUB was a common euphemism for "to impregnate." The British prefer pudding, but another food metaphor for pregnancy is TO HAVE A BUN IN THE OVEN or TO HAVE ONE IN THE OVEN. Since the eighteenth century, the word "oven" has been a vulgarism for the pudendum. Eric

---

Partridge thinks that this expression for pregnancy may be related to a proverb used from the sixteenth through nineteenth centuries: "He (or she) that has a bun in the oven knows where to go for a son (or daughter)." If, as some people say, the expression is still a vulgarism, it is certainly a cosy, domestic one. An American variant that we believe is Southern in origin is TO HAVE ONE or A WATERMELON ON THE VINE or TO SWALLOW A WATERMELON SEED. Nancy, in William Faulkner's short story of the 1930s "That Evening Sun," is in just that DELICATE CONDITION. She might also be described as FRAGRANT, not an aromatic blossom but a near or close rhyme for "pregnant."

CLUCKY Pregnant. In Australia this euphemism comparing a pregnant woman to a brooding hen has been used by women since 1941. Our American equivalent is ON THE NEST. A more jocular British variant slyly alludes to pregnancy as THE RESULT OF A LARK IN THE PARK AFTER DARK (pub slang, ca. 1930).

DELICATE CONDITION, IN A Pregnant. In 1850, Dickens's Mrs. Micawber (*David Copperfield*) found herself in A DELICATE STATE OF HEALTH or DELICATE CONDITION. In other words, she was GONE—as in SIX MONTHS GONE. More recent British women have described themselves as FALLEN, perhaps in a vestigial tribute to the Victorian FALLEN WOMAN (see **HOOKER**, FALLEN WOMAN), and the expression I FELL is widely used. Since 1796 Americans would say that a pregnant woman was IN A FAMILY WAY. A delicate way of indicating that an EXPECTANT MOTHER (see **EXPECTING**) is soon to be delivered is to say that HER TIME IS NEAR.

ENCEINTE Pregnant. One of the most elegant ways of evading an earthy truth is to say it in French. This English and American euphemism for pregnancy was current as early as the nineteenth century and still is. However, in the United States, with its disdain for affectation and its incompetence at foreign accents, ENCEINTE became a source of humor when it was used on a Hallmark greeting card: "I knew you were no dilettante!/Glad to hear you're *enceinte!*" As a legal term in

English, the word dates from 1599, when it appears in a will as: "If my wife be *insented* with a manchild. . . . " Another Frenchification that is still used to disguise the process of childbearing is the French word for "lying-in," ACCOUCHEMENT (in use in England since ca. 1809). At least from 1759, the era of the bungling Dr. Slop in Lawrence Sterne's *Tristram Shandy*, a male midwife was called an *accoucheur*.

EXPECTING, EXPECTANT Pregnant. By 1862 the term EXPECTANT FATHER was in use, and by the 1880s EXPECTANT MOTHER was current. A somewhat more elegant form of EXPECTING is ANTICIPATING. A positively regal term—coined by American maternity shops in the 1950s and 1960s—is LADY-IN-WAITING. Among plain folks an EXPECTANT lady is A WAITING WOMAN. In Britain, she is A MUM-TO-BE and, in America, a MOTHER-TO-BE.

HOLE OUT IN ONE, A A pregnancy as a result of one's first sexual experience. The origin of this Australian euphemism dating from 1901 is obviously golf. Other expressions for getting pregnant, not necessarily with beginner's luck, are to be IN TROUBLE (British and American since 1891) and TO BREAK or SPRAIN YOUR ANKLE. The latter also means to have an abortion.

INFANTICIPATING Pregnant. This American euphemism reflects the self-conscious cleverness fashionable in the early 1940s. It labored and brought forth a family of equally nauseating cutenesses designed to be tactful. Anyone desiring to inquire if a woman is pregnant or FULL OF HEIR may ask if she is: RATTLE SHOPPING, PREPARING THE BASSINET, REHEARSING LULLABIES, KNITTING, WAITING FOR THE PATTER OF LITTLE FEET, EATING FOR TWO or if she and her husband will BE A TRIO, HAVE A LITTLE TAX DEDUCTION, DECLARE A DIVIDEND, RING THE STORK BELL, LEARN ALL ABOUT DIAPER FOLDING or PUT ON HEIRS. After enduring this barrage, one wonders why they would ever want TO PLAY A RETURN ENGAGEMENT or give birth to a second child.

IRISH TOOTHACHE, AN Pregnancy. This lower-class English

euphemism was coined in about 1909 when it was also used as the initials ITA. One of the many British jokes at the expense of the Irish, it was a jab at Irish Catholicism and its censure of birth control. Thus the phrase hints that, in Ireland, pregnancy is as routine an event as a toothache. Amusingly, AN IRISH TOOTHACHE is also used to refer to PRIAPISM. Other terms relating to pregnancy that have additional or double meanings are MISS and ACCIDENT. In both England and America, a woman who involuntarily aborts a child is said to have had A MISS or MIS (miscarriage) or AN ACCIDENT. A "miss," used in England since 1527, is also used now in both Britain and America to refer to a suspected pregnancy because a woman misses her PERIOD (see Chapter 3, MENSTRUATION, **FLOWERS**, PERIOD). An ACCIDENT also refers to an unplanned or illegitimate child.

LOVE CHILD, A   An illegitimate child. In 1805 the term LOVE CHILD was coined to refer more politely to a child who was either LOVE-BEGOTTEN or A LOVE BRAT. Not until the 1850s, however, did Dickens's Micawber of *David Copperfield* feel tolerant enough to opine that "accidents will happen in the best regulated families." In our more casual contemporary American society, the BIRTHPARENTS (1980s, biological parents of an illegitimate child) might admit that they CHEATED THE STARTER. There are even terms for special kinds of illegitimate children such as A TRICK BABY, one fathered by a prostitute's client during one of her professional engagements (see PROFESSIONAL SEX, **TRICK**).

8

The Language of Government: Bureaucratese and Urbababble

Every government has its linguistic protocol. The American government has been described as an assembly of those speaking bureaucratese, Pentagonese, State-Departmentese, gobbledygook and a local city dialect called "urbababble." The British have gone so far as to list categories of words, and words themselves, that may not be uttered in Parliament, thus inadvertently encouraging British statesmen to coin new euphemisms. May's *British Parliamentary Process* informs us that Members of Parliament may make no disloyal or disrespectful reference to the Queen, her family, the Lord Chancellor, the governor general of an independent territory, the Speaker, the chairman of Ways and Means, Members of either house of Parliament, judges of the superior courts and so on down to the humble recorder in a county court. Nor may "opprobrious reflections" be cast on sovereigns and nations friendly to or allied with the United Kingdom or on their representatives. While these prohibitions leave little latitude for the abusive tendencies native to human nature, they are often honored more in the breach than in the observance. Indeed, Members of Parliament have been known to use such officially forbidden, unparliamentary expressions as "blackguard," "blether," "cheeky young pup," "guttersnipe," "humbug," "hypocrite," "jackass," "Pharisee," "ruffian," "slanderer," "stool pigeon," "swine," "villain" etc.

In addition, the poor repressed MPs are not allowed to misrepresent the language of another or charge another with uttering a deliberate falsehood, although the word "calumnious" has been generally approved as "in order." Still worse, they are prohibited from using abusive and insulting language and from hissing, booing and interrupting speakers on the floor. May notes to his horror that Members are often rowdy; on March 19, 1872, the galleries had to be cleared and notice had to be taken of "the crowing of cocks and other disorderly noises proceeding from the Members." It still surprises non-Britishers to hear the ordinary sounds of the House of Commons—hisses, boos, table thumping and cries of "Hear! hear!"

It is an equal shock to non-Americans to watch the U.S. Congress in action. American legislators may be less vocally insulting, but they have been known to read newspapers, stroll about the chambers, whisper, shout and insist that the *Congressional Record* (the account of congressional actions) include local baseball scores and favorite recipes for chocolate cake. Filibustering, the ultimate vulgarism—even when used for just purposes—is one of the rights of senators. It seems to illustrate the fact that, even though there is U.S. government protocol, it is extremely flexible and that free speech is guaranteed by the First Amendment to the Constitution. But senators and representatives still so rarely describe each other in four-letter words that when they do so it shocks colleagues and the public. When President Harry Truman called a columnist an SOB, clean-tongued Americans were deeply offended. But, then, he was from Missouri!

Whatever their individual codes, all governments are gold mines of euphemism. They use it primarily for the purposes of defending and rationalizing their actions and for disguising or diminishing their failures or unpopular proposals and policies. Yet, no matter how innocent the material under discussion seems to be, it is the nature of government to convert clear language to bureaucratese and gobbledygook. Less colorful than the euphemistic vocabulary of many other subjects, government language works by depersonalizing and generalizing or abstracting. Thus a Cuban or Frenchman is A FOREIGN NATIONAL or UNITED STATES NON-NATIONAL, and one who has a U. S. work permit is A GREEN CARDER or DOCUMENTED WORKER. Even an innocent tree is not a tree; it is A REFORESTATION UNIT .

Pentagonese is the most popular and widely disseminated of the dialects invading government language, public conversation and the media. Gliding close behind is State-Departmentese, described by Arthur Schlesinger Jr. as "a bureaucratic patois borrowed, in large part, from the Department of Defense." When a member of the State Department informs you that there is "a need for more fully informed judgments," he is diplomatically saying, "You don't know your elbow from a hole in the ground." Knowing the language not only tells you when you are being insulted, but it also establishes your credentials as a member of the in-group (as in crime; see introductory essay to Chapter 6). Perhaps killing gobbledygook is so difficult because its use creates a sense of belonging and importance. William Safire wrote that the opening phrase of the Gettysburg Address, "We are now engaged in a civil war," would be better understood by Washingtonians if rendered into bureaucratese as "We have entered upon a period of uncertainty involving fairly high mobilization." A cake recipe translated into bureaucratese would speak of "interfacing" the ingredients in a "given time frame" and making sure that the "infrastructures" are smooth.

Because the most popular subjects of current discussion are diplomacy, economic problems and social legislation, our entries are concentrated in these areas. Diplomats are a rich source. Because they often seek to minimize international tensions, they frequently obfuscate both their true motives and their real failures. Only the cognoscenti recognize that A USEFUL AND BUSINESSLIKE

MEETING between two diplomats is one at which nothing is accomplished and that A SERIOUS AND CANDID DISCUSSION is actually a major disagreement. In domestic and international economics "depression" is a taboo word. Thus it is known as DEFLATION, DISINFLATION, and, ingeniously, ROLLING READJUSTMENT. The unemployment that results from it is UNDERUTILIZATION, an expression supposed to comfort and pacify THE ECONOMICALLY DISADVANTAGED INDIVIDUALS (the poor) who suffer because of it.

Although "the poor we shall always have with us," they may soon no longer be called THE ECONOMICALLY DISADVANTAGED. Governmentese changes so rapidly that some of the euphemisms recorded here have already been superseded and others may soon be. In the future the poor may be termed "those of nascent means"; the old, now THE LONGER LIVED or SENIOR CITIZENS, may be elevated to "quasi-centurions" or the "ultra-mature"; and even what is now called BUREAUCRATESE may change its name to "agenciola" or, better still, to "speakease."

BALLOONING Deliberately leaking information to determine national attitudes toward a potential course of action. This government technique of obtaining information in an indirect way is equivalent to the old meteorological practice of SENDING UP A TRIAL BALLOON to test wind currents and weather conditions. SENDING UP A TRIAL BALLOON rapidly became a figurative expresssion for pre-testing or political opinion polling. The public relations world tests marketability of an idea or product by RUNNING IT UP THE FLAGPOLE TO SEE WHO SALUTES. If the results of any of these tests indicate a hostile reception, particularly to a phenomenon that already exists, COSMETIC measures (those devised to cover up or conceal defects) may be necessary. An excellent example of governmental COSMETIZING appeared in a letter written by John T. Connolly to the *New York Times* in July 1970: "Attorney General John Mitchell's expressed preference for the term 'quick entry' over the scorned catchword 'no knock' provides glaring evidence of the way in which government currently uses words as cosmetics to delude the public and even itself."

BENIGN NEGLECT Non-intervention and non-interference, particularly in the affairs of colonies or ethnic minorities. Daniel Patrick Moynihan originated this term in his famous report, *The Negro-American Revolution* (1964), a discussion of the lives of ethnic minorities with special attention to New York. He suggested that governmental attitudes toward racial minorities had been and should continue to be those of BENIGN NEGLECT (leaving people alone to seek their own solutions to their problems). In *Doublespeak in America*, Mario Pei says that the phrase is originally English (from 1839), when the Earl of Durham suggested that Canada, which had become strong and self-reliant "through many years of benign neglect by the British," should become self-governing. The doctrine of benign neglect would be automatically opposed to such programs as AFFIRMATIVE ACTION or EQUAL OPPORTUNITY (making all employment accessible to members of ETHNIC minorities and females and specifically seeking them out for positions).

BIOSPHERE OVERLOAD Overpopulation. Ronald Ziegler, President Nixon's press secretary, is responsible for this American euphemism of the early 1970s. OVERLOAD is also called by government officials DEMOGRAPHIC STRAIN. It is particularly prevalent in DISTRESSED URBAN AREAS (poor and rundown sections of cities). Among the solutions proposed to alleviate this problem have been URBAN HOMESTEADING (1974, buying an abandoned or burnt-out house for a small fee in exchange for repairing, restoring and living in it and receiving a tax abatement for one's labors) and, in general, helping the CATEGORICALLY NEEDY, that is, those eligible to receive welfare, the aged, the blind and the dependent.

BROAD GAUGE THINKER, A One concerned with broad policy rather than detail. William Safire suggests that the term BROAD GAUGE THINKER comes from the seven-foot gauge railroad track of the Victorian civil engineer Isambard Kingdom Brunel, who created track larger than the standard gauge. The expression, used in government, business and academia, indicates a theoretician and overall policy maker. As Safire notes, only such a person would come up with an expression like THE SOCIAL SAFETY NET. This phrase, defined by David Stockman, was used early in the 1970s to mean what we think of as Social Security, unemployment compensation, Medicare and Medicaid. Safire thinks the expression is based on a circus image—that of a trapeze artist's safety net.

CONGRESSIONAL OVERSIGHT   The provision by the Legislative Reorganization Act of 1946 that each standing committee of either House of Congress "shall exercise continuous watchfulness of the execution of any laws the subject matter of which is within the jurisdiction of the community." CONGRESSIONAL OVERSIGHT, the obligation and power to oversee legislative action, is often executed by PUBLIC TRUSTEES (a watchdog commission). Among the duties of such a commission may be the supervision of AD HOCCERY, a slang term coined to describe policy, rules or committees set up on an ad hoc basis. If a large number of agencies are acting on such a basis, government by them may be called an AD HOCRACY —a term made popular by Anthony Wedgewood Benn (who now prefers to be known as Tony Benn) in 1970.

CROSS-CULTURAL COMMUNICATIONS   Conversation between at least two people, particularly political, social or intellectual leaders, from different countries. No one, in the United States government at least, ever merely talks. When any two government representatives meet, they may have EXCHANGES OF IDEAS or FACE-TO-FACE DIALOGUES, SHARE IDEAS or ENGAGE IN A DIALOGUE. When the discussants are from different countries, they are engaged in CROSS-CULTURAL COMMUNICATIONS, very often with the purpose of persuading other leaders to think favorably of their nation. Our diplomats attempt to COMMUNICATE EFFECTIVELY (persuade, sometimes forcefully) and to avoid both A USEFUL AND BUSINESSLIKE MEETING (one in which no agreement is reached and nothing is accomplished, 1980) and A SERIOUS AND CANDID DISCUSSION (serious disagreement). The results

---

of all meetings, particularly HIGH-LEVEL BILATERAL MEETINGS (meetings between two upper-level diplomats or civil servants representing two governments) will often be leaked by A RELIABLE SOURCE (a source of information whose name is concealed, 1958) unless they are kept OFF THE RECORD (secret or confidential in news jargon).

DETENTE The softening of international tensions; more specifically, political cooperation or harmony between the United States and the Union of Soviet Socialist Republics. Theodore Sorensen, President Kennedy's advisor and speechwriter, used the term EMERGING DETENTE in the late 1960s, but DETENTE has meant the easing of strained international political relations since 1908. The golden age of DETENTE occurred in 1972–73 when Henry Kissinger used the term frequently. During that time, DETENTE was seen as an alternative to CONTAINMENT (forced isolation of enemy nations) and COLD WAR HOSTILITIES (hostile relations without overt military actions, from THE COLD WAR with the USSR beginning after World War II). DETENTE officially eschews DESTABILIZATION (a CIA term for the overthrow of a foreign government) and prefers to cement relations by FOREIGN POLICY TOOLS (resources such as military, financial and trade assistance employed to influence foreign nations favorably).

DEVOLUTION Decentralization by the delegation of greater powers to local authorities. When the British term DEVOLUTION is used, it means decentralization of government and the strengthening of local power. William Safire indicates that the word was first popularized in the Irish Home Rule controversy, but it has since been used in England, America and Canada. In its less euphemistic meaning of decentralization, DEVOLUTION may involve the act of REPRIVATIZING. TO REPRIVATIZE, according to the Reagan administration, is to reduce systematically the federal government's intrusion in (and contribution to) the private sector. CLIENTS or CLIENT STATES, dependent states or governments (1970), may find that REPRIVATIZATION makes them freer but poorer.

DOROTHY DIX(ER), A   A planted question, usually asked by a member of the government party to elicit an answer that has been prepared by a minister to promote his government. Australians have been speaking of A DOROTHY DIX(ER) since the 1960s, when they read the advice column "Dear Dorothy Dix" in their newspapers. Other political phenomena that take their names from those of actual people are the British POWELLISM (an economically conservative, politically isolationist and socially racist policy) named after the British minister Enoch Powell, and the American term WALLACEISM. (See **STONEWALL**.) WALLACEISM, from George C. Wallace (1919–), governor of Alabama, implies populism, support of STATES RIGHTS (often a euphemism for racial discrimination) and opposition to racial integration.

ENERGY RELEASE   Radiation released from a nuclear reactor. ENERGY RELEASE, a 1970 euphemism, operates by omitting any mention of the fact that the energy released is radioactive. The lack of specificity in identifying the nature of a product released or generated is typical of the names for nuclear energy, nuclear devices and nuclear waste sites, which are called HAZARDOUS WASTE SITES. When a nuclear reactor is in danger of exploding or melting down, for example, it is described as ABOVE CRITICAL. New programs to alleviate the fuel problems in the United States have led both federal and state agencies to utilize ALTERNATE ENERGY SOURCES (meaning non-oil sources and including nuclear fuels).

EYES ONLY   Top secret. EYES ONLY is a security classification in the United States for a document that merits the highest order of secrecy and may not be shared; it suggests that a TOP SECRET document should be seen and not heard. Lower in the rank of classified documents are those that are SENSITIVE, that is, SECRET CLASSIFIED—a euphemism for classified as secret or simply embarrassing to the government if revealed. SECRET SENSITIVE means highly secret, and NOFORM means no foreign dissemination of the materials or their contents.

FOG   Frequency of gobbledygook in government publications, etc. Both the British and United States governments have

---

spawned various bureaucratic languages that have been described as gobbledygook, a term coined in 1944. The FOG index determines how much gobbledygook a particular government publication contains. Not to be outdone by the "feds," the city governments throughout the United States have generated their own variety of gobbledygook known as URBABABBLE. While the government in Washington, D.C. specializes in BUREAUCRATESE and PENTAGONESE, a name for the jargon of the American military industrial complex that entered the language in 1952, the language of the British government is criticized and corrected by the Plain English Society, which deplores gobbledygook.

FOGGY BOTTOM   The United States Department of State. Since 1930, the United States State Department has been jocularly called FOGGY BOTTOM because of the fogginess of its official language (see **FOG**). Among the expressions that it may have perpetrated are: IN THE EARLY STATES OF FINALIZATION (not finished), FINALIZED (finished), SEMI-FINALIZED (half-finished). FOGGY BOTTOM, however, is not responsible for the navy's description of high waves as CLIMACTIC DISTURBANCES AT THE AIR-SEA INTERFACE nor can it be blamed for EMPOST (British governmentese for mail). The British alone are to be held responsible for such far-fetched titles as THE URBAN CONSERVATION AND ENVIRONMENTAL AWARENESS WORK PARTY (the name of an anti-vandalism committee of the Wolverhampton District Council).

FOREIGN NATIONALS   Foreigners. At least since the 1950s, the U.S. government has officially upgraded the pejorative term "foreigner" to FOREIGN NATIONAL. This process operates on the model of an earlier coinage from World War II— DISPLACED PERSONS (refugees) or DPS, used to improve the status of those whose national and social identities had been obliterated by prison camp sentences, widespread bombings, FORCED EVACUATIONS (see Chapter 9, PLAYERS, **INTERNEE**)—especially those suffered at the hands of the Nazis. Another term, "backward nations" (poor ones), has been successively upgraded to UNDERDEVELOPED NATIONS,

LESSER-DEVELOPED NATIONS, and now DEVELOPING NATIONS. In turn, DEVELOPING NATIONS are being replaced by EMERGENT or EMERGING NATIONS—outgrowths of the term FLEDGLING NATIONS ascribed to Eleanor Roosevelt in the 1950s.

FOURTH OF JULY SPEECH, A   An emotional or flag-waving political speech. American politicians have been accused of BLOVIATION (pompous oratory, formed from the verb TO BLOVIATE) and a favorite time to BLOVIATE is on American Independence Day. The most famous parody of a Fourth of July speech (American, 1879) is e.e. cummings' satire: "Next to, of course God, America I/love you, land of the Pilgrims and so forth, oh/say can you see by the dawn's early/my country t'is of. . . ."

GREEN CARDER, A   A foreign worker who has "legal alien" status in the United States. A GREEN CARD or American alien registration card for NON-NATIONALS is a valuable commodity, and a foreign worker who holds one is considered extremely fortunate because it permits him or her to work legally in the United States. A green carder avoids the difficulty of being AN UNDOCUMENTED PERSON or WORKER (illegal alien, see **FOREIGN NATIONALS**). America attempts to control the flow of illegal aliens, as they are non-euphemistically called, over its borders. South Africa speaks more euphemistically of its internal INFLUX CONTROL (1973, a body of government restrictions designed to prevent Black Africans from entering urban areas without working or other permits).

GREY AREA, A   A geographical area with low employment that is still not poor enough to merit government assistance. In 1970, the *Times* of London asserted that "the future of GREY AREAS —places which have fallen between the two stools of prosperity and real depression—is of great importance in this corner of Britain." British inhabitants living in GREY AREAS may or may not be eligible for NON-CONTRIBUTORY INVALIDITY BENEFITS (welfare disability payments) sometimes known in the United States as INCOME TRANSFER PROGRAMS (welfare subsidies). In the United States, a heated battle over the issue of welfare payments has led government officials to suggest that increased welfare would require RECEIPTS STRENGTHENING (a tax increase, 1981), an expression coined by Lawrence Kudlow, the chief economist of the Office of Management and Budget. Current government consensus is that most welfare recipients are NEGATIVE SAVERS (people who spend more than they make) and that the LEVEL OF SUPPORT (budget) is inadequate to maintain such programs.

HIGH PROFILE   Visibility, being in the public eye. HIGH PROFILE, now used particularly in politics and public relations for one who is IN THE LIMELIGHT (from the intense white light produced by heating lime in an oxyhydrogen flame, a technique discovered by William Drumond in 1826), was probably derived from naval jargon. A ship with a high profile is a moving target while one with a low profile is safe. The term VANISHING SILHOUETTE—derived fom both HIGH and LOW PROFILE—refers to impotence of power or loss of prestige and influence.

JOB TURNING   The process by means of which jobs begin to lose the authority and salary usually associated with them. In 1980, Sheila Rule used the government employment euphemism JOB TURNING to describe what happens when positions formerly occupied by men begin to become available in large numbers to women. The result is a degradation of authority and a diminution of salary for once highly paid and powerful positions. This situation is certainly one that the ECONOMIC DETERMINISTS (Marxists) did not foresee in their programs for greater employment equality for women.

KNOCKING ON DOORS   Lobbying or asking for political favors. KNOCKING ON DOORS is a Washington expression for lobbying or attempting to influence policy. It is one way of not UTILIZING NORMAL PROCEDURES, that is, avoiding regular government channels and hierarchies. Washington politicians and lobbyists have also been known to GET TOGETHER (make a business deal). When lobbyists or other witnesses are called before congressional committees to testify, they have been known to request that their expenses be PROCESSED

EXPEDITIOUSLY (that they receive their reimbursements quickly). All of the above expressions were heard at the Senate Judiciary Subcommittee's hearings on the contacts between Robert L. Vesco and officers and employees of the United States in October 1980.

LIQUIDITY CRISIS, A A severe shortage of liquid assets or expendable funds. Americans have been suffering from and expressing the reality of A LIQUIDITY CRISIS since 1970, when Federal Reserve Board Chairman Arthur Burns warned businessmen that they were living in a monetary desert. This metaphor, linking money with water, is utilized by present-day businesses experiencing A CASH FLOW PROBLEM (a situation in which available cash is scarce, or sometimes a euphemism for a lack of funds in any form). During this PERIOD OF ECONOMIC ADJUSTMENT (see **REFLATION**), otherwise known as RECESSION (sometimes a euphemism for a depression), many businesses and governmental agencies have found themselves suffering under BUDGET CONSTRAINTS (low and limited funds). Part of the problem has been blamed upon A REVENUE GAP (a situation in which projected expenditures exceed projected revenues) necessitating EXTENDING RESOURCES and ATTRACTING ASSISTANCE (getting more money) so that more projects, sometimes including cultural ones, can be MADE POSSIBLE (funded) at the lowest level. Money must be made available so that employees receive REMUNERATION and EMOLUMENTS (pay, wages, salary, incomes etc.).

MANAGED NEWS Slanted or "doctored" information generated by the United States government for its own purposes. This American euphemism is a result of the Cuban missile crisis of 1962. NEWS MANAGEMENT, as the activity is called, appears to be AN ONGOING SITUATION (bureaucratese for a continuing issue or problem). MANAGED NEWS will avoid discussing such an event as A WARRANTLESS INVESTIGATION (an illegal investigation by the FBI, 1978). MANAGED NEWS is associated by many with support for internal LAW AND ORDER (a term that to many means emphasis not only on strong police powers but also on political or social repression). This last euphemism is an old one and stems from a conservative law and order party formed in 1842. Britain's form of managing the news is often THE DEFENSE NOTICE or D NOTICE, a government memorandum requesting newspapers not to publish specific items in the interest of national security (1960s).

MR. CLEAN, A A politician whose campaign methods and fund raising techniques are impeccably honest. MR. CLEAN has become an epithet for an extremely honest American politician and, by extension, for any honest official. Its source is probably the household cleaning product of the same name, which was advertized by a tall, bald man named Mr. Clean, who wore one gold earring and snow-white clothes (1960s). While a political MR. CLEAN would have no objection to setting up A CITIZENS COMMITTEE (a quasi-independent association for members of the opposite party and political independents who wish to support him but not necessarily his party), he would object to LAYING PIPES and providing STREET MONEY. The former has meant political bribery in the United States since 1850. It originated in the fact that Irish workers in America were persuaded to sell their votes in exchange for employment laying pipes in waterworks. More recent equivalents to LAYING PIPES are PULLING WIRES (1862) and PULLING STRINGS (bringing influence to bear). STREET MONEY (1976) is another phrase for WALKING AROUND MONEY—legal but questionable payments made to volunteers and precinct workers on or just before election day. Although the date at which this expression entered American political jargon is uncertain, the phrase was popularized in the early 1960s. Although a MR. CLEAN would lend himself to COATTAILING (being used to bring weaker candidates to electoral victories by joining with them on a ticket), he would eschew all of these other more questionable practices in order to maintain high CANDIDATE CREDIBILITY, a phrase coined by Senator Eugene McCarthy to indicate believability and virtue.

NECKTIES AND TURBANS Liberals and religious

conservatives in Iran. When, in 1979, members of the United States diplomatic corps were imprisoned for ransom in Iran, American newspapers began to observe Iranian political parties more closely than before. They coined this euphemism to describe not only the loyalties but the archetypal dress of Iranian liberals and conservatives. International crises have broadcast foreign euphemisms in translation throughout the United States. For example, in 1977, the American public read of Idi Amin's STATE RESEARCH BUREAU (secret police), and for more than two decades American newspaper readers have been familiar with the South African term PLURAL RELATIONS for APARTHEID.

NEEDY AND DEPENDENT PERSONS Welfare recipients. In a 1980 statement introducing welfare and Medicaid fiscal assistance programs (WAMFAP), Senator Daniel Patrick Moynihan spoke eloquently about the needs of ECONOMICALLY DISADVANTAGED INDIVIDUALS (the poor). Among these are, of course, what Stewart Alsop termed ETHNICS (minority or national groups) in 1972. Moynihan noted that those who lived in HIGH BENEFIT STATES (states with large welfare payments and progams) were more likely to be the beneficiaries of INCOME MAINTENANCE (welfare). It was hardly necessary to mention the fact that a large concentration of NEEDY AND DEPENDENT PERSONS will be found in the INNER CITY (a 1950s expression for the central and usually poor section of town). Believing that the ECONOMICALLY DISADVANTAGED we shall always have with us, the Reagan administration has sought to avoid SUPPLEMENTAL APPROPRIATIONS (additional funds given when the budget is insufficient to meet proposed costs) for such programs.

NORMALIZATION OF RELATIONS Resumption of political contacts with or recognition of a foreign government with which relations had been severed. The reestablishment of political relations with the government of the People's Republic of China (PRC), formerly called "Red China," is responsible for this euphemism of 1979. The term functions by suggesting that tension or strife is an abnormality, and it is a more fastidious way of referring to what in the 1950s and 60s was also called THE TWO-CHINA POLICY (recognition of both Chiang Kai-shek's nationalist Republic of China on Taiwan and the PRC). That such a NORMALIZATION could be achieved was due in part to PING-PONG DIPLOMACY, a Cold War term (post-World War II) for implementing relations between China and the United States through the exchange of ping-pong teams. PING-PONG DIPLOMACY itself was a later phase of the Cultural Presentations Progam of the late 1950s, which exchanged entertainers, musicians and art exhibitions between the USSR and the United States in an attempt to alleviate Cold War tensions. The United States considered such exchanges IN ITS NATIONAL INTEREST (beneficial to American goals and needs) and felt that its contributions helped to PROCLAIM THE AMERICAN MESSAGE (propagandize).

ONE HOUSE BILL, A   A piece of legislation passed by either the House of Representatives or the Senate for public relations purposes. A ONE HOUSE BILL, which never becomes law, is one of the ways in which the United States Congress maintains its popularity, since legal lip service is paid to popular projects that no one really wishes to see brought to fruition. Congress tends to avoid both acting in a way and using language that will bring public censure; thus Congress seldom kills a bill. Instead, it RECOMMITS it, that is, sends it back to the committee that proposed it in the first place, thus effectively preventing its passage. It does not speak of taking a vacation but instead of entering A DISTRICT WORK PERIOD (a congressional recess during which a congressman ostensibly returns to take care of local interests in the district that has elected him). Congress does not openly provide patronage; instead a congressman or senator may give a loyal aide or campaigner A PLUM (a profitable or prestigious political position as a reward for service).

PEOPLE'S CAPITALISM   The American public's participation in the stock market. PEOPLE'S CAPITALISM is the New York Stock Exchange's revenge against PEOPLE'S DEMOCRACIES (q.v.). In the freedom-loving United States, Wall-Streeters used the expression in the early 1950s to indicate the vast extent of stock ownership among the ordinary American people.

PEOPLE'S DEMOCRACY, A A Communist nation. A PEOPLE'S DEMOCRACY, perhaps redundant since *demos* means people, is a favored Communist euphemism for a Marxist state. It is interchangeable with the equally euphemistic PEOPLE'S REPUBLIC but earlier in origin, since the term was first used in 1911 by Dr. Sun Yat-sen. But even PEOPLE'S DEMOCRACIES have been known to seek and obtain A SPHERE OF INFLUENCE, that is, a smaller or weaker nation or nations dominated by a more powerful one. A more recent variation on SPHERE OF INFLUENCE is SPHERE OF INTEREST (area of operations), more directly called SPHERE OF ACTION. PEOPLE'S DEMOCRACIES, as well as Western nations, have been known to seek A POLITICAL SOLUTION to their international problems. This doublespeak phrase may mean a military solution. When it does, it creates A CREDIBILITY GAP (the refusal to believe a political leader or nation, a phrase popularized in the Lyndon Johnson administration ca. 1964).

PERSONNEL CEILING REDUCTIONS Employment cutbacks. This bureaucratese of the 1970s masks the harsh reality of qualified candidates being unable to obtain government employment. Another disguise in the realm of government employment is embodied in the expression TO RIF, a 1960s acronym for "reduction in force"; originally a Washington expression, RIF has now spread to state capitols and other governmental centers. When employment or other problems affect entire government agencies, causing them to be subsumed by other bureaus or agencies, the process of losing autonomy is called A REDUCTION IN SELF-CONTAINED POWER CENTERS.

PUBLIC DIPLOMACY Information gathering from and influencing of foreign public opinion through non-official channels, a form of spying. A USIA (United States Information Agency) term for ascertaining and shaping foreign public opinion, PUBLIC DIPLOMACY is joined by FISH AND CHIPS DIPLOMACY, an American expression for making foreign nations buy United States fish products in exchange for allocating them surplus fish from United States fisheries. FISH AND CHIPS DIPLOMACY may be more generally understood as import-export quid pro quo relations.

QUARANTINE, A A unilateral embargo. When President John F. Kennedy used this euphemism for a blockade during the Cuban missile crisis (1962), he was drawing upon a much older tradition and meaning of the term. In 1937, Harold Ickes spoke of facism as a disease, which, he said, should be "quarantined." "Quarantine," familiar to English speakers as a word for a forty-day period of isolation to prevent those exposed to an infectious disease from contracting or spreading it, has been used since 1663. The oldest appearance of the term in English, however, dates from 1609, when it was used to describe a forty-day period following the death of her husband during which a widow had a right to remain in the "chief mansion house." Among the alternatives to quarantine as a political strategy is QUIET DIPLOMACY, a term coined in 1976 by Henry Kissinger to describe private or behind-the-scenes diplomatic relations.

RED TAPE Excessively elaborate and complex bureaucratic procedures required before an action much simpler than the procedure can be performed. Although RED TAPE is now a general metaphor for government forms and procedures that impede rather than permit actions, particularly bureaucratic ones, it is derived from the use of actual red tape to bind English government documents into packets. A stock item in the United States *Defense Supply Catalogue*, it is still described there as "Tape, pressure sensitive, adhesive, ¼ inch wide, 72 yards, 3 inch core, red. No. 634-3264. $1.14 per roll." RED TAPE is associated, particularly by anti-bureaucratic people, with THE ESTABLISHMENT (power structure, 1968). It is, in fact, endemic to all complex forms of organized government. The British, who invented RED TAPE, suffer from its linguistic offshoots when they deal with such procedural terms as EMPLOYER'S CERTIFICATE (pay form) and ENTITLEMENT (the right to money or money itself, also used in the United States).

REFLATION "Inflation on top of inflation." This definition by Margaret Thatcher describes a phenomenon that is current in America and England and is the mother of many euphemisms. Because countless nations are now suffering from DEFLATION (1919, U.S. term for what we now call A RECESSION), they have coined such terms as DISINFLATION (1947), STAGFLATION (somewhat pejorative and a coinage of the late 1960s meaning rising inflation combined with a stagnant economy and high unemployment), RECESSION (a 1950s American expression for an economic slump) and the ingenious ROLLING READJUSTMENT (a late 1970s term for recession). To combat such economic disasters many experts have suggested COUNTERCYCLICAL measures (a late 1970s American expression for anti-recessionary measures). All of these terms are meant to conceal that we are now living in A LEANER SOCIETY (Senator Gary Hart's 1980 expression for a country in the midst of a depression).

ROSE GARDEN STRATEGY, A The refusal of a United States president to participate in internal political activities while an international crisis is breaking. Already in the process of assuming a more general meaning, the phrase THE ROSE GARDEN STRATEGY originated during the Iranian hostage crisis of 1977. Senator Edward ("Ted") Kennedy accused President Carter of STAYING IN THE ROSE GARDEN (the famous White House garden) and refusing to debate American political problems until the hostages were free—in order to avoid jeopardizing his chances in the coming battle for the Democratic nomination. THE OVAL OFFICE, a metonymy for the president since the 1970s and as popular as the older WHITE HOUSE, might well have insisted that he needed to be close to his HOT LINE—the famous international telephone used for emergencies.

SCENARIO, A A scheme or plot. This American euphemism for a dangerous charade was used by John Dean III in his book *Blind Ambition* to describe the planned sequence of events in the Watergate break-in. During this episode, G. Gordon Liddy hung a sign on his door saying "plumbers" to conceal the activities of his group and disguise the break-in in which these agents participated to obtain the information. This small group of burglarizing spies was a part of A SPECIAL INVESTIGATORS UNIT, organized by John Ehrlichman for the purpose of stopping leaks of top-secret information to newspapers. It is probable that, had THE PLUMBERS obtained the documents they sought, they would have STERILIZED, SANITIZED or DECONTAMINATED them (i.e., effaced any identifying marks before using or circulating the materials). In the case of extremely dangerous or deleterious materials, they might have had TO DEEP SIX them (a term Ehrlichman used in 1973 when he advised Nixon to destroy evidence in the case). The Watergate PLUMBERS, like the CIA, went to great lengths to protect their FAMILY JEWELS (1977, most embarrassing secrets; see also Chapter 1, MALE GENITALS, JEWELS).

SCRUB, TO To censor or edit, particularly a political statement, for public consumption. In February 1982 President Reagan's press secretary excused some of the President's less pleasing and politic remarks by arguing that he MISSPEAKS (literally, "says what he does not mean" but actually "commits verbal indiscretions") because his speeches are sometimes not SCRUBBED (pre-screened). SCRUBBING is less serious than SANITIZING (removing damaging statements in a document, 1975) or LAUNDERING (whitewashing, deleting or covering illegal actions). People may also be SANITIZED—made to appear innocent when they are possibly guilty. When this failed in the case of Nixon's attorney general John Mitchell, Mitchell was forced to hire protection for both his MISSPEAKS and misdeeds. He sought the protection of what he called, for the first time, A SECURITY COORDINATOR (a bodyguard) and what we now call (1981) A PERSONAL SECURITY FORCE (group of bodyguards).

SPLENDID OSCILLATION Indecisiveness or ostrichlike disregard for a problem. In his speech on President Carter's foreign policy, then Senator George Bush coined this term to indicate that the President's behavior was a combination of oscillation and isolationism. To the South, the word

OSCILLATIONIST (pronounced in a Southern accent like "isolationist") means head-in-the-sand behavior. To the North, it means indecisiveness. To many, Woodrow Wilson seemed to be practicing a form of indecisive politics when he coined the phrase WATCHFUL WAITING (1913) to announce the importance of delaying any action that would draw the United States into war with Mexico. By 1936 any party member who did not agree with party policy would adopt a more extreme form of response by TAKING A WALK (Al Smith's expression for leaving the party when Roosevelt was nominated over him).

STONEWALL, TO   To obstruct justice, to cover up or conceal. This eponymous American euphemism is derived from Stonewall Jackson (1824–63) and the first Battle of Bull Run (1861), when a fellow officer described Jackson as "standing like a stone wall against his opponents." A STONEWALLER is one who obstructs and blocks his opponents with dogged determination. The expression has also been used in England, where it is associated with a stubborn defense in cricket, and in Australia and New Zealand, where it is associated with parliamentary filibustering. The phrase was repopularized (with the meanings listed in the definition above) in 1973 when President Nixon, in a recorded conversation, allegedly said, "I don't give a shit what happens. I want you all to stonewall it." One who neither STONEWALLS nor actively supports a measure is said in England to HOLD THE RING. At least since 1970, this has meant to stand by a conflict, political or military, without taking a stand or interfering. Barnhart suggests that its origin lies in boxing. One who HELD THE RING was part of a ring of onlookers at a fight. Another pugilistic metaphor lies behind the British euphemism FREE-FOR-ALLER, otherwise known as A DONNYBROOK. At least since 1968, the expression has been applied to politicians and others who ignore rules and regulations for their own advantage.

SUNSHINE LAW, A   A law requiring that deliberations of a legislative or administrative body be open to the public and press unless privacy or security dictate otherwise. In 1976 a GOVERNMENT IN THE SUNSHINE LAW was signed. This law, applying to all agencies headed by presidentially appointed commissioners, required free public and print media access to non-classified deliberations of the governing bodies. An expression that is metaphorically related but very different in actual meaning is SUNSET LAW. A SUNSET LAW requires that specified agencies disband at the end of a stipulated period; before they may resume their activities, they must justify their continuance. In short, this law limits the time period during which agencies or groups may operate. It requires that after the stipulated period, the agency in question must show cause why it should be reconstituted.

UDI; UNILATERAL DECLARATION OF INDEPENDENCE A declaration of national sovereignty and independence by a colony or territory without the consent of the mother country. UDI is one of the most delicate British euphemisms for what might be considered a political rebellion or revolution. It consists of a series of loaded terms. The first, of course, is unilateral, which literally means one-sided and has been used in the legal sense of a UNILATERAL AGREEMENT, for example, since 1802. A UNILATERAL AGREEMENT is not really an agreement but an independent decision of one party exclusive of the desires of the other. A declaration of independence, including the one related to THE MINOR INCIDENT of 1776, means a usurpation of the powers of the mother country, amounting to home rule. Sometimes, instead of UNILATERAL AGREEMENTS or declarations, nations will attempt to reach a modus vivendi through PROXIMITY TALKS. These are diplomatic negotiations carried on by a third party when the two nations in question do not have, or have broken off, diplomatic relations.

UEY, TO DO A To change one's political point of view. In Australia, since 1976, politicians who change their stripes have been accused of DOING A UEY or MAKING A U TURN. Diplomats, protected by their license plates, do indeed make U turns where others may not, and they have also been known TO WALK BACK THE CAT. This is American foreign service slang (1977) for retreating from a diplomatic position in negotiation or reducing one's demands. It is the diplomatic equivalent to the military STRATEGIC WITHDRAWAL TO THE REAR (retreat; see Chapter 9, STRATEGIES, **ROUTE OF EGRESS**) and may be the result of POLICY GUIDANCE, a polite way of describing orders given to one government agency by another and more powerful one. A longer-lived and still more common expression for DOING A UEY is DOING A FLIP-FLOP.

UNDEREMPLOYED PERSON, AN A person who does not hold a job commensurate with his ability. This phrase was developed by the government and the business world during the recent decade when thousands of highly educated people entered the employment market at the moment when the number of jobs for them declined drastically. UNDEREMPLOYED or UNDERUTILIZED PEOPLE are sometimes less euphemistically referred to as OVEREDUCATED.

VICUNA COAT, A An influence peddler. During the Eisenhower administration, presidential advisor Sherman Adams accepted a vicuna coat in payment for exercising his influence. Adams was forced to resign, but the term VICUNA COAT (1950s) lives on. Lobbying, sometimes conducted on the thin edge of legality, has been disguised as LEGISLATIVE ADVOCACY LEADERSHIP (1970s) and lobbyists who are powerful enough to be successful in the desert of Washington have been called RAINMAKERS since 1959.

9

The Game of War:
The Players, the Props,
the Strategies

"Retreat?" said a U.S. Pentagon official. "We don't have a word for that! We call it exfiltration, an adjustment of the front or a route of egress." "Well, we don't use that term," said his British counterpart, "but we are less euphemistic about it than you Americans are." He was right—to some extent at least—although the growth of shared international alliances like NATO and SEATO has eroded some of the distinctions in national vocabularies—if only on the official level. For example, in any country military officials know that A CONVENTIONAL WEAPON is a non-nuclear one and that AN ANTI-PERSONNEL WEAPON is one that destroys people, whether soldiers or civilians, rather than structures or installations, considered more strategically impressive.

The examples above illustrate one purpose of military euphemism, that of slanting language to minimize defeats, destruction, and the violence of war. Pentagonese, the official language of the Department of Defense, known in its own circle as the DOD, specializes in neologisms and mysterious sounding acronyms like ICBM, MIRV and MAD. Like the language of government, it depersonalizes, generalizes and abstracts.

The ordinary British TOMMY or American GI slogging his way through the muddy battlefield uses another language in addition to Pentagonese. He has his own brand of linguistic minimalization. Motivated by fear of the horrors he faces, he resorts to gallows humor. In his military euphemisms, a dead comrade has BOUGHT THE FARM, and friends who are injured beyond hope are sent to a division of the military hospital called by marines THE WHITE LIE WARD. Enlisted men create a psychological support system for themselves by sentimentalizing or humanizing their weapons with names. (We all remember the women's names painted on World War II planes like the Enola Gay.) And he will rename or nickname the military unit to which he belongs, often giving it an ironic title, as did THE RANCH HANDS—the Air Force defoliation unit in Vietnam, which adopted the motto, "Only you can prevent forests."

Although ordinary fighting men themselves tend to "christen" their implements of war, English officials tell us that, while the American Pentagon numbers and letters its weapons, like the M-109 tank, the British typically name them. The British equivalent of the M-109 is THE ABBOT. Perhaps this is because, as the British say, the American military establishment is newer, larger and more impersonal. The British war vocabulary, much of which was transmitted to America, is surprisingly old. RECONNAISSANCE, for example, is from 1810. Some terms date from the sixteenth century, and some were even adopted from ancient Roman military language. Part of the British military vocabulary is a survival of the army's days in India, beginning in the eighteenth century. The Englishman who serves tea to officers and soldiers may still be called the "char wallah."

Since the beginning of the nuclear age, vast efforts have been devoted to disguising the almost unbearable threat of human annihilation. Such efforts have raised euphemism to new heights, and it is significant that the multitudinous terms for nuclear strategies and techniques like DETERRENCE and FIRST STRIKE

CAPABILITY never mention the word "nuclear" or the implied possibility of extinction.

Attempts to avoid an all-out war have been partly responsible for the creation and growth of an elaborate military INTELLIGENCE (i.e., spying) organization. These aristocrats of strategy have coined their own complex language of PSYOP (psychological operations). Better known to the public than most military language, PSYOP terminology has been used and popularized in hundreds of spy novels. Furthermore, the media, in officially sponsored attempts to avoid full-scale war by minimalizing our "minor" military or spying operations, call a bloody battle on a national border AN INCIDENT. Francis Gary Powers's famous spying mission over Russia was euphemistically reduced to AN OVERFLIGHT.

It is the nature of the beast that all nations attempt to create the impression of innocence by justifying their military actions. In its own eyes no nation is ever the aggressor. Until the day when we beat our swords into ploughshares, we shall have an increasingly elaborate and ever-expanding lexicon of "justifying" euphemisms.

PLAYERS

ARMAMENT COMMUNITY, THE Weapons experts and purveyors. What used to be called MUNITIONS INTERESTS came, under the pressure of protest against the Vietnam War, to be called THE ARMAMENT COMMUNITY. (See **DEFENSE INTELLECTUALS**.) This United States community, particularly the nuclear power portion of it, was responsible in the late 1960s and 1970s for coining such terms as A RAPID OXIDATION for a fire and ENERGETIC DISASSEMBLY (1979) for an explosion, particularly a nuclear explosion. In the same terminology AN ALL OUT STRATEGIC EXCHANGE is a pleasanter way of discussing total nuclear war. Those British who are interested not only in nuclear war but in military strategy in general have reversed the usual American linguistic practice of making work seem like play by suggesting that the frivolous-sounding WAR GAMES (mock military maneuvers and engagements) be called by a more serious name—WAR STUDIES.

BEST; BEHAVIORAL SKILLS TRAINING, A U.S. Navy program for incompetent and unproductive sailors. Sailors in the U.S. Navy who are, to paraphrase *All Hands* (the Navy in-house magazine), incapable of "completing their enlistment" or not up to "acceptable levels of performance" are remediated through this program and can now meet requirements presumably as the BEST. This is a military equivalent of the civilian practice of calling slow learners EXCEPTIONAL CHILDREN (1960s) and dubbing their schools SPECIAL (1960s) or DEVELOPMENTAL (1970s).

BOUGHT IT Died in action. The origin of the British and American expression is uncertain, but it probably comes from the English phrase for paying a penalty BOUGHT IT DEARLY, which appears as early as 1250. An American variant is TO BUY THE FARM (pre–World War II), which is fully explained in e. e. cummings' poem "nobody loses all the time," in which "uncle sol," a failure at every farm he buys in life, succeeds only after death by starting a worm farm. Both these terms reflect the servicemen's feelings that they are considered EXPENDABLE (W. H. White, *They Were Expendable*, U.S., 1942)—a depersonalization of the dead, who were referred to in eighteenth-century English sailors' jargon as EXPENDED. Another expression for dead with financial undertones is the current United States military euphemism ACCOUNTED FOR or killed, as in the phrase "Ten were accounted for."

CASUALTY, A A wounded or dead person in a war; a dead soldier. This euphemism, which has made a statistic of the American dead since the Civil War, has been used to designate military losses by death, desertion or sickness since 1494. However, since World War II, United States armed forces have encountered more cold-hearted terms for death. The Nazis acquainted the world with THE FINAL SOLUTION, EVACUATION, SPECIAL TREATMENT and RESETTLEMENT for genocide. Vietnam familiarized us with FRAGGING (see **FRAG**).

The nuclear establishment has coined the term MEGADEATH—the death of a million—since 100 MEGADEATHS sound much less serious than what they equal—one hundred million people dead.

COMPANY, THE The Central Intelligence Agency. THE COMPANY, an informal name for the CIA, is based, Hugh Rawson says, on the older name for the British Secret Intelligence Service or SIS, THE FIRM or THE OLD FIRM—a term that the readers of John le Carré know well. *Cia* is also the Spanish abbreviation for "company." The jargon of THE INTELLIGENCE SERVICES—be they the CIA or the British MI 5 (known to fans of James Bond)—is, as might be expected, always covert. For example, the acronym for AGENTS (spies) favored by THE INTELLIGENCE COMMUNITY is HUMINT. Those whom AGENTS watch, whose phones they tap and whose mail they open, are TARGETS. In intelligence lingo AN ASSET is not the opposite of a liability but the INTELLIGENCE COMMUNITY's term for such SURVEILLANCE (spying) devices as LISTENING POSTS and MONITORING STATIONS (places close to hostile countries in which radar and other technical means may be used for spying). A SHEEP DIP or SHEEP DIPPING is the use of a military person or instrument in a civilian capacity or under civilian COVER. Safire notes that the term SHEEP DIPPING is also used for the placing of individuals in organizations or groups in order to collect information about them or similar groups. MAIL COVER is postal spying, in effect the opening of mail. All of these activities are performed by what are now called OPERATIVES. AN OPERATIVE, the newer form of OPERATOR, is of course a spy or secret agent and was originally associated with the Pinkerton agency, which used it in 1905 to replace the more vulgar "detective." INTELLIGENCE is itself a euphemism that has meant the secret communications of spies or secret or private agents since 1587. United States OPERATIVES are entitled to some protection or COVER; therefore they receive INTELLIGENCE IDENTITY PROTECTION under House Bill 5615. Those TARGETS they trap are less fortunate and are ILL (arrested on suspicion or for interrogation or jailed) or IN THE HOSPITAL (in jail).

DEFENSE INTELLECTUALS   Policy makers and strategy planners of our DEFENSE ESTABLISHMENT (see **NOTIONALS**). The role of America's DEFENSE INTELLECTUALS was described by Herman Kahn, the social scientist, as THINKING ABOUT THE UNTHINKABLE (pondering and planning total nuclear war). America's DEFENSE INTELLECTUALS have consisted of such formidable scientists as the father of the atom bomb, J. Robert Oppenheimer, the father of the hydrogen bomb, Edward Teller, and social scientists Kissinger and Wohlstetter. Among the strategies that might be originated by DEFENSE INTELLECTUALS are DECOUPLING (a British euphemism for separating and isolating a nation from its allies) and TRIAGE. TRIAGE (from the French *trier*, to pick or cull) is a word whose original meaning was innocent but later assumed more sinister implications. In the eighteenth century it meant to sort according to quality and was applied to wool, coffee and other inanimate objects. By World War I, it had come to mean a method for deciding which of the wounded would benefit from, and should therefore be administered, the limited treatment available. A TRIAGE was a sorting station for the wounded where they were divided according to the severity of their wounds (1930). Since 1976, TRIAGE has meant deciding, on the basis of their strength, which nations will be politically and militarily aided and which will be left to destruction.

FIRE BRIGADE, A   A military unit that is extremely mobile and is therefore designed to handle emergencies such as sudden enemy attacks. In U.S. military slang, particularly since the Vietnam era, A FIRE BRIGADE has been the euphemism describing a unit that, like firemen, can be rushed to any location where there is trouble. The related but less euphonious British term is SNATCH SQUAD or ADVANCE SQUAD—a group organized to put down a riot by capturing (snatching) its leaders. Equally mysterious is the British MONITORING FORCE comprised of security troops who enforce a cease-fire (see **SOURCE**, MONITORING).

FIRST SKIRT, THE   The commanding officer in a WAC

(Women's Army Corps) company. In these days of an increased female component in the armed services, women have created their own equivalents for the older male military euphemisms. THE FIRST SKIRT in a WAC company is, of course, the female version of THE TOP BRASS in a male army unit. *SSAM* (*Soldier, Sailor, Airman, Marine,* September 1980), a newspaper for enlisted persons, reports that the old male NCO boast, "I'm not afraid of any colonel, he puts his pants on the same way I do," has a very contemporary female version, "I don't sweat the first skirt, she puts her pantyhose on the same way I do." The former WAVES, now the Women's Naval Corps, a unit of the U.S. Navy, may share the euphemism FIRST SKIRT for CO (commanding officer), but they have a special nautical euphemism for an NCO (noncommissioned officer). Although we assume that not every wave is a big shot, since World II a naval NCO has been called A RIPPLE.

FRAG, TO To kill a fellow soldier or officer by setting off a fragmentation grenade. FRAGGING or murdering one's officers by means of A FRAGMENTATION DEVICE was a frequent occurrence in both the Korean POLICE ACTION (so called because the United States Congress never declared war) and the Vietnamese CONFLICT. It differed from TAKING (SOMEONE) OUT since the latter means to destroy the enemy rather than one's unpleasant, fellow countrymen.

FREE A MAN FOR DUTY, TO To use women in non-combatant roles. This military evasion of both truth and the responsibility for it implies that duty is only active and that women who serve in non-combatant capacities are there to make useful people available. It is current.

FREEDOM FIGHTER, A A guerilla, an "irregular" soldier. One man's guerilla is another man's FREEDOM FIGHTER, and the latter term, in use since 1942, has largely replaced the older euphemism PARTISAN, which dated from 1692 (and was replaced by guerilla only after World War II). Guerilla itself, now thought of as non-euphemistic, was originally used by the Duke of Wellington between 1810 and 1815 (as an adjective modifying war) to mean a small war, rather than as a noun to mean a soldier (*guerrillero*) who fought it. In addition to FREEDOM FIGHTERS, men who soldier in wars may be CIVILIAN IRREGULAR DEFENSE FORCES (mercenaries, a word dating from 1583 for professional soldiers serving a foreign power for payment). Hiring mercenaries has been called GREENBACKING, since GREENBACKS are United States dollars and were used for paying some of the soldiers (from any nation) who were hired by the United States to fight in Vietnam.

INTERNEE, AN A prisoner, civilian or military, in a prison camp. INTERNEES or INTERNS were those, mainly second-generation Japanese Americans, who were imprisoned, usually on suspicion alone, in RELOCATION CENTERS or INTERNMENT CAMPS during World War II. Disgraceful as it was, INTERNMENT was not as destructive as the more innocent-sounding PROTECTIVE CUSTODY, from 1933 on a German euphemism for imprisonment in a concentration camp. The British DETAINED (imprisoned) aliens and suspected spies during World War II, and both they and other nations have used the technique of TRANSFER OF POPULATION—mass eviction or deportation—popularized if not coined by George Orwell in "Politics and the English Language" (1946). However, when British citizens were endangered by falling bombs, they were EVACUATED to ALTERNATIVE ACCOMMODATION UNITS, the less frightening term in 1940s bureaucratese for accommodations or areas in less danger of bombing.

KATE KARNEY Army; also a member of the British army. The British army itself and a member of it are, in rhyming slang, KATE KARNEY. The ordinary British infantryman—brother or at least cousin to the American GI JOE (World War II)—is A TOMMY or TOMMY ATKINS (1883, at first in the form THOMAS ATKINS, the specimen name on official army forms since 1815; the British JOHN DOE). A Canadian soldier of the same rank and status has been called A JOHNNY CANUCK at least since the 1950s—the name is also a personification of Canada similar to America's UNCLE SAM—and Canadians call a new recruit A JOHNNY RAW, a term that was formerly used in the British army (see Kipling). The opposite of a JOHNNY RAW in the

United States is A LIFER. This term for a career soldier or officer who expects to spend his life in the armed services is derived, amusingly, from the prison term for a person serving a life sentence in an American prison (early 1800s).

MEMORIAL SERVICES The U.S. Army department in charge of registering and keeping account of army graves throughout the world. MEMORIAL SERVICES, a name much in keeping with undertakers' euphemisms, is a new official title of the department formerly called Graves Registration. Yet another new official U.S. Army term is DINING FACILITY. It replaces the older and certainly more graphic "mess hall."

MP Military Police. *SSAM* (*Soldier, Sailor, Airman, Marine,* August 1980) cities the *Acronyms, Initialisms and Abbreviations Dictionary,* which lists over seventy meanings for the abbreviation MP. It can even mean MELTING POINT—the point at which a prisoner breaks down after being grilled by a military policeman. POV can mean plane of vibration or peak of operating voltage as well as privately owned vehicle. In military language, where acronyms abound, a single one can have several meanings—even DOD. This customary acronym for the Department of Defense has at least seven other military meanings, among which are died of disease and depth of discharge. Acronyms constitute such a large portion of military speech that a conversation may be as unintelligible to the ordinary civilian as the one *SSAM* reports: "Hey, the CO [see **FIRST SKIRT**] wants to see the PFC [Private First Class] down at the MP shack about a DWI [driving while intoxicated] in a POV [privately owned vehicle]." In many of these cases, acronyms are not merely abbreviations but disguises for illegal, frightening or secret references; therefore they function as euphemisms.

NOTIONALS Fictitious companies or businesses that serve as COVERS for intelligence agents. THE INTELLIGENCE COMMUNITY (1976), itself a euphemism for our espionage bureau, earlier called THE INTELLIGENCE ESTABLISHMENT (see **DEFENSE INTELLECTUALS**), has found it necessary to provide fictitious identities and occupations for the spies it employs. Through a technique called BACKSTOPPING, it gives AGENTS seemingly true but really false identities and occupations and thus provides them with credibility. It may do this through the creation of NOTIONALS or of PROPRIETARIES. The latter are real companies capable of doing business, but they serve and may be controlled by the intelligence agency. A more concrete form of protection is the creation of A SAFE HOUSE. Known to every reader of spy stories, this is a residence that looks innocent but is "in reality" a safe meeting place for spies.

OLD NEWTON TOOK HIM or GOT HIM He died in a military airplane crash. Since 1925, this has been one of the RAF's more ingenious expressions for death from the pull of gravity. A contemporary American expression for the same fate is THUD. In American Army parlance since World War II, HE BOUGHT IT or ONE has been a clear albeit somewhat indirect way of saying "He was killed" or, more brutally, ZAPPED. If the soldier was killed by a bullet, probably the indirect referent of "it" or "one," his fellow soldiers might say IT HAD HIS NAME ON IT. Today, a member of the Air Force can be sure that he will never BUY ONE if there are CLEAN SKIES—the condition of the airways after the enemy air force has been obliterated.

PVS; POST-VIETNAM SYNDROME Serious readjustment problems. At the end of 1981, Time magazine interviewed some twenty-five members of a U.S. Army unit to determine how they had fared since their return to America after the Vietnam War. The overwhelming response to questions was that their lives had been altered irrevocably, usually for the worse. Many had nightmares, others were violent or self-destructive and many could not adapt to civilian life. The catchall phrase for the devastation they experienced is PVS. A related term, used much earlier and in England, is SERVICE CONNECTED or SERVICE RELATED DISABILITY. This neutralizing phrase initially meant a war injury but was later expanded to include any permanent disabling injury or disease incurred while on or aggravated by active duty.

QUEEN'S SHILLING, TO TAKE THE   To enlist in the British armed forces. British soldiers have TAKEN THE QUEEN'S SHILLING since the time of Queen Elizabeth I, when they were paid a shilling for their military services. If a soldier changed his mind and wished to leave, he had to repay both the enlistment shilling and twenty others as his SMART MONEY (damages or forfeit). Nowadays, British soldiers stationed in INSECURE AREAS (embattled regions) or undeclared combat zones like Northern Ireland are likely to find a shilling insufficient pay indeed, hence it has become merely a symbol.

RALLIER or RETURNEE, A   A Viet Cong deserter. Those who betrayed or left the Viet Cong and RALLIED to the Allied side in the Vietnam War were considered, by the Pentagon, people who had at last COME ROUND or RETURNED TO THE FOLD (late 1960s).

RANCH HANDS, THE   The name of the special Air Force unit that flew defoliation missions in South Vietnam. Michael Herr publicized this in-group name in his brilliant and plain-talking book *Dispatches* (1977). He explains that the name of the unit arose from the fact that their motto was: "Only you can prevent forests." Defoliation, a much-favored military term during the Vietnam War, is itself obfuscating. Although it describes the removal of leaves from trees, it ignores the destruction of other living things within a forested area and the permanence of such destruction. We are, however, PACIFIED (see STRATEGIES, **PACIFY**) by two brilliant definitions in the *Dictionary of Military and Associated Terms* (the official Pentagon lexicon known as *DMAT*). "Defoliant operations" are "the employment of defoliating agents on vegetated areas in support of military operations"—in other words, clearing away the forests so you can see the trees. "A defoliating agent" is defined as "a chemical which causes trees, shrubs, and other plants to shed their leaves prematurely." Such premature aging looks to the naked eye like permanent winter.

REGIMENTAL RESTAURANT, THE   The mess hall house. In Britain what American military official language calls "the mess hall" or, more recently, THE DINING FACILITY, has been lately transformed from a mess house or cook house to A REGIMENTAL RESTAURANT. British military washing rooms are elegantly described as ABLUTIONS FACILITIES. The British soldier who does KP is AT DUTIES or, less frequently, AT DIXIE (a large metal cooking pot). But these evasions are minor compared to the official but almost never used American terms for shovel: A COMBAT EMPLACEMENT EVACUATOR, A DIGGING INSTRUMENT or AN ENTRENCHING TOOL.

SERVICES NO LONGER REQUIRED Dishonorable or other than honorable discharge. Ever since 1943, when either an Australian or British serviceman has been sent back from the war as a failure, he has been able to resort to this term. But an Australian sent home for a misdemeanor is called A SNARLER. Both British and American servicemen who are LET OUT under less than ideal circumstances undergo AN OTHER THAN HONORABLE DISCHARGE or LESS THAN HONORABLE DISCHARGE. The reasons for being RIFFED, an acronym for REDUCTION IN FORCE (meaning fired or discharged in American English), may be manifold. They may include failure to pass HEALTH, WELFARE AND MORALE INSPECTIONS (an American expression for barracks bed-check) or more heinous violations of the military code for which American sailors, for instance, might be confined to the CORRECTIONAL CENTER (brig) and subsequently subjected to A GENERAL DISCHARGE (bad conduct discharge). A far preferable way to leave the service is by getting AN EARLY OUT, leaving the service before one's term is over, especially on medical grounds.

SOURCE, A The intelligence community term for a spy or a person who provides secret information. This word is an American and British euphemism for AN AGENT (itself a euphemism from "secret service agent," British by 1900). Usually a foreigner, A SOURCE is always engaged in COVERT OPERATIONS or OBSERVATION (spying). He is part of a larger non-official network of communication called THE BACKCHANNEL (Henry Kissinger favored this term but it was in official use by about 1971). Among the techniques sources may use to gain information are: MONITORING (eavesdropping, spying), often conducted by means of various forms of TECHNICAL SURVEILLANCE (spying by using technological devices such as TELEPHONE LISTENING DEVICES or bugs which may be DEMUTED or turned up to a higher volume); LONG RANGE SURVEILLANCE (watching or spying by means of radar); and telemetry (monitoring radio signals of missiles and using satellites to photograph unfriendly territory). TECHNICAL SURVEILLANCE, which is also called ELECTRONIC PENETRATION, is distinguished by United States government agents who use the term both from simple SURVEILLANCE (spying) and from the more direct TECHNICAL TRESPASS (a break-in by U.S. agents, late 1970s and probably of Watergate origin). All of the preceding operations are part of TECHNICAL COLLECTION SYSTEMS (non-human mechanical spying devices). Surveillance (1815) and OBSERVATION (1836) are nineteenth-century British military terms for spying upon or closely watching an enemy.

WHITE LIE WARD, THE   The Marine Corps name for the Danang hospital ward devoted to hopeless cases. Michael Herr (*Dispatches*, 1977) points to the irony of this name for the segment of the hospital where "they take cases so bad that they will never be the same again." We assume that the doctors and other officers were not guilty of cruel deception but were attempting to be kind when they told the patients LITTLE WHITE LIES. On the same humane principles, when an American serviceman died, his mother became A GOLD STAR MOTHER (since World War II). If a South Vietnamese soldier was killed, his family was honored with A CONDOLENCE AWARD—COMPENSATION or what, in the earlier times of primitive blood feuds and battles, was called "blood money" (Old English, *wergilt*, literally "man money").

PROPS

ANTI-PERSONNEL WEAPON   A weapon directed against enemy soldiers or populace. The *Dictionary of Military and Associated Terms* (U.S. Pentagon), NATO and SEATO currently define ANTI-PERSONNEL MINES as mines "designed to cause casualties to personnel." The linguistic trick here is that of disguising human beings as faceless collective PERSONNEL. Collective nouns, not people, are thus destroyed. In Vietnam, special bombs designed to explode (often at waist level) and send thousands of flechettes into the victim(s) were called ANTI-PERSONNEL BOMBS.

BLACK RADIO Radio broadcasts in which one nation in conflict with another masquerades as the voice of its opponent. This American euphemism for one technique of psychological warfare was used by Major General Rollen in a memo during 1964 in which he reported the repetition of thirty-minute daily programs allegedly broadcast by dissident elements in North Vietnam. Actually, the broadcasters were Americans and their allies. One possible consequence of such a measure is BLOWBACK, coined in an analogy to "feedback" in electronics and to "blowby" in the automotive industry. BLOWBACK is more crudely described in America as BLACK PROPAGANDA or DISINFORMATION (from the Russian *desinformatsiya,* 1960s and 1970s), deliberate falsehoods that get back to and are believed by the country of their origin. BLOWBACK is also known as FALLOUT and DOMESTIC REPLAY. The GRANNY SYNDROME, a British euphemism, is an example of MISINFORMATION rather than DISINFORMATION. It is a euphemism for incorrect intelligence materials, particularly those that come from the GRAPEVINE (originally a gossip network but, by the late 1970s and the Rhodesian civil war, used to mean friends and associates).

CONVENTIONAL WEAPON, A A non-nuclear weapon. Among the British names for CONVENTIONAL or non-nuclear WEAPONS are those for types of planes—THE NIMROD (after the mighty biblical hunter), THE HAWK and THE TORNADO; and those for tanks: THE ABBOT (equivalent to the American M-109), THE CHIEFTAIN, CHALLENGER, CONQUEROR, CENTURION and FOX. Although Americans tend to number rather than name their weapons, they do tend to name ships and missiles, and we are all acquainted with THE POSEIDON (after the Greek sea god), TRIDENT and POLARIS submarines and THE MINUTE MAN, SENTINEL, ATLAS and TRITON missiles. A favorite American device for concealing the nature of a given weapon is to coin an acronym. SAMs are surface to air missiles; HARMS (HIGH SPEED ANTIRADIATION MISSILE SYSTEM) are missiles that home in on a radiation source; FOBS (fractional orbital bombardment systems) are nuclear weapons in which warheads are delivered to targets on earth from an orbiting space satellite; and MIRVs (MULTIPLE INDEPENDENTLY TARGETED REENTRY VEHICLES) are missiles that have more than one warhead, each of which can be aimed at a separate target.

COUNTERFORCE WEAPONS Nuclear missiles to be used against enemy forces. This current American euphemism has a companion in COUNTERVALUE WEAPONS, which are nuclear missiles aimed at cities. Those that might be called HEAVY (MISSILES) have a heavy THROW WEIGHT (the amount of THE PAYLOAD—megatons of actual nuclear material that can be sent aloft). In 1981, President Reagan proposed RACETRACKING—the moving of missiles to various American launching emplacements in random and unpredictable ways—a program that would be an MBS (multiple base system) entailing the shifting of missiles from one SILO (underground missile storage site) to another. However, the DELIVERY VEHICLES and SYSTEMS (missiles and other machines for carrying nuclear warheads and bombs) have not yet been RACETRACKED; therefore, most of them remain in HARDENED SILOS (heavily reinforced underground launching sites).

DERRY AND TOMS Bombs. This British rhyming slang expression was popularized during World War II and the London Blitz. The allusion here is to a famous but now defunct London store of that name; however, TO DERRY and TO HAVE A DERRY ON mean to dislike or hate. More dangerous than being hit by an ordinary DERRY AND TOM is encountering AN ENHANCED RADIATION WEAPON or A CLEAN BOMB (an Americanism for the neutron bomb which leaves everything standing and destroys only people). CLEAN BOMB, a weapon with RADIATION ENHANCEMENT, won the 1977 Doublespeak Award of the National Council of Teachers of English for its skillful evasion of the neutron bomb's ORDNANCE SUCCESS (efficacy of destructiveness). Bomb squads are still called, in the American armed forces, EOD MEN. Their area of expertise is in EXPLOSIVE ORDNANCE DISPOSAL. ORDNANCE itself is an ancient word for military materials, stores or supplies (1390) and RECOVERED ORDNANCE is a term still used for the bombs that the EOD finds and defuses. The British version of a bomb squad has been a UXB (unexploded bomb) SQUAD or BRIGADE since the 1940s. The exploits of such a group have recently been popularized in a television series entitled "Danger: UXB."

ECM; ELECTRONIC COUNTERMEASURES This American euphemism for spying by electronic means (also known as ELECTRONIC RECONNAISSANCE) includes such techniques as ELECTRONIC DECEPTION (using technical means to mislead the enemy by tampering or interfering with his own electronic equipment) and jamming. (For further material, see PLAYERS, **SOURCE**.) The information gained is not part of THE BOOK, information about the enemy found in open sources, a still current expression probably originating in the police term THE BOOK (see Chapter 6, COPS AND ROBBERS, **PAT DOWN**, THROWING THE BOOK AT).

FRIENDLY GRENADE, A A grenade inadvertently thrown or dropped by one's own troops and often on them. Mario Pei, in his book *Doublespeak,* notes that a friendly grenade is just as dangerous as a hostile one. FRIENDLY GRENADES are but one example of what the British call DROPPING SHORT (dropping ammunition into one's own lines). A British informant argues that for a gunner A DROP SHORT is not a euphemism (see STRATEGIES, **NEGLECT**). More euphemistic but equally deadly, though much quieter, is the NONDISCERNIBLE MICRO-BIONOCULATOR, a poison dart gun developed by the CIA. It is silent, electronically operated, and (Rawson says) can shoot a dart about 100 meters.

NERVE AGENT, A A gas or other substance that attacks the nervous system, used in chemical warfare. NERVE AGENT is one of a number of British military euphemisms in use since about 1970 for chemical weapons. The British refer to CW AGENTS (chemical warfare agents) and describe them as PERSISTENT, meaning lasting, and NONPERSISTENT, meaning temporary. One specific agent, tear gas, is known in England (since 1968) as CS. It is from the compound orthochlorbenzalmalontrie, first synthesized in the United States in the 1920s. In general, the British refer to their capacity for conducting chemical and germ warfare as THE OFFENSIVE CHEMICAL CAPABILITY. Americans speak of SELECTIVE ORDNANCE. This last term is specifically used for various compounds utilizing napalm such as incendijel and incinderjell. Incinderjell is a combination of jellied gasoline and napalm and is used in flame throwers and fire bombs. All these compounds would be called, in American military slang, INCAPS, a shortening of incapacitating chemical agents or drugs (1968), and to protect one's soldiers from them, one would place them in FULL MOPP. MOPP, an abbreviation of MISSION ORIENTATION PROTECTIVE POSTURE, might include both weapons and a special suit, boots, gloves, protective mask and helmet (1970s).

STRATEGIES

ACTIVE AIR DEFENSE   Keeping enemy planes out of one's area by attacking them or defending the area with planes. The Pentagon's *Dictionary of Military and Associated Terms*, a complete manual of the art of making war, defines ACTIVE AIR DEFENSE as the "employment of a limited offensive action and counterattacks to deny a contested area or position to the enemy." In simple language, this means attacking and destroying an adversary before he can get you. The action is always aggressive and may be offensive, but it is always referred to as "defense." A similar euphemistic effect is achieved by another Department of Defense expression, CLOSE AIR SUPPORT. This term, which means supporting allied troops by bombing nearby enemy planes or ground troops with your planes (1974), stresses its supportive rather than destructive functions. Other military expressions that became euphemistic because of what they do not mention are STRATEGIC LIFT OPERATIONS and PREPOSITIONING. The former, indeed, suggests that men and supplies will be transported. It does not, however, indicate that their destination is a battle. PREPOSITIONING, or moving heavy equipment and supplies to a potential crisis area, again does not indicate the purpose of such movement, a possible attack.

ADJUSTMENT OF THE FRONT, AN　A retreat. Hugh Rawson notes that in about 250 B.C., the Macedonian commander Antigonus Gonatas refused to admit that he had retreated and described his actions as A STRATEGIC MOVEMENT TO THE REAR. This term is still in use (see **ROUTE OF EGRESS**) and is now often also described as AN ADJUSTMENT TO THE FRONT. Since the 1950s, our army, which never retreats, has conducted RETROGRADE MANEUVERS or WITHDRAWALS, REDEPLOYED ITS FORCES and even RETIRED with dignity intact. When surrounded or trapped by a hostile enemy, our army does not panic, it EXFILTRATES (from infiltration in a military sense, 1930s, and the action or process of filtering out, 1897). This recently coined military antonym of "infiltrate" has been in use since the 1960s as a description of a stealthy escape from an enemy zone.

AIR TO AIR ENCOUNTERS　What, in World War II, was called a dogfight (two planes shooting it out). In the United States–Libya incident in 1981 this was called an AIR TO AIR ENCOUNTER. GROUND TO AIR ENCOUNTERS occur when anti-aircraft missiles shoot at planes or airborne weapons or missiles. AIR TO GROUND ENCOUNTERS occur when missiles are fired from planes to the ground. To avoid the need for all of the above, American military strategists suggest AIR INTERDICTION. This elaborate circumlocution means preventive long-distance bombing or shooting from the air by defeating an enemy and destroying his air and ground weapons before one's own troops are close enough to be injured or hit by FRIENDLY FIRE (see PROPS, **FRIENDLY GRENADE**).

ASYMMETRIC CAPACITY　The condition that exists when

another nation (or nations) has a greater nuclear striking force than ours has. The term ASYMMETRIC CAPACITY is but one of the many that disguise the blatant fact that *they* have more weapons than we have. In this case, the weapon superiority is A COUNTERFORCE CAPABILITY (see **SECOND STRIKE CA-PABILITY** and PROPS, **COUNTERFORCE WEAPON**), that is, the ability to strike back after being attacked with nuclear weapons. The United States is now engaged in A STRATEGIC COMPETITION (arms race) in preparation for a possible BI-POLAR SUPERPOWER CONFRONTATION (a nuclear war between two major, i.e., nuclear powers).

BORDER INCIDENT, A A brief military confrontation, frequently involving casualties, somewhere near national boundaries. The U.S. Pentagon's *Dictionary of Military and Associated Terms* and the military publications of all countries in the inter-American system of military alliances define INCIDENTS as "brief clashes or other military disturbances generally of a transitory nature and not involving protracted hostilities." During some recent BORDER INCIDENTS in Afghanistan and Israel, nationals on both sides were maimed and killed. The euphemism disguises the violence and fatality by substituting the word INCIDENT for "bloody battle"; it attempts to reassure us that quicker is not merely better but negligible. The word "border," although sometimes used to designate an area one hundred miles or more inside the country, allays our fears that the consequences may be fatal or major.

COLLATERAL DAMAGE The unintentional destruction of civilians in a nuclear attack. Since 1374, "collateral" has meant that which is aside from the main subject, line of action or purpose of something. In the nuclear era, COLLATERAL DAMAGE means the destruction of people, cities and resources as a result of nuclear fallout, imprecise targeting or plain error. The MEGADEATHS (millions of deaths) that COLLATERAL DAMAGE may entail are not represented in the term.

FLUTTERING An INTELLIGENCE COMMUNITY term for administering a lie detector test to one's own agents to determine their loyalty. It is often given to ascertain if an agent is a MOLE—a foreign spy deliberately placed in one's own national intelligence agency. Safire says that the term was either coined or reported by John le Carré in his espionage novel *The Spy Who Came in from the Cold*.

FORCE DE FRAPPE or DE DISSUASION   A striking force, especially a nuclear one. Even a destructive capability can sound attractive if it is discussed in French. These two expressions, the second of which is more euphemistic, mean a striking force and a force capable of what in America is called "unfriendly persuasion." They are part of the body that implements the concept of DETERRENCE (see **SECOND STRIKE CAPABILITY** and **MAD**). This term goes back as far as 1916 despite the fact that it is generally thought to be of recent origin. Such forces as those striking bodies described above are of paramount importance in MEETING ENGAGEMENTS (collisions between opposing forces in which speed is the principal requirement for victory). The same kind of thinking that created FORCE DE FRAPPE and FORCE DE DISSUASION has produced the euphemism for a hostile act (bombing, invasion etc.), PROTECTIVE REACTION. This 1960s term was used to describe offensive as well as defensive acts.

INCREMENTALISM   The gradual build-up of military attacks. Since 1966, TO ESCALATE has lost its primary meaning (to increase) and become a military euphemism for intensifying activities in war. INCREMENTALISM is really gradual ESCALATION, and it was used by Lyndon Johnson's administration (1963–69) to describe attacks made in Vietnam to persuade the enemy to make peace. More recently, the ESCALATION of the production of armaments has been described as a STRATEGIC MODERNIZATION PROGRAM. Again, the euphemism does not mention that many of the arms updated and manufactured are nuclear. A STRATEGIC MODERNIZATION PROGRAM is expected to result in SYSTEMATIZED INCREMENTAL CAPABILITIES, a planned, orderly military build-up that will conclude in HORIZONTAL ESCALATION—widening warfare.

MAD   MUTUAL ASSURED DESTRUCTION. This American term

was coined by Donald Brennan of the Hudson Institute in 1969 to stand for an all-out bilateral nuclear war and its consequences. The elegant and genteel name for an all-out nuclear attack is DOCTRINE OF DETERRENCE, and it has many advocates who consider the strategy sane (see **SECOND STRIKE CAPABILITY**). In practice, the DOCTRINE OF DETERRENCE would not simply create A CENTER OF ASPIRATIONS, Nixonese for "target," or concentrate upon SURGICAL or PRECISION BOMBING (neither surgical nor very precise, perhaps accurate but very messy). It would be no PROTECTIVE REACTION (the 1970 military term for bombing raids against anti-aircraft installations). Instead, it would mean UNACCEPTABLE DAMAGE. This is destruction from an enemy second strike sufficiently massive to prevent retaliation. It is presumably total destruction as opposed to ACCEPTABLE LOSSES and ACCEPTABLE DAMAGE, casualties that would still leave our army standing.

NEGLECT The command to disregard the last firing order executed and wait for a new one. In official parlance (*Dictionary of Military and Associated Terms*), NEGLECT is defined as "a report to the observer or spotter to indicate that the last round was fired with incorrect data and that the round(s) will be fired again, using correct data." What "neglect" really means is: "We gave you the wrong information, fellas, so you hit the wrong and/or missed the right target. Forget it and wait for new orders!" In the armed forces such a situation might be called a SNAFU—one of the military acronyms for a mistake (see **TOFU**).

OVERFLIGHT, AN An illegal flight, often for the purpose of espionage, over hostile territory. The most famous OVERFLIGHT was that made by Francis Gary Powers in the U-2 plane flying over Russia (1960), but the euphemism had been used earlier (1949) by the CIA. OVERFLIGHTS are more difficult when there are NATIONAL TECHNICAL MEANS OF VERIFICATION or devices such as spy satellites and long-range radar that can monitor all planes to ascertain that the country's security agreements are being complied with.

PACIFY, TO   To lay waste or destroy territory in a war. An American euphemism created during the Vietnam War, PACIFICATION is anything but peaceful since it implies bombing, defoliation and the forcible evacuation of native populations. The Vietnam War, officially known as the Vietnam POLICE ACTION (a term popularized by Harry Truman to describe the Korean War, which could not be called a war because it was never legally declared by Congress) was more than AN INCIDENT (1937, see **BORDER INCIDENT**). It is more accurately classified as a LIMITED WAR (an American expression for an OVERT MILITARY CONFRONTATION or OVERT MILITARY CONFLICT, that is, a war) since its size and intensity is controlled by the opponents. For some Americans " 'Nam" seemed only AN UNFORTUNATE INTERRUPTION. This expression was originally coined by the Germans speaking of World War II, which they thought of as causing A TEMPORARY BREACH in their relations with the British (Jane Kramer, *New Yorker* 3:20, 1978).

PRE-EMPTIVE STRIKE, A   A surprise attack. A sneak attack is just not cricket, but describing it as A PRE-EMPTIVE STRIKE makes it a little more acceptable. This term, popularized by President Kennedy in the Cuban missile crisis of 1962, is one of many designed to remove the responsibility from the attacking nation. In 1966 Israel's Foreign Minister Abba Eban used the elegantly vague DEMONSTRATIVE DETERRENCE to describe an Israeli attack on a Jordanian village thought to harbor terrorists, but, by 1967, he preferred to use PRE-EMPTIVE STRIKE. One never invades; if one is British one TAKES AN INITIATIVE or PREVENTIVE INITIATIVE or A LIMITED AGGRESSIVE ACTION. In any event, in both Britain and America, war is generally described as a PREVENTIVE ACTION (see **PREVENTIVE WAR**), a term in use as early as 1639.

PRE-STRIKE RECONNAISSANCE   Aerial spying forays. According to the Department of Defense *Dictionary of Military and Associated Terms*, an official government publication compiled by the Joint Chiefs of Staff (1979), PRE-STRIKE RE-CONNAISSANCE is a mission "undertaken for the purpose of obtaining complete information about known targets for use by the strike force." Although this term has undergone various obfuscatory changes within the last thirty years, any discerning American can piece together the real meaning of both the term and the elements of its definition. PRE-STRIKE RECONNAISSANCE is a spying mission aimed at determining the most vital sites for bombing and/or ground action. In 1960, Francis Gary Powers flew A RECONNAISSANCE MISSION in a U-2 plane (U abbreviates "utility") and was charged by the Russians with espionage; the American media dubbed THE U-2 INCIDENT AN OVERFLIGHT (q.v.). The term RECONNAISSANCE, from the French *reconnoitre*, has meant a survey of enemy positions or strength conducted to determine the lay of the land or enemy power since 1810. In that year the Duke of Wellington complained, "It was a dark and foggy day, and the reconnaissance which I was able to make of the place was very imperfect." The word RECONNOITER was itself used in 1799 by General George Washington, who wrote of a "reconnoitre of the seaboard to St. Mary's." As a verb, meaning to observe the enemy, it was first used in English in 1707.

PREVENTIVE WAR   War of aggression disguised as defensive action. Safire says that this expression—used during the 1960s by Sorenson and President Kennedy, but first used by Bertrand Russell in 1948—means war. Actually the term, in the form PREVENTIVE ACTION, was first used in 1639. Today A PREVENTIVE WAR is one waged on the philosophy that "we should make war on them before they make war on us." The general concept underlying this euphemism is that no war started by oneself or one's allies is really AN INCURSION (an offensive invasion popularized in 1971 in relation to Vietnam, but in English since 1432 meaning a hostile invasion or a sudden attack). A PREVENTIVE WAR is, perhaps, the one kind of war of which A DAWK (U.S. slang for a person who is neither a hawk nor a dove, disapproving of war but unwilling to propagandize actively against it, 1966) would disapprove. In recent years CONFRONTATIONS (wars) have been known as BORDER INCIDENTS (q.v.), LIMITED ENGAGEMENTS, BORDER

INCURSIONS (all terms activated by the Vietnam War)—all forms of ACTIVE DEFENSE (offense, used in 1978 by Menachem Begin about the PLO).

PSYOP; PSYCHOLOGICAL OPERATION An action or operation in psychological warfare. This American euphemism was patterned after an earlier abbreviation, "psywar" (for psychological warfare). One of the less subtle techniques of PSYOP is known as THE BELL TELEPHONE HOUR, that is, torture time. It takes its name from a famous radio program of classical music ("The Bell Telephone Hour") that opened with soprano Helen Traubel singing "If I could tell you of my devotion," and, more directly, from the fact that the wires of field telephones were used to deliver shocks to the breasts and genitals of suspected Viet Cong. The term also derives from the earlier TUCKER TELEPHONE, a form of torture practiced at the Tucker State Farm (prison) in Arkansas. An earlier form of torture was THE WATER CURE, used by the United States Army in the Philippines at the beginning of the twentieth century. Another part of PSYOP is the more general category of PROGRAMMING TECHNIQUES—propaganda and less gentle forms of PERSUASION such as INTERROGATION (questioning, often by means of torture) and DEEP INTERROGATION (brainwashing).

RECONNAISSANCE IN FORCE Search and destroy. This euphemism is among the many for the unpleasant military practice of searching an area and destroying presumed enemies within it. (See **PRE-STRIKE RECONNAISSANCE.**) Since the 1960s and the Vietnam War, American military forces have described RECONNAISSANCE IN FORCE as: SEARCH AND CLEAR (an expression that won a "doublespeak" award), SEARCH AND SWEEP (even cleaner) and A SWEEPING OPERATION. A SWEEPING OPERATION might include H AND I, an abbreviation of HARASSMENT AND INTERDICTION (U.S., 1960s), that is, random firing, especially at night, to deter possible enemies from action.

ROUTE OF EGRESS Defensive retreat or withdrawal. There is no Department of Defense term for defeat. The closest approximation to such an admission is the above euphemism for a defensive withdrawal. Literally, this expression refers to the route or course the armed forces take in leaving an embattled area. In fact, it disguises a "hasty exit" or a "rout" in the earlier days of plainer talk. We suspect that other nations have equally circumlocutory phrases for the same military humiliation.

SECOND STRIKE CAPABILITY The capability of a nation to retaliate with nuclear weapons after a surprise enemy nuclear attack. All the major powers or SUPERPOWERS, as those who have nuclear weapons are called, have FIRST STRIKE CAPABILITIES, nuclear weapons that may be openly deployed and are designed for an initial attack against an enemy. SECOND STRIKE CAPABILITY is a description of hidden weapons and of a nation's ability to strike back even after nuclear attack (see **MAD**). Both of these terms conceal the fact that the strikes mentioned will be made with nuclear weapons. Both are considered parts of the key United States concept of DETERRENCE, itself a euphemism since it means massive utilization of nuclear weapons. Strikes (always nuclear; see also **PRE-EMPTIVE STRIKE** for non-nuclear) may take various and harmless sounding forms. They may be COUNTERFORCE—attacks aimed at an enemy's missiles and military installations—or COUNTERVALUE—attacks aimed at an enemy's cities and industries. They may be SURGICAL (see **MAD**), air attacks that supposedly obliterate only what they aim to obliterate, SELECTIVE (causing less than total devastation) or simply MASSIVE. (See also PROPS, **COUNTERFORCE WEAPONS**.)

SINGLE INTEGRATED OPERATIONS PLAN, A A list of nuclear targets in the USSR, described by Senator Daniel Moynihan in 1980. This hit list is kept at the headquarters of SAC (Strategic Air Command) in Omaha, Nebraska.

TERMINATION WITH EXTREME PREJUDICE Assassination. This CIA euphemism from the 1970s is an elaboration rather than the expected shortening of an older underworld expression for murder—TERMINATE. Rawson has noted a number of governmental variations on the theme: EXECUTIVE ACTION (which also means a coup in which a foreign leader is removed) and NEUTRALIZING (TERMINATING lower level personnel). The special assassination unit of the CIA has been called THE HEALTH ALTERATION COMMITTEE (1976).

TOFU Things ordinary: fucked-up. In American military parlance TOFU is not a name for high-protein, low-calorie bean curd, but one of the many acronyms based on SNAFU. SNAFU (situation normal: all fucked up) was originated, according to Partridge, by the British army in about 1940, but was soon also used by the American armed forces. Perhaps even earlier is MFU (military fuck-up), which Partridge finds in use in 1939. Among the many variations on SNAFU, Rawson lists: FUBAR (fucked up beyond all recognition), GFU (general fuck up, usually applied to an inept individual), JANFU (joint Army-Navy fuck-up), SAMFU (self-adjusting military fuck-up, British), SAPFU (surpassing all previous fuck-ups), SNEFU (situation normal: everything fucked up, British), SUSFU (situation unchanged: still fucked up), TARFU (things are really fucked up) and TUIFU (the ultimate in fuck-ups). In polite company, all the above may substitute FOUL-UP for "fuck-up." One may also describe a military mess-up still more euphemistically as A GLITCH.

VIETNAMIZATION The removal of American troops and their replacement by Vietnamese forces as a means of withdrawing from the war. VIETNAMIZATION is one of the more infamous euphemisms coined during the period of the Vietnam War. It replaced the earlier and more direct term DE-AMERICANIZATION (the reduction of American military involvement in Vietnam), used from about 1966. VIETNAMIZATION (1968) was most aptly described by Senator Eugene McCarthy as "changing the color of the bodies." As part of this process, RUFF PUFFS or members of the South Vietnamese regional forces and popular forces (the euphemism was coined from the abbreviation of these words to "rf" and "pf") were substituted for American troops in this CONFRONTATION with the CHARLIES. A CHARLIE, a Viet Cong guerilla or Viet Cong soldier, is a shortening of VICTOR CHARLEY (or CHARLIE), the communications code name for the VC or Viet Cong.

Bibliography

Adams, Ramon F. *Western Words: A Dictionary of the American West*. New ed. Norman: University of Oklahoma Press, 1968.

Adelman, Clifford. *Generations*. New York: Praeger, 1972.

Airman: Official Magazine of the U.S. Air Force. Vol. 24, No. 4, April 1980; No. 8, August 1980; No. 9, September 1980, *passim*.

All Hands: Magazine of the U.S. Navy. No. 759, April 1980; No. 761, June 1980; No. 775, August 1981, *passim*.

American Heritage Dictionary of the English Language. Boston: Houghton Mifflin Co., 1976.

Anderson, Annelise G. *The Business of Organized Crime*. Stanford, Calif.: Hoover Institution Press, 1979.

Avis, Walter S., and Charles Crate, eds. *A Dictionary of Canadianisms on Historical Principles*. Toronto: n.p. 1967.

Barnhart, Clarence L., Sol Steinmetz and Robert K. Barnhart. *A New Dictionary of English*. London: Longman, 1972.

Barrère, Albert, and Charles G. Leland. *A Dictionary of Slang, Jargon and Cant*. 2 vols. London: George Bell & Sons, 1897.

Beeching, Cyril Leslie. *A Dictionary of Eponyms*. London: Clive Bingley, 1979.

Beekman, Eric. *The Criminal Justice Dictionary*. Ann Arbor, Mich.: Pierian Press, 1979.

Beeton, Douglas Ridley. *A Dictionary of English Usage in South Africa*. Cape Town: Oxford University Press, 1975.

Bernbach, Lisa. *Preppy Handbook*. New York: Workman Publishing, 1980.

Berrey, Lester V., and Melvin Van Den Bark. *The American Thesaurus of Slang*. New York: Thomas Y. Crowell, 1953.

Bickerton, Anthea. *CB Radio English*. Wick, Scotland: Abson Books, 1981.

Branford, Jean. *A Dictionary of South African English*. Cape Town: Oxford University Press, 1978.

Bremer, John B. *Words on Words*. New York: Columbia University Press, 1980.

Brewer, E. Cobham. *The Dictionary of Phrase and Fable*. New York: Avenel Books, 1978.

Century Dictionary and Cyclopedia. 12 vols. New York: Century Co., 1911.

Clemmen, Donald. *The Prison Community*. New York: Holt, Reinhart & Winston, 1940.

Congressional Record. August 4, 1980; August 5, 1980; August 6, 1980; September 23, 1980.

Corrections Magazine. Vol. 7, June 3, 1981, *passim*.

Cressey, Donald R. *Organized Crime and Criminal Organizations.* Cambridge, Mass.: Heffer and Sons, 1971.

_____, and Robert A. McDermott. *Diversion from the Juvenile Justice System.* U.S. Department of Justice, Law Enforcement Assistance Administration, January 1974.

Cutts, Martin, and Chrissie Maher. *Writing Plain English.* (Pamphlet.) United Kingdom: Plain English Society, 1980.

Daily Mail (London), *passim.*

Daily Telegraph (London), *passim.*

De Sola, Ralph. *Crime Dictionary.* New York: Facts On File, 1982.

Dictionary of American English on Historical Principles. Edited by Sir William Alexander Craigie and James R. Hulbert. 4 vols. Chicago: University of Chicago Press, 1936–44.

Dictionary of Military and Associated Terms. Department of Defense, Joint Chiefs of Staff, June 1, 1979 (J.C.S. Pub. 1).

Dillard, Joey Lee. *American Talk: Where Our Words Came From.* New York: Random House, 1976.

_____. *Black English: Its History and Usage in the United States.* New York: Random House, 1972.

_____. *Lexicon of Black English.* New York: Seabury Press, 1977.

"The Euphemism: Telling It Like It Isn't." Time essay, *Time* magazine. September 19, 1969.

Farmer, John. *Americanisms Old and New: A Dictionary of Words, Phrases and Colloquialisms.* London: Thomas Poulter & Sons, 1889. Reprint. Gryphon Books, 1971.

Farmer, John S., and W. E. Henley. *Slang and Its Analogues.* 7 vols. New York: Kraus Reprint Corp., 1965.

Fleming, John, and Hugh Honour. *Dictionary of the Decorative Arts.* New York: Harper & Row, 1977.

Franklyn, Julian. *A Dictionary of Rhyming Slang.* 2nd ed. London: Routledge & Kegan Paul, 1961.

Franzblau, Rose N. *The Middle Years.* New York: Holt, 1971.

"Glossary of Terms and Slang Common in Penal Establishments." London: British Home Office, n.d.

Goldin, Hyman E., and Frank O'Leary. *American Underworld Lingo.* New York: Twayne, 1950.

Golding, William Gerald. *Rites of Passage.* New York: Farrar Straus Giroux, 1980.

Gordon, James D. *The English Language: An Historical Introduction.* New York: Thomas Y. Crowell, 1972.

Gowers, Sir Ernest. *The Complete Plain Words.* London: Her Majesty's Stationers, 1954.

Grose, Francis. *A Classical Dictionary of the Vulgar Tongue.* (1796). Edited by Eric Partridge. New York: Barnes & Noble, 1963.

Gunner (Magazine of the Royal Artillery). No. 111, February 1980, *passim.*

Hargrave, Basil. *Origins and Meaning of Popular Phrases Including Those Which Came into Use During the Great War.* Detroit: Gale Research Company, 1968.

Hart, James. *The Oxford Companion to American Literature.* New York: Oxford University Press, 1948.

Hayakawa, S. I. *Language in Thought and Action.* New York: Harcourt, Brace, 1949.

Herr, Michael. *Dispatches.* New York: Alfred A. Knopf, 1977.

Hogan, P. "Pentagonese," *Colliers,* November 24, 1951.

Homer, Frederic D. *Guns and Garlic: Myths and Realities of Organized Crime*. West Lafayette, Ind.: Purdue University Studies, 1974.

Howard, Philip. *New Words for Old*. New York: Oxford University Press, 1977.

———. *Weasel Words*. New York: Oxford University Press, 1979.

Kett, Joseph F. *Rites of Passage: Adolescence in America 1870 to the Present*. New York: Basic Books, 1977.

Knopf, Olga. *Successful Aging*. New York: Viking Press, 1975.

Kornbloom, Allen N. *The Moral Hazards: Police Strategies for Honesty and Ethical Behavior*. Lexington, Mass.: D. C. Heath, 1976.

Kramer, Jane. "A Reporter in Europe: Hamburg." *New Yorker*, March 20, 1978.

Laqueur, Walter. *A Dictionary of Politics*. Rev. ed. New York: Free Press, 1973.

Le Shan, Eda J. *The Wonderful Crisis of Middle Age*. New York: McKay, 1973.

Lewis, Gerald E. *How to Talk Yankee*. (Pamphlet) n.p.: Thorndike Press, 1979.

Little, William, et al. *The Oxford University Dictionary on Historical Principles*, revised and edited by C. T. Onions, 3rd ed. revised with addenda. Oxford: Clarendon Press, 1955.

Londy, Eugene. *The Underground Dictionary*. New York: Simon & Schuster, 1971.

The Louisiana State Penitentiary Dictionary of Slang. Duplicated. N.p., n.d.

Mager, N. H., and S. K. Mager. *Encyclopedic Dictionary of English Usage*. Englewood Cliffs, N.J.: Prentice-Hall, 1974.

Major, Clarence. *Dictionary of Afro-American Slang.* New York: International Publishers, 1970.

Marckwardt, Albert H. *American English.* 2nd ed., revised by J. L. Dillard. New York: Oxford University Press, 1980.

Marine Corps Gazette. October 1980, *passim.*

Marples, Morris. *Public School Slang.* London: Constable and Co., 1940.

_____. *University Slang.* London: Williams and Norgate, 1950.

Martin, Julian. *Law Enforcement Vocabulary.* Springfield, Ill.: Charles C Thomas, 1979.

Mathews, M. M. *A Dictionary of Americanisms.* Chicago: University of Chicago Press, 1951.

Maurer, David W. *The American Confidence Man.* Springfield, Ill.: Charles C Thomas, 1974.

_____. *The Big Con.* New York: Pocket Books, 1949.

May, Erskine. *A Treatise on the Law, Privileges, Proceedings & Usage of Parliament.* 19th ed. Edited by Sir David Lidderdale, K.C.B. London: Butterworths, 1976.

Mencken, H. L. *The American Language: An Inquiry into the Development of English in the United States.* New York: Alfred A. Knopf, 1936.

Mitford, Jessica. *The American Way of Death.* New York: Simon & Schuster, 1963.

Morris, William and Mary. *Harper Dictionary of Contemporary English.* New York: Harper & Row, 1975.

_____. *Morris Dictionary of Word and Phrase Origins.* New York: Harper & Row, 1977.

National Advisory Council on Adult Education. *Report.* Washington, D.C.: Government Printing Office, July 1980, *passim.*

Neaman, Judith S., and Carole G. Silver. Notes taken on testimony before the U.S. Senate Judiciary Committee subcommittee hearings on the Robert L. Vesco case, October 10, 1980, *passim*.

Newman, Edwin. *A Civil Tongue*. Indianapolis, Ind.: Bobbs-Merrill, 1976.

———. *Strictly Speaking*. Indianapolis, Ind.: Bobbs-Merrill, 1974. *New York Times, passim*.

Oxford Companion to English Literature. 3rd ed. Edited by Sir Paul Harvey. Oxford: Clarendon Press, 1960.

Oxford English Dictionary. 2 vols. Oxford: Clarendon Press, 1971.

Partridge, Eric. *A Dictionary of Catch Phrases, British and American, from the Sixteenth Century to the Present Day*. New York: Stein & Day, 1977.

———. *A Dictionary of Slang and Unconventional English*. New York: Macmillan Co., 1961.

———. *Origins*. 2nd ed. New York: Macmillan Co., 1959.

———. *Shakespeare's Bawdy*. New York: E. P. Dutton, 1960.

Pearl, Anita. *The Jonathan David Dictionary of Popular Slang*. Middle Village, N.Y.: Jonathan David, 1980.

Pei, Mario. *Doublespeak in America*. New York: Hawthorn Books, 1973.

Phythian, B. A. *A Concise Dictionary of English Slang and Colloquialisms*. 2nd ed. Boston: The Writer, Inc., 1976.

Powis, David. *The Signs of Crime: A Field Manual for Police*. London: McGraw-Hill Limited, 1977.

Random House Dictionary of the English Language. College ed. Edited by Laurence Urdang. New York: Random House, 1968.

Rawson, Hugh. *A Dictionary of Euphemisms and Other Doubletalk*. New York: Crown Publishers, 1981.

Roget's International Thesaurus. Rev. ed. New York: Thomas Y. Crowell, 1953.

Ross, Thomas W. *Chaucer's Bawdy.* New York: E. P. Dutton, 1972.

Rosten, Leo. *The Joys of Yiddish.* New York: McGraw-Hill, 1958.

Russell, Willis, and Mary Gray Porter. "Among the New Words." *American Speech,* Vol. 55, No. 1, Spring 1980.

Safire, William. "On Language." *New York Times Magazine.* March 4, 1979; April 8, 1979; July 18, 1980; September 20, 1981; October 4, 1981.

_____. *Safire's Political Dictionary: An Enlarged Up-to-date Edition of the New Language of Politics.* New York: Random House, 1978.

Sagarin, Edward. *The Anatomy of Dirty Words.* N.p.: Lyle Stuart, 1962.

Salerno, Ralph, and John S. Tompkins. *The Crime Confederation.* Garden City, N.Y.: Doubleday, 1969.

Samovar, Larry, and Fred Sanders. "Language Patterns of Prostitutes." *Et Cetera,* Vol. 35, No. 1, March 1978.

Screw magazine, "Carnal Classified." No. 714, November 8, 1982.

Severn, Paul. *People Words.* New York: Washburn, Inc., 1966.

Sheehy, Gail. *Passages: Predictable Crises of Adult Life.* New York: E. P. Dutton, 1976.

Shipley, Joseph T. *In Praise of English.* New York: New York Times Books, 1977.

_____. *Playing with Words.* Englewood Cliffs, N.J.: Prentice-Hall, 1960.

Shorter Oxford English Dictionary on Historical Principles. Edited by William Little, H. W. Fowler, and J. Coulson. Revised and edited by C. T. Onions. Oxford: Clarendon Press, 1956.

Sisson, A. F. *Sisson's Synonyms, An Unabridged Synonym and Related-Terms Finder.* West Nyack, N.Y.: Parker Publishing Co., 1969.

Soldier (British). Vol. 37, No. 3, March 1981; Vol. 37, No. 7, July 1981, *passim.*

Soldier News (British). No. 38, October 17–30, 1980; No. 55, June 26–July 9, 1981, *passim.*

Soldiers: The Official U.S. Army Magazine. Vol. 35, No. 6, June 1980, *passim.*

Spergel, Irving. *Racketville, Slumtown, Haulburg.* Chicago: University of Chicago Press, 1964.

SSAM (Soldier, Sailor, Airman, Marine). No. 22, July 1980; No. 23, August 1980; No. 24, September 1980; No. 25, October 1980; No. 37, October 1981, *passim.*

Stirling, Nora. *Your Money or Your Life.* Indianapolis, Ind.: Bobbs-Merrill, 1974.

Supplement to the Oxford English Dictionary. Edited by R. W. Burchfield. 2 vols. Oxford: Clarendon Press, 1972–1976.

Sykes, Gresham M. *The Society of Captives: A Study of a Maximum Security Prison.* Princeton, N.J.: Princeton University Press, 1958.

U.S. Congress. House of Representatives, Committee on Interstate and Foreign Commerce, Subcommittee on Health and the Environment. *A Descriptive Dictionary of Health Care.* Washington, D.C.: Government Printing Office, February 1976.

U.S. Congress. House of Representatives, Select Committee on Aging, Subcommittee on Retirement Income and Employment.

Midlife Women: Policy Proposals on Their Problems. Summary of papers submitted. Comm. Pub. No. 96–180. Washington, D.C.: Government Printing Office, April 1979.

U.S. Congress. Senate, Committee on Labor and Human Resources. Report on the Health Sciences Promotion Act of 1980. Washington, D.C.: Government Printing Office.

U.S. Department of Health, Education and Welfare. *How to Select a Nursing Home.* G.P.O. Stock No. 017-022-00502-6. Washington, D.C.: Government Printing Office.

Vallins, George Henry. *Better English.* London: Deutsch, 1955.

Ware, J. Redding. *Passing English of the Victorian Era, A Dictionary of Heterodox English Slang and Phrase.* London: George Routledge and Sons Ltd.; n.d.

Wentworth, Harold, and Stuart Berg Flexner. *Dictionary of American Slang, Second Supplemented Edition.* New York: Thomas Y. Crowell, 1960.

Whorf, Benjamin Lee. *Language, Thought, and Reality.* Edited by J. B. Carroll. New York: John Wiley and Sons, 1964.

Wilkes, G. A. *A Dictionary of Australian Colloquialisms.* London: Routledge & Kegan Paul, 1978.

Williams, Joseph M. *Origins of the English Language.* New York: Free Press, 1957.

Williams, Vergil L. *Dictionary of American Penology: An Introductory Guide.* Westport, Conn.: Greenwood Press, 1979.

Wright, Peter. *Cockney Dialect and Slang.* London: B. T. Balsford Ltd., 1981.

Index

Catalog

If you are interested in a list of fine Paperback
books, covering a wide range of subjects
and interests, send your name and address,
requesting your free catalog, to:

McGraw-Hill Paperbacks
1221 Avenue of Americas
New York, N.Y. 10020